Jennifer Bryan.

AAT Tutorial Text

Intermediate
Units 7 & 8
Cost Accounting II

First edition 1993
Second edition August 1994

ISBN 0 7517 6027 7 (previous edition 0 7517 6008 0)

British Library Cataloguing-in-Publication Data

A catalogue record for this book
is available from the British Library

Published by

BPP Publishing Limited
Aldine House, Aldine Place
London W12 8AW

We are grateful to the Lead Body for Accounting for permission to reproduce extracts from the Standards of Competence for Accounting.

Contents

Preface

For years the market leader in targeted study texts and practice and revision material for the AAT qualification, BPP has built on its extensive experience in the field of publishing for professional qualifications in producing material specifically for the AAT's new Education and Training Scheme. The scheme has accreditation from the National Council for Vocational Qualifications (NCVQ) and the Scottish Vocational Education Council. The aim of the new scheme is to ensure that aspiring accounting technicians at different levels (NVQ/SVQ levels 2, 3 and 4) can demonstrate that they are qualified to do the tasks they perform by the achievement of certain recognised standards of competence.

BPP's study material for Units 7 and 8 of the Intermediate stage comprises a *Cost Accounting II* Tutorial Text and an accompanying Workbook. The Tutorial Text covers what the student needs to know and how tasks need to be performed, based on the standards of competence for the units, which are set out on pages (viii) to (xiv). The *Cost Accounting II* Workbook contains extensive Exercises, Assignments and Central Assessment Exercises on which to practise relevant skills and techniques.

BPP's study material has the following features.

- It takes a practical, active approach to teaching, centred on what the student needs to be able to do at the end of the learning and practice process.
- It emphasises the importance of understanding the practical nature of assessment and provides students with plenty of opportunity to practise for such assessments.
- It can be linked into a college course by being used as course material.

The August 1994 edition of this Tutorial Text

This edition of the Tutorial Text has been updated and improved in the following ways.

(a) New material has been added on cost codes.
(b) A number of sections have been revised, including those on graphs and time series.
(c) The VAT part has been fully updated for all changes in VAT law and practice.

BPP Publishing
August 1994

For details of the other BPP titles relevant to your studies for Units 7 and 8 and for a full list of books in the BPP AAT range, please turn to pages 253 and 254. If you wish to send us your comments on this Tutorial Text, please turn to page 255.

How to use this Tutorial Text

This *Cost Accounting II* Tutorial Text covers Unit 7: *Preparing reports and returns* and Unit 8: *Preparing VAT returns*. It is designed to be used alongside BPP's *Cost Accounting II* Workbook. The Workbook provides Exercises on the material covered in this Tutorial Text, together with Assignments (longer case study simulations of the devolved assessment type) and exercises of the types which may be included in the Central Assessment for Unit 7.

As you complete each chapter of this Tutorial Text, work through the Exercises in the corresponding session in the *Cost Accounting II* Workbook. Once you have completed all of the Sessions of Exercises, you will be in a position to attempt longer Assignments in the Workbook in preparation for devolved assessment in Units 7 and 8. Bear in mind that the tasks involved in simulations varies in length and complexity; there may be more than one 'scenario' involved in the tasks on which the devolved assessment for a unit is based.

If you complete all of the Exercises and Assignments in the *Cost Accounting II* Workbook, then you will have gained practice in all parts of the elements of competence included in Units 7 & 8.

You will also want to practise the kinds of task which will be set in the Central Assessment for Unit 7. Central Assessment Exercises are provided in the Workbook for this purpose. These include the contents of Central Assessments set by the AAT together with suggested solutions prepared by BPP.

Preparing reports and returns: introductory points

Unit 7: Preparing reports and returns involves:

(a) preparing periodic performance reports; and
(b) preparing reports and returns for outside agencies.

Before you start the main part of this Tutorial Text, you should note the following points on studying Unit 7.

Periodic performance reports are reports required by management which give management information about how well a business, or a division or department, is performing. Accounting and other quantitative information needs to be compiled and presented in a clear and intelligible way.

The ways in which the information is compiled will depend on how the accounting system of the organisation is organised. Different organisations will also have different ways of measuring how well organisational units are doing: in other words, there will be various performance measures or performance indicators. Measuring or quantifying performance in a government agency processing benefit claims will demand rather different measures or indicators than would be used in a factory manufacturing glass containers, for example.

Whatever the organisation, there need to be agreed methods covering various aspects of accounting for and reporting on performance of the organisation and the units (eg divisions or departments) making it up. Agreed procedures are important so that there is as much consistency as possible. If different accounting methods and performance measures were used from one period to the next, it would become difficult (or impossible) to make comparisons of results between the different periods. In medium-sized or large organisations, as well as in many well established small organisations, the agreed methods and procedures will be recorded in documentation.

The reports and returns required from an organisation by outside agencies are of various types and of varying complexity. One such return is the VAT return, which is covered in Unit 8: *Preparing VAT returns* and is dealt with in Part B of this Tutorial Text.

Although it is important to have a general awareness of the variety of reports and returns which outside agencies of various kinds require, you should not attempt to learn the requirements for all the reports, returns and forms you come across (except where this is specifically required, as in the case of VAT returns, covered in Unit 8). What is important is that you should develop the ability to complete any report or return which you might be presented with in your work as an Accounting Technician using appropriate information for the organisation's or the external agency's requirements.

This means developing skills in identifying and collating information. Such skills may be needed to find out exactly what an external agency's requirements are. For example, if you were asked to complete a form required by the Registrar of Companies (Companies House), you might need to consult a textbook on company law to check some particular point, as well as whatever instructions are provided with the form itself. You will also need to collect together the information which needs to be entered on the report or return. Techniques in presenting information are important here. Although many forms and returns require information to be presented in a prescribed way, in other cases there will be more flexibility about the ways in which the information can be presented.

It can be appreciated from the above that there are certain general skills involving identifying, compiling and presenting information which are common to periodic performance reports and reports and returns for external agencies. The way this Tutorial Text is organised reflects this. When you are studying these various techniques (for example, tables and charts in Chapter 4, or graphs in Chapter 5), be prepared to apply them in either type of task.

Standards of competence

Introduction

The new competence-based Education and Training Scheme of the Association of Accounting Technicians (AAT) is based on an analysis of the work of accounting staff in a wide range of industries and types of organisation. The Standards of Competence for Accounting which students are expected to meet are based on this analysis.

The Standards identify the *key purpose* of the accounting occupation, which is to 'operate, maintain and improve systems, to record, plan, monitor and report on the financial activities of an organisation', and a number of *key roles* of the occupation. Each key role is subdivided into *units of competence.* By successfully completing assessments in specified units of competence, students can gain qualifications at NVQ/SVQ levels 2, 3 and 4, which correspond to the AAT Foundation, Intermediate and Technician stages of competence respectively.

Intermediate stage key roles and units of competence

The key roles and unit titles for the AAT Intermediate stage (NVQ/SVQ level 3) are set out below.

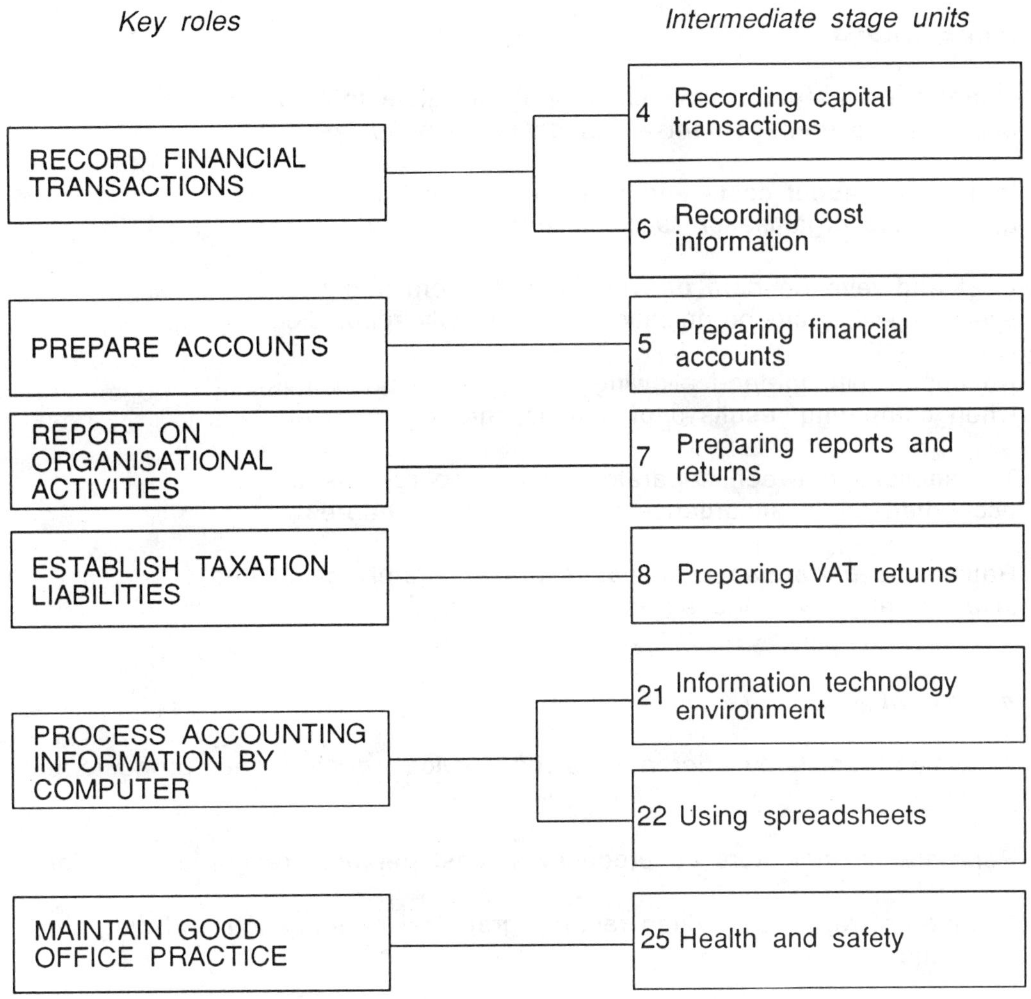

Units and elements of competence

Units of competence are divided into *elements of competence* describing activities which the individual should be able to perform.

Each element includes a set of *performance criteria* which define what constitutes competent performance. Each element also includes a *range statement* which defines the situations, contexts, methods etc in which the competence should be displayed.

Supplementing the standards of competence are statements of *knowledge and understanding* which underpin competent performance of the standards.

This Tutorial Text covers Unit 7: *Preparing reports and returns* and Unit 8: *Preparing VAT returns*. The elements of competence for these units are set out below. Performance criteria and areas of knowledge and understanding are cross-referenced below to chapters in this Tutorial Text, which correspond with sessions of exercises in the companion *Cost Accounting II* Workbook.

Unit 7: Preparing reports and returns

Element 7.1 Prepare periodic performance reports

	Performance criteria	*Chapters in this Text*
1	Reports are prepared in a clear and intelligible form and presented to management within defined timescales	2-6, 8
2	Information about costs and revenues derived from different units of the organisation is consolidated in standard form	9, 10
3	Cost and revenue data derived from different information systems within the organisation are correctly reconciled	9, 10
4	An appropriate method allowing for changing price levels when comparing results over time is agreed and used	7
5	Transactions between separate units of the organisation are accounted for in accordance with agreed procedures	10
6	Ratios and performance indicators are accurately calculated in accordance with the agreed methodology	9, 11

Range statement

1 Analysis of results by different divisions, services, departments, products, processes or sales areas

2 Performance indicators of: productivity, cost per unit, resource utilisation, profitability

3 Methods of reporting: written reports, graphical presentation and diagrams (bar charts, pie diagrams), tables

Knowledge and understanding

The business environment

1	Main sources of government statistics	2
2	Awareness of relevant performance and quality measures	9, 11

Accounting techniques

1	Use of standard units of inputs and outputs	9
2	Time series analysis	6
3	Use of index numbers	7
4	Main types of performance indicators (see Range statement)	9, 11
5	Graphical and diagrammatic presentation (see Range statement)	4, 5
6	Tabulation of accounting and other quantitative information	4

		Chapters in this Text
The organisation		
1	Background understanding that the accounting systems of an organisation are affected by its organisational structure, its administrative systems and procedures and the nature of its business transactions	1
2	Background understanding that recording and accounting practices may vary in different parts of the organisation	1

Element 7.2 Prepare reports and returns for outside agencies

Performance criteria

1	The conventions and definitions used by the external agency are correctly used in preparing the report or return	2
2	Relevant information is identified, collated and presented in accordance with the external agency's requirement	2, 8
3	Calculations of ratios and performance indicators are accurate	9, 11
4	The report/return is presented in accordance with the external agency's deadline	2, 8

(*Note.* This is a 'generic' competence for organisations in both the public and private sectors, eg returns to trade associations, reports to government grant awarding agencies, statutory returns to DOE by local authorities, returns to Department of Health by Health Authorities.)

Range statement

1 Returns on standard forms
2 Written reports on specific issues
3 Graphic and diagrammatic presentation of information
4 Tabulation of accounting and other quantitative information

Knowledge and understanding

The business environment		
1	Main types of external organisations requiring reports and returns:	
	(a) regulatory	2
	(b) grant awarding	2
	(c) information collecting	2
2	Main sources of government statistics	2
3	Trade associations	2
Accounting techniques		
Methods of presenting information (see Range Statement)		3-5, 8

		Chapters in this Text
The organisation		
1	Background understanding that the accounting systems of an organisation are affected by its organisational structure, its administrative systems and procedures and the nature of its business transactions	1
2	Background understanding that a variety of outside agencies may require reports and returns from organisations and that these requirements must be built into administrative and accounting systems and procedures	1

Unit 8: Preparing VAT returns

Element 8.1 Prepare VAT returns

Performance criteria

1	VAT returns are correctly completed from the appropriate sources and submitted within the statutory time limits	12
2	Relevant inputs and outputs are correctly identified and calculated	13
3	VAT documentation is correctly filed	12
4	Submissions are made in accordance with currently operative VAT laws and regulations	12
5	Discussions with VAT inspectors are conducted openly and constructively to promote the efficiency of the VAT accounting system	12, 13

Range statement

1 Exempt supplies, zero rated supplies, imports and exports

Knowledge and understanding

The business environment

1	Basic law and practice relating to all issues covered in the range statement and referred to in the performance criteria. Specific issues include:	
	(a) the classification of types of supply	13
	(b) registration requirements	12
	(c) the form of VAT invoices; tax points	12
2	Sources of information on VAT: Customs and Excise Guide	13
3	Administration of VAT; enforcement	13

		Chapters in this Text
The organisation		
1	Background understanding that the accounting systems of an organisation are affected by its organisational structure, its administrative systems and procedures and the nature of its business transactions	1
2	Background understanding that recording and accounting practices may vary in different parts of the organisation	1

Assessment structure

Devolved and central assessment

The units of competence in the AAT Education and Training Scheme are assessed by a combination of devolved assessment and central assessment.

Devolved assessment tests students' ability to apply the skills detailed in the various units of competence. At the Intermediate stage, evidence is collected in an Accounting Portfolio. Devolved assessment may be carried out by means of:

(a) simulations of workplace activities set by AAT-approved assessors; or
(b) observation in the workplace by AAT-approved assessors.

Central assessments are set and marked by the AAT, and concentrate on testing students' grasp of the knowledge and understanding which underpins units of competence.

The Intermediate stage

Units of competence at the AAT Intermediate stage (NVQ/SVQ level 3) are tested by central assessment (CA) and devolved assessment (DA) as follows.

Unit number	*Unit title*	*CA*		*DA*
4	Recording capital transactions	√	CA3	√
5	Preparing financial accounts	√		√
6	Recording cost information	√	CA4	√
7	Preparing reports and returns	√		√
8	Preparing VAT returns			√
21	Information technology environment			√
22	Using spreadsheets			√
25	Health and safety			√

CA4

Central Assessment CA4 covers underpinning knowledge and understanding for Units 6 and 7. Unit 6 is covered in BPP's *Cost Accounting I* Tutorial Text and Workbook. CA4 is 3 hours long and is divided into parts as follows.

Part 1 Practical tasks
Part 2 Short answer questions
Part 3 Calculations and report

The main topics to be assessed are: the objectives of cost accounting and budgeting, cost behaviour, elements of cost, principles of cost collection, objectives of overhead apportionments, and principles of standard costing and variance analysis.

PART A
Unit 7: Preparing reports and returns

1. The organisation, accounting and reporting

1. **Organisations and their structure**
2. **Accounting practices in different parts of the organisation**
3. **Internal and external reports**

1. Organisations and their structure

Introduction

1.1 If you examine the descriptions of the *knowledge and understanding* required for all of the units of competence at the AAT Intermediate stage (NVQ level 3), you will find that you are required to have a:

> 'Background understanding that the accounting systems of an organisation are affected by its organisational structure, its administrative systems and procedures and the nature of its business transactions.'

This is identical to what is required at Foundation stage.

1.2 At Intermediate stage, then, you require the same knowledge and understanding of organisational structure as at Foundation stage. Furthermore, both Units 7 and 8 at the Intermediate stage require:

> 'Background understanding that recording and accounting practices may vary in different parts of the organisation'.

1.3 Unit 7 also requires:

> 'Background understanding that a variety of outside agencies may require reports and returns from organisations and that these requirements must be built into administrative and accounting systems and procedures'.

1.4 The aims of this chapter are:

(a) to revise some of the ideas covered at Foundation stage;

(b) to introduce some ideas about different ways of dealing with financial information within the organisation.

Organisations

1.5 There are many different kinds of organisation, from an aircraft manufacturer to a bank to a government department to a hospital to a corner shop.

1.6 As we saw at the Foundation stage, it is possible to distinguish organisations from each other in a number of ways, so that the many different types of organisation can be fitted into a number of categories. Ways of classifying and distinguishing organisations include the following.

(a) *By type of activity.* Here are some examples.

- (i) Retailers (eg greengrocer, supermarket chain)
- (ii) Manufacturers (eg of painkillers, ballbearings, cars)
- (iii) Service organisations (eg restaurants, schools)
- (iv) Contractors (eg power station building)

(b) *By size of business.* A large supermarket would have more in common with another large organisation than with a small grocer's shop.

(c) *Profit orientated or non profit orientated.* An organisation in existence to make a profit seeks to maximise the difference between what it receives in revenue, and what it pays out in expenses. The surplus, or profit, is distributed to the owners to do with as they please. A charity, on the other hand, is a non profit making organisation. Public sector organisations are funded from general taxation to provide services, not, generally speaking, to make a profit.

(d) *Legal status and ownership.*

(i) The business affairs of sole traders are not distinguished from their personal affairs in the eyes of the law.

(ii) A partnership is an agreement (normally documented) between two or more individuals, but the partners are still personally liable for the debts of the business.

(iii) A *limited company* on the other hand is a separate legal personality in the eyes of the law, and is a separate legal entity from its owners (shareholders). (A UK limited company can be identified by the words Limited or public limited company, or the letters Ltd or plc after its name - there are equivalents for Welsh companies.)

(iv) Some organisations (eg hospitals) are owned and funded by central or local government. These are public sector organisations.

(v) Some private sector organisations (eg British Telecom) are partly government owned, in that the government is a shareholder.

Organisation structure

1.7 Organisations are often so large that there have be formal and defined relationships between the persons within the organisation. This is because:

(a) there is a large number of *tasks* that have to be done, involving several people, and these activities have to be coordinated in some way;

(b) there is often a large number of *people* who have to be coordinated and motivated.

1.8 Many large organisations have a person or committee at the head who is responsible, in the last instance, for the direction the organisation takes and its policies and strategies (for example, what to sell and which countries to trade in). An individual might be called *Chief Executive,* or *Managing Director.* A committee might be called a *Board of Directors* or an Executive Committee.

1.9 In a large organisation, the Board's decisions will 'cascade' down for detailed implementation, and *information* about performance will rise up. Each person on the top will have a number of people reporting to him or her, and in turn these other people will have their own subordinates, and so on. This is the *management hierarchy,* in which a person's position and responsibilities are defined in relation to other people's positions and responsibilities.

1.10 Another aspect of organisation structure, which depends on its size as much as anything else, is how it is arranged.

(a) For example, say you work for an organisation which manufactures a range of cars and buses. These are both manufactured and sold in Europe and Asia. The company has its head office, and most of its research facilities in the UK. It is a UK registered company, and has no shareholders outside the UK. The company employs 20,000 people. If you work for a large organisation, you will be familiar with the fact that some people work in marketing and selling, others work in production and still more in finance and administration.

(b) Such a company is likely to be quite complex. There is bound to be a central committee of top executives in charge of the overall running of the business, but how about the rest of the business? There are a number of ways by which it could be organised.

(i) Would the business be structured geographically, like this?

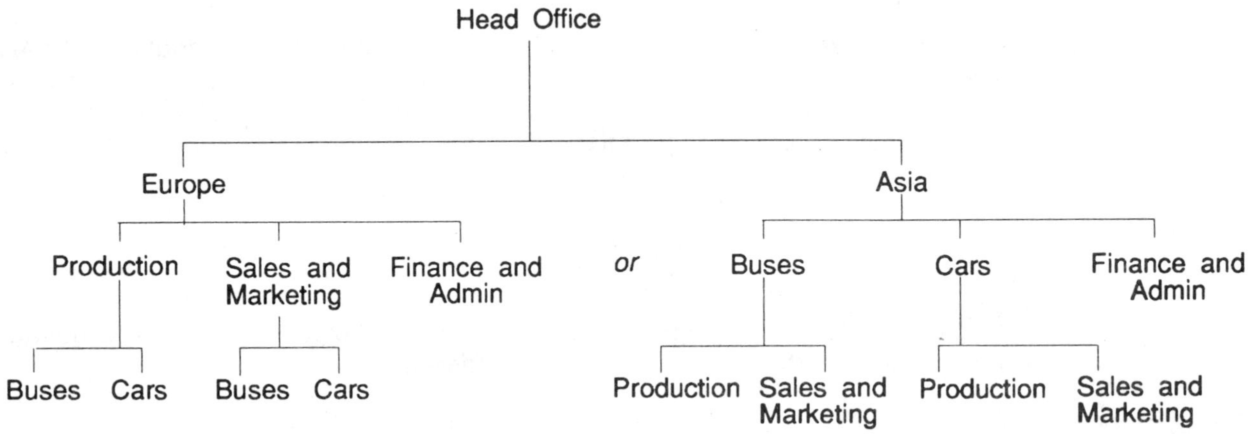

In this *geographical organisation structure* the responsibility for all the activities of the company is divided on an area basis. The manager for Asia is in charge of producing and selling products in that area.

(ii) Would the business be structured on a product-divisional basis, like this?

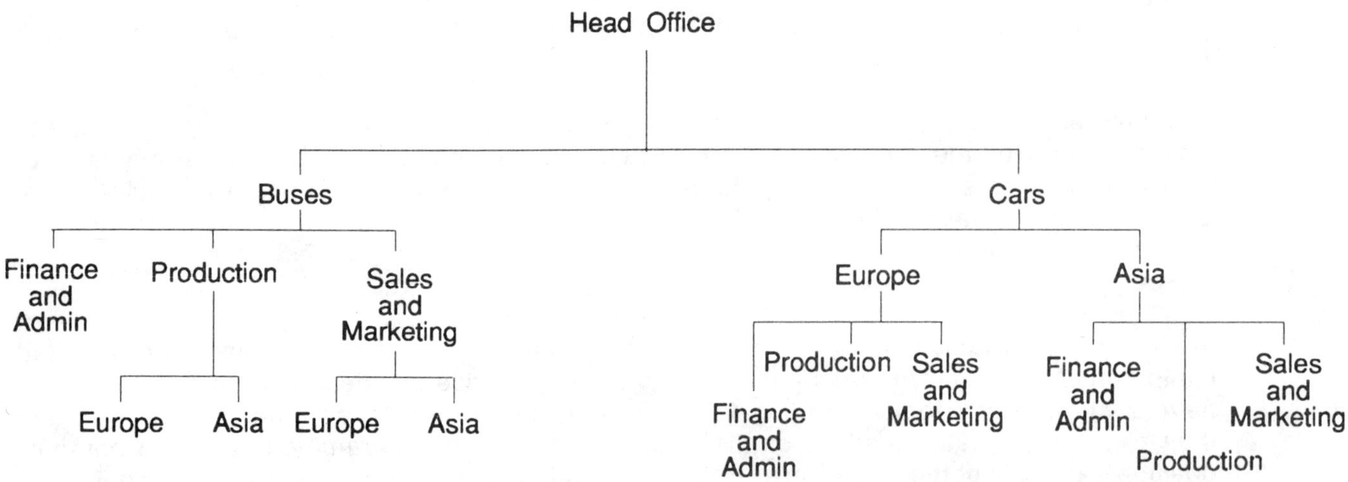

In this *product-division structure* the responsibility for buses worldwide, and cars worldwide are each given to one individual.

(iii) Or would the business by structured on a functional basis, like this?

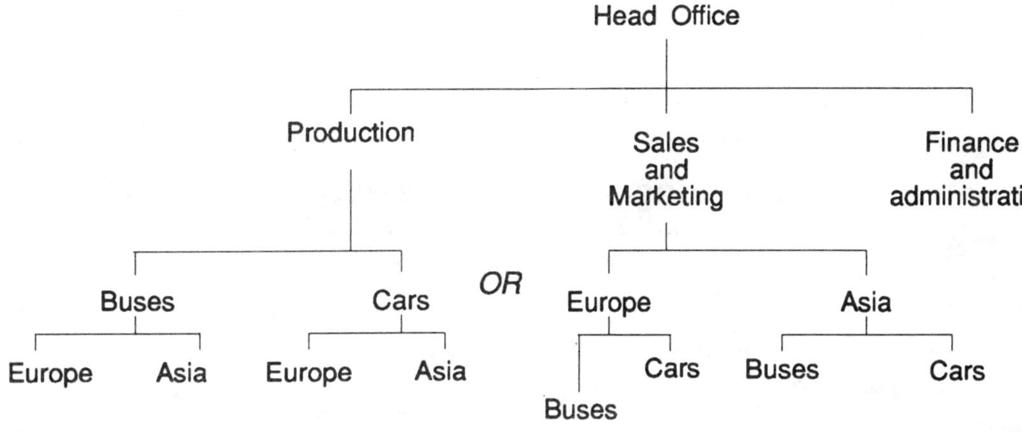

In this *functional organisation structure*, worldwide control of production is vested in one person, as is the case with sales and marketing.

(iv) Or would the business be structured on a matrix basis, like this?

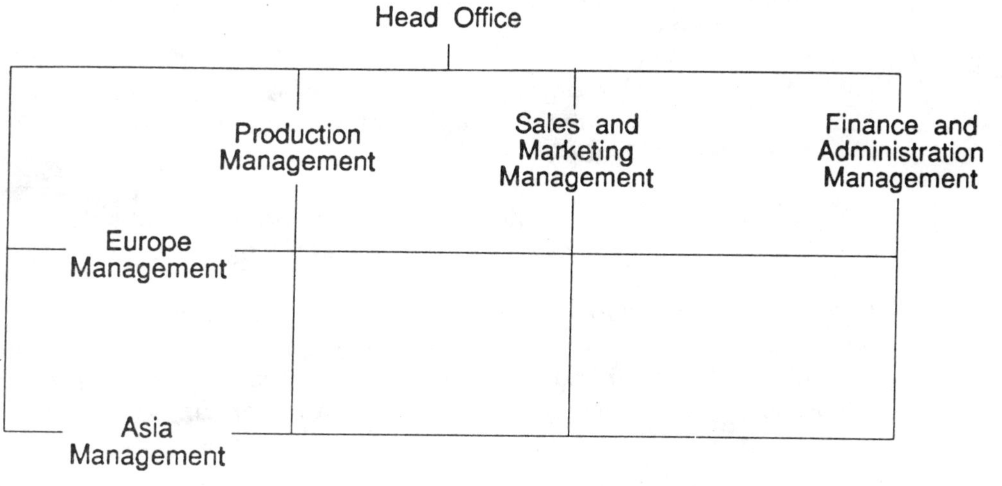

In a *matrix organisation structure*, somebody involved in production in Europe has to report equally to the European manager and to the production manager.

1.11 There are many arguments for and against each structure, and it is not our purpose to rehearse them here. However, they do have a direct effect on the accounting system. They determine:

(a) how information is collected, and by whom;
(b) how information is sent up the management hierarchy;
(c) how the information is aggregated and summarised.

1.12 In short, the information gives managers a 'view of the world', and the decisions they take are influenced by the information they receive about the organisation and the wider social environment in which it operates.

2. Accounting practices in different parts of the organisation

2.1 It was emphasised at the AAT Foundation stage that an organisation's accounting systems are affected by the nature of its business transactions and the sort of business it is.

(a) *Size.* A small business like a greengrocer will have a simple, cash-based accounting system, where the main accounting record will probably be the till roll. A large retail business, such as a chain of supermarkets, will have elaborate accounting systems of some technological complexity covering a large number of product ranges and sites.

(b) *Type of organisation.*

(i) A *service business* might need to record the time employees take on particular jobs. Accounting on a job or client basis might also be a feature of service businesses.

(ii) A *public sector organisation,* such as a government department, may be more concerned with the monitoring of expenditure against performance targets than recording revenue.

(iii) *A manufacturing company* will account both for unit sales and revenue, but needs to keep track of costs for decision-making purposes and so forth.

(c) *Organisation structure.* Accounting information can influence the structure of the organisation as the way in which accounting information is aggregated and summarised will reflect the reporting structure of the organisation. For example, in a business managed by area, accounts will be prepared on an area basis.

2.2 We can take the point in paragraph 2.1(c) a bit further to discuss the different accounting procedures in different areas of the organisation, on the bases outlined in section 1 of this chapter.

2.3 Remember, of course, that nearly all organisations will have some sort of functional reporting (eg revenue and production), but differ in the extent to which these form the basis for analysing the performance of the organisation at a higher level.

2.4 From this we can deduce that accounting procedures relate to both:

(a) collecting and *recording* accounting data; and
(b) providing and *reporting* accounting information.

Accounting procedures and geographical structure

2.5 An organisation's geographical structure poses a number of issues.

(a) It might be dispersed over several different countries in the world. Of course this might be true of a functional organisation as well, but we can deal with the special problems of accounting in different countries here.

(b) It might also be very decentralised in each country.

2.6 Taking the idea of an organisation spread over many different countries, and organised on an area basis, there are a number of ways in which the accounting procedures will be specifically affected by geography.

(a) *Different currencies.* The accounting system must accept the existence of foreign exchange.

(i) *Recording information.* Customers might want to pay in local currency, but it is possible that some elements of the product might be imported from another country, which have been paid for in a different currency.

(ii) *Reporting information.* If you wanted to compare the performance of a Belgian subsidiary company with that, say, of a subsidiary in Uruguay, you would have to firstly convert the results to a common currency (eg US dollar), and then isolate the difference thus caused by the changes in exchange rates alone.

(b) *Different legal and accounting requirements.* Many countries have completely different legal standards and requirements for recording accounting information. In some countries, the state issues a chart of accounts, down to minute detail. In the UK, on the other hand, companies can prepare accounts as they wish providing that those which are published for the benefit of shareholders conform to the Companies Act 1989: in other respects, the auditors assess whether the accounts give a true and fair view.

(c) *Different ways of doing business* (for example, the length of credit normally allowed), might mean that the emphasis of the accountant's job differs from country to country. In a country in which payments are made by cash, management of debtors is likely to take up far less time and effort than in a country where extended credit periods are the norm.

(d) There might be a number of factors relating to the political, economic, social and technological factors which can affect a country's accounting practices.

For example, some economies have had persistently high rates of inflation (Bolivia once had an inflation rate of 1000% per year, and some other countries still have inflation rates of over 100% per year). This can have a significant effect on pricing and on measuring performance.

Accounting procedures and product information

2.7 Information is sometimes reported on a product basis.

2.8 This involves both recording and reporting issues. This is because the functional activities of buying and selling, paying expenses and so forth are still the same, but the resulting information is grouped in a particular way to highlight revenue earned and costs incurred by a particular product. It is possible, then, that the product divisional basis will affect the coding system of the company.

2.9 Recording accounting information relating to revenue is usually easy. An individual product has a price, and it is relatively simple to record unit sales.

2.10 Costs are more problematic. After all, electricity expenses can be incurred making a number of products. Material might be divided between products. Some companies have elaborate coding systems which track individual items of expenditure and allocate them between products. (This is the purpose of *standard costing systems.*)

2.11 The importance of cost information is not just a feature of a product-division structured organisation, as this information is necessary for decision making in any organisation.

2.12 In a product-division structure, administrative functions are carried out by individual product divisions. However, there will still be some areas (eg research and development) which are shared by all divisions, and it might not be easy to allocate these common costs.

Accounting procedures and business functions

2.13 The following relates not just to functionally structured organisations, of course, as all organisations will have different procedures for sales and marketing, finance and accounting, and each department has different requirements for recording and reporting information.

2.14 For convenience, we can identify the following functions.

(a) *Sales and marketing.* This includes sales order processing, distribution, invoicing, credit control, and the management of debtors. In addition, on the marketing side, there is market research, advertising and so forth.

(b) *Production.* This can include purchasing, stock control of raw materials and finished goods, costing, capital equipment purchasing.

(c) *Finance and administration.* This includes the accounting function, treasury functions and so forth (which might also include credit control and the management of debtors and creditors). This function can also include personnel management.

(d) There are also business activities which perhaps cross the divide between various functions.

   (i) *Research and development* of new products and processes is mostly under the control of the production function. However, the marketing function is also concerned, as the marketing function perhaps determines what new products and services customers actually desire.

   (ii) *Personnel* issues might also be the concern of the individual functional departments. For example, the production function will know which staff are needed for particular jobs. In some instances, they will need to assess whether someone is technically competent.

(iii) *Information management.* Some organisations have an Information Director on the Board of Directors, to manage issues relating to information technology.

(iv) The functions of the organisation need to be integrated in some way, and their activities planned and coordinated. This might be achieved by the executive board, or there might be a small *corporate planning department* which will plan the direction the organisation should take, in consultation with the other functional departments.

Sales and marketing

2.15 If you have completed Unit 2 of the AAT Foundation stage, you will have some idea about the roles and procedures of the sales and marketing function.

2.16 The selling and marketing activity ensures that a commercial organisation earns its keep. Sales and marketing staff have a direct relationship with the customer. Quick and speedy satisfaction of customer orders is therefore a prime requirement for this function.

2.17 The accounting procedures will involve the following.

(a) Receipt of orders, perhaps over the phone. These requests from customers must be converted into a form suitable for input to the accounting system.

(b) Accounting information will thus relate to both:

(i) the order; and
(ii) the customer.

(c) The order must relate to a real item of product or service that the organisation provides. Details of availability might be found from stock records.

(d) Perhaps more effort will go into the accounting procedures relating to customers. For credit sales, orders and invoices are but the beginning of a *relationship* between supplier and customer.

(e) Many of the accounting procedures in the selling and marketing function will relate to the management of debtors.

(i) Matching invoiced amounts to orders, and cash receipts to invoiced amounts, so that the organisation receives money owed. To this end, it is possible that invoice lists will be prepared, and also the sales ledger reviewed, every month.

(ii) Reviewing unpaid amounts and chasing them. A regular procedure is the preparation of a debtors age analysis.

(iii) Estimating discounts and so forth is necessary to find the right amount to invoice.

(f) As well as recording information about sales and cash receipts, accounting information in the sales and marketing function might be information which managers use to take decisions, and to monitor the performance of the business eg:

(i) sales of particular products;
(ii) sales in a region or area;
(iii) the efficiency of the organisation of the sales function.

(g) Other accounting information in sales and marketing will relate to advertising expenditure, distribution, the calculation of commission for sales staff and so on. In these cases, accounting information is used for the purposes of cost control.

Production

2.18 Accounting procedures in the production function are probably more varied than in the sales function, simply because the variety of activities in developing a product or service is greater than in selling it.

2.19 *Purchasing goods and services.* Accounting procedures relating to purchases include:

(a) recording the purchase invoice in the appropriate expense and creditor accounts;
(b) ensuring that bills are paid when they fall due, or on the terms agreed with the supplier.

In some respects, the accounting procedures for creditors are similar to those for debtors, in terms of matching invoices with goods received. The total level of creditors must be kept under control.

2.20 *Stock control.* Stock control also affects the sales and marketing function in relation to finished goods, but also involves the *timing* of the purchases mentioned above, especially of raw materials. Enough stock, neither too much nor too little, must be available for production.

2.21 Production control is involved in monitoring the progress of production. Obviously, this is less of a problem with service industries, which do not make complex manufactured products. One of the purposes of production control is to ensure that materials costs are minimised, subject to required standards of quality.

2.22 Accounting procedures might involve a standard costing system, to keep track of costs and unexpected variances in prices and usage of the inputs necessary for production. (Recording cost information is the subject of Unit 6.)

2.23 Wages and salaries, as you should recall from the Foundation payroll unit, are an important part of the total costs an organisation incurs on production. However, the payroll is likely to be run by the accounts department. The production function will keep details such as timesheets, job sheets and so forth, on which the necessary information can be recorded for further use.

Finance and administration

2.24 The finance function runs the accounting systems for all the other functions, so that the debtors or sales ledger may well come into the remit of the accounts department.

2.25 The accounts department integrates the financial activities of the rest of the organisation, being specifically responsible for receipts and payments, for managing working capital (such as debtors and creditors) and trying to ensure that there is a sufficient flow of funds at the right times to ensure that bills can be paid.

2.26 The accounts department will also be involved in the preparation of the payroll of the business. Certain information is provided by the personnel department, and some by the production function (eg about hours worked), but the accounts department eventually ensures that people get paid.

2.27 The finance function is responsible for the management of the organisation's relationship with financial institutions such as banks.

2.28 In short, the accounts department work is comprised of the regular production of reports and accounting information (eg every month).

2.29 The accounts department also checks the integrity of accounting data. Control accounts help to ensure that errors or inconsistencies in accounting data are identified.

Summary

2.30 Accounting activities in an organisation relate to both the recording of information and the reporting of information.

(a) Recording transactions data is necessary so that all revenues, expenses, assets and liabilities are captured by the accounting system to give a representation in numerical form of the activities of the organisation.

(b) Reporting information is necessary to make more use of this basic data.

2.31 Accounting recording practices differ in different parts of the organisation, depending on the type of activities carried out in that part of the organisation.

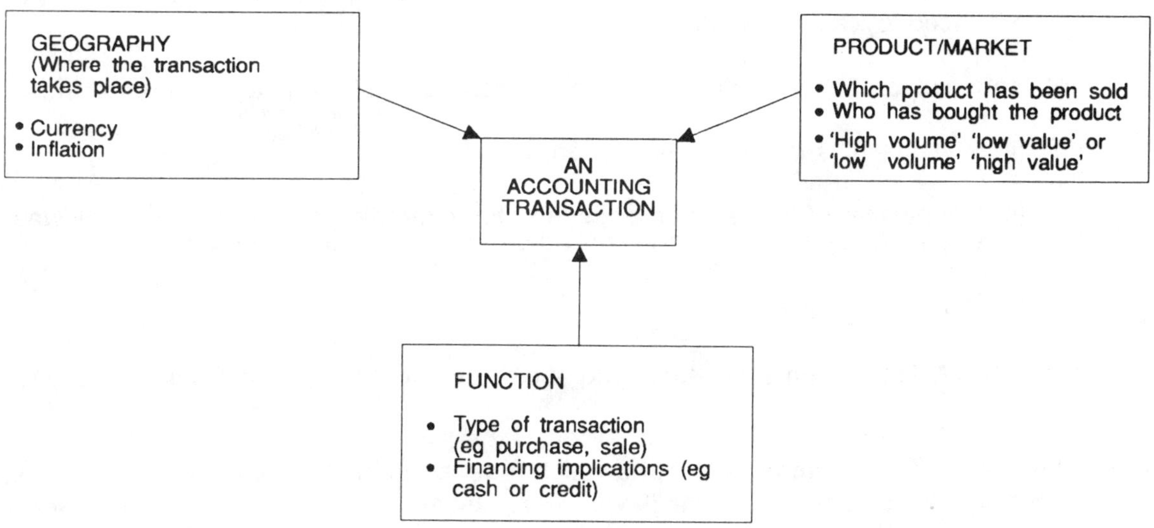

3. Internal and external reports

3.1 At Foundation stage, the basic documentation for an accounting system was covered (eg invoices, credit notes and timesheets) in the course of learning about credit transactions, cash transactions and payroll transactions. As we have seen above, this is, by and large, a matter of recording information.

3.2 The next question relates to what do you do with the information once it has been recorded, in the ledgers and various books of account. (What follows is an introduction to the subject of reporting.)

3.3 The basic accounting information is generally aggregated, summarised, and analysed into *reports.* You saw, briefly in the early parts of this chapter, some of the reports produced by the accounting system.

(a) A debtors age analysis provides a listing in which the age of the debts owing is made clear, so the organisation knows the proportion and the amount of debts 30 days old, 60 days old and so forth.

(b) Unit 5: *Preparing financial accounts* involves preparation of the trial balance of a trading enterprise. The trial balance is a summary of the balances on the nominal ledger, and from the trial balance is extracted the following two reports.

- (i) The *balance sheet* is like a 'snapshot' of what an organisation owns (assets), and what it owes (liabilities and capital) at a particular point in time.
- (ii) The *profit and loss account* is a statement describing what a business has earned and what expenses have been incurred in a particular period.

(c) A payroll summary, detailing how much a company has paid in wages, and how this cost is allocated between departments for a particular period is another type of report produced by an accounting system.

(d) You can probably think of even more reports, but here are some examples.

- (i) A list of sales revenue by area.
- (ii) Analysis of costs over a period (for example, how much in total was spent on telephone bills).
- (iii) Profit by division.
- (iv) A list of items in stock and their valuation to give a total value.

3.4 There are a large number of reports which must be submitted to external agencies, too. This concept will be familiar to you if you were assessed at the Foundation stage.

(a) There are a large number of returns to be sent to the Inland Revenue, in relation to PAYE and deductions for National Insurance.

(b) Returns have to be sent to HM Customs & Excise for Value Added Tax. (The returns you send to the VAT office are assessed in Unit 8: *Preparing VAT returns.*)

(c) Every year, a limited company must prepare financial statements for submission to shareholders. These financial statements comprise a balance sheet, a profit and loss account, and a statement detailing the flows of cash in and out of the organisation.

The rules for preparing financial statements for publication to shareholders are quite strict. This is so that management have as little latitude as possible to massage the numbers to overstate the organisation's performance.

Also, financial statements provide necessary information to debtors and creditors of the business. (Do you remember that a limited liability company is one whereby the owners are not liable for the debts of the business?)

(d) If a business has borrowings from the bank, especially if they are significant, then the bank will want to see proof that the business is generating enough cash to pay interest on its loans. A bank might wish to see cash flow statements on a regular basis.

(e) Some kinds of organisations are required to file special returns on a regular basis to the authorities. This is particularly true of banks and financial services companies. Banks must report details of assets and liabilities and so forth to the Bank of England to assess their solvency. Other companies, for example those which sell investment schemes or which give 'financial advice', must report to a 'Self Regulatory Organisation'.

3.5 The requirements of these reports can sometimes be quite onerous, especially as the consequences for filling them in wrongly can be quite severe. (For example, there are heavy penalties for errors in VAT returns.)

3.6 There are advantages, then, in an accounting system in which these external reporting requirements are embedded in the way that information is collected and treated, and the ease with which it can be manipulated.

3.7 In practice, this means that when the accounting system is devised, a number of the following options might be taken.

(a) Ledger accounts can be set up for those assets, liabilities and items of income or expenditure which need to be reported.

(b) Memorandum accounts can be establish to record this information specifically (for example, the memorandum sales ledger details individual debtor accounts).

(c) An appropriate coding system is devised, especially in a computer system, so that the relevant data can be easily extracted from the accounting records.

3.8 It is possible, however, that these reporting requirements, especially if they are complex, will not be embedded in the accounting system. Moreover, information of a non-accounting nature might also be required to complete the report.

3.9 In many cases, it is possible that the information for the reports will be separately extracted from the accounting records and relevant files, and a model made. In a computer system, this will mean that data extracted from the records might have to be input manually into a spreadsheet model so that it can be manipulated in the right format.

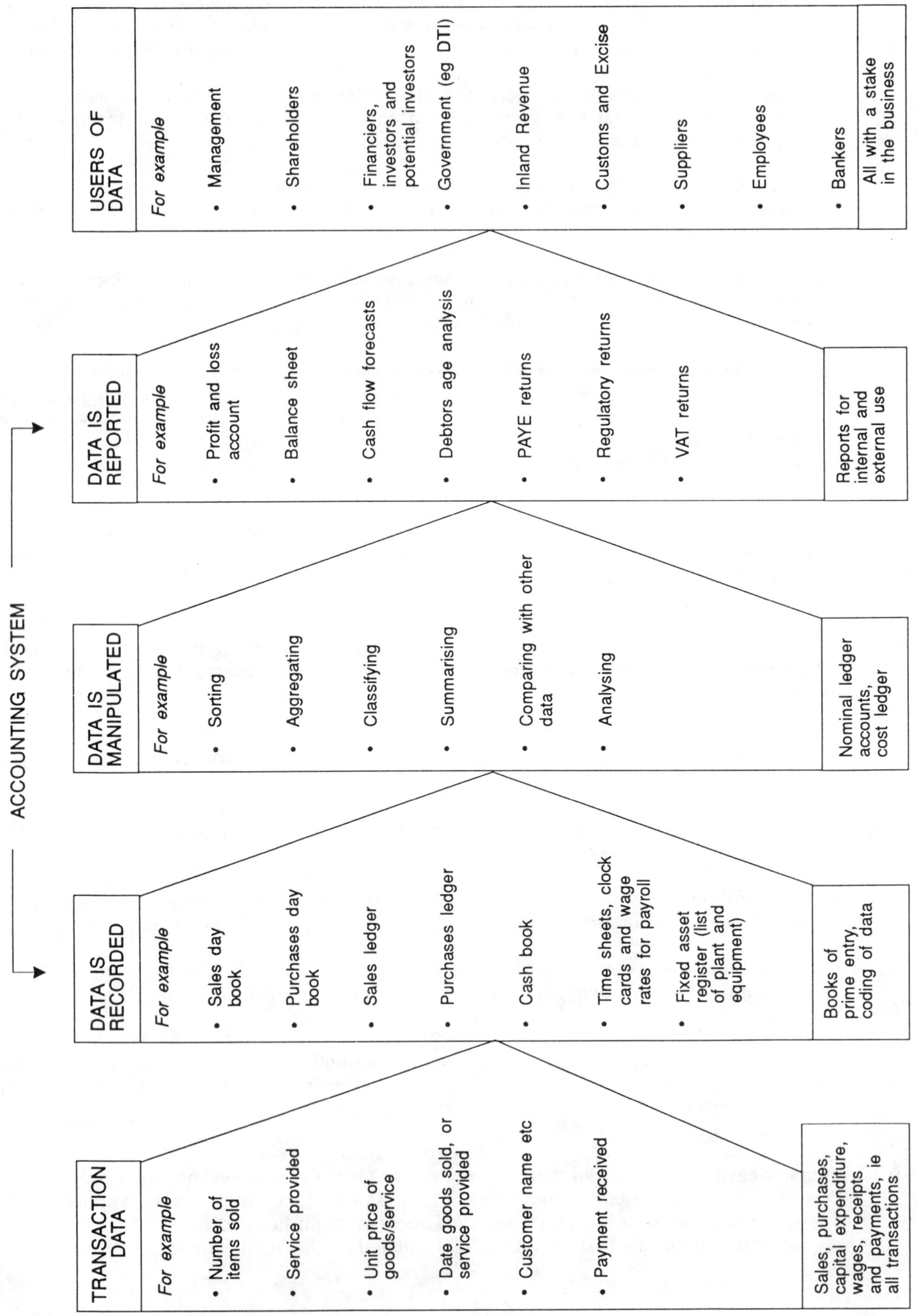
ACCOUNTING SYSTEM
TRANSACTION DATA
For example
• Number of items sold
• Service provided
• Unit price of goods/service
• Date goods sold, or service provided
• Customer name etc
• Payment received
Sales, purchases, capital expenditure, wages, receipts and payments, ie all transactions
DATA IS RECORDED
For example
• Sales day book
• Purchases day book
• Sales ledger
• Purchases ledger
• Cash book
• Time sheets, clock cards and wage rates for payroll
• Fixed asset register (list of plant and equipment)
Books of prime entry, coding of data
DATA IS MANIPULATED
For example
• Sorting
• Aggregating
• Classifying
• Summarising
• Comparing with other data
• Analysing
Nominal ledger accounts, cost ledger
DATA IS REPORTED
For example
• Profit and loss account
• Balance sheet
• Cash flow forecasts
• Debtors age analysis
• PAYE returns
• Regulatory returns
• VAT returns
Reports for internal and external use
USERS OF DATA
For example
• Management
• Shareholders
• Financiers, investors and potential investors
• Government (eg DTI)
• Inland Revenue
• Customs and Excise
• Suppliers
• Employees
• Bankers
All with a stake in the business

3.10 So, we can surmise that the problems of reporting for external agencies are as follows:

(a) identifying the data in the first place, as it falls from the transaction itself into the accounting system;

(b) tagging the data as it flows round the accounting system;

(c) pulling this data out of the accounting system, together with other data of the same type;

(d) aggregating, analysing and rearranging the data in a format suitable for the report.

Key points in this chapter

- This chapter has described some of the variety and types of organisation.
- Accounting systems have two main purposes:
    - to record information relevant to business transactions;
    - to report this information to management and other interested parties in a variety of formats.

For practice on the points covered in this chapter, you should now attempt the Exercises in Session 1 of the Cost Accounting II Workbook

2. Business and accounting information

1. **Business information**
2. **Accountants as information providers**
3. **Management information systems**
4. **The qualities of accounting information**

1. Business information

Identifying the information you need

1.1 Whether you are preparing reports for the internal purposes of your organisation or preparing reports, returns or forms for outside agencies, you will need to be able to identify the information which is relevant to the requirements of what you are doing. Various questions may arise. What is meant by information? What is the purpose of information? What is good information?

1.2 The process of assessment for which you are preparing may be based on your *receiving* a certain amount of information from the assessors, *selecting* essential and relevant items from that information, and manipulating those items to formulate a communication of your own which is *sent* - supposedly - to other people in the given situation, and - in fact - to the assessor. If you are assessed directly on your performance in your workplace, then the process is essentially similar, except that the communication which you prepare and on which you are assessed is sent to the people for whom it is actually intended.

1.3 This Tutorial Text works on the same basis. You may *receive* all the information that this text offers you, but it will be of little practical value to you, unless you understand, select, record, remember and use that information to develop useable skills. You must make it your own, ie 're-process' it for your own purposes.

1.4 The ways in which information is presented and the ways people select information can have important implications for which pieces of information they use. Some readers of this Tutorial Text will probably begin their study of Unit 7 by going to the start of Chapter 1 on page 3. If they do, they will have missed some introductory notes on the Unit which are included at page (vii). (If you did miss these points, you are advised to have a look at them now.) Other readers will review the introductory pages before starting Chapter 1 and will therefore note the introductory points covered there.

The purpose of the information

1.5 The information you need will depend upon the purpose for which the information is needed. The manager or supervisor may be required to make reports and returns of various kinds. Some reports and returns may be required by parts of the organisation for which the manager works. Examples include a branch expected to make returns to its head office, and a company in a group which is required to make reports and returns to the 'parent' company or 'holding' company which owns it. The chief purpose of these internal reports and returns is to help in making business decisions.

1.6 Other reports and returns are required by external agencies or organisations. For example, in the UK, regular returns must be made, on time, to HM Customs & Excise by VAT-registered businesses so that it can decide how much VAT (value added tax) the business is liable to pay over. (Preparing VAT returns is covered in Part B of this Tutorial Text.) Someone applying for a government grant will need to get together data of various kinds, perhaps including forecast data about how a business is expected to progress in the future, to support its application for a grant. A trade association to which a business chooses to belong might expect regular returns to be made by members so that it can be sure that the member business is continuing to meet its conditions of membership.

1.7 From the point of view of the manager or supervisor, the purpose of collecting together and presenting the information needed by the external organisations is mainly to *comply* with the requirements of that organisation, with regulations or with the law.

Defining 'information' and 'data'

1.8 'Information' is 'telling': by extension it also means 'what is told' – items of knowledge, news or whatever.

1.9 You will probably have heard the word 'data' (plural of 'datum') used in scientific or business contexts (as in 'data processing'). Data are the raw materials (facts, figures etc) which become *information*, when they are processed so as to have meaning for the person who receives them, leading to action or decision of some kind. The processing itself may involve classifying, selecting, sorting, analysing, calculating and various means of communicating.

1.10 For example, train departure times are 'data': a schedule which groups those times according to destination and lists them in order of departure is 'information' for a potential passenger on one of the trains.

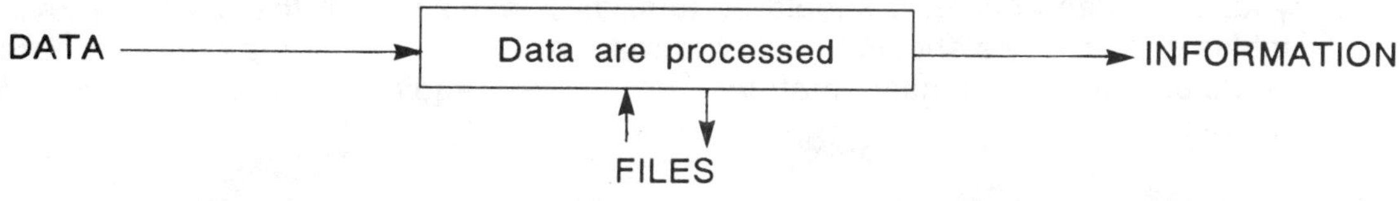

(Files are used to provide data for processing and to store data/information after processing)

What is good information?

1.11 There are some general principles as to what makes good information. Good information will:

(a) be relevant to a user's needs.

This means:

(i) *identifying the user.* Information must be suited and sent to the right person, ie one who needs it to do his job, make a decision etc;

(ii) *getting the purpose right.* Information is effective only when it helps a user to act or make a decision. If you ask someone the way to the nearest train station, you do not expect or need to be told that the weather is fine, or even that there is a very interesting train station in another town some miles away;

(iii) *getting the volume right.* Information must be complete for its purpose, ie not omitting any necessary item: it should also be no *more* in volume that the user will find helpful or be able to take in.

Consider information as the answer to a particular enquiry or problem, anything else being strictly 'icing on the cake', and you will not fall into the trap of irrelevance.

(b) *be accurate within the user's needs.* Downright falsehood and error are fatal to effective communication of any sort. It may, however, be impossible - or at least time-consuming and expensive - to gather, process and assimilate information that is minutely detailed. An approximation or an average figure is often sufficient to our needs. If you asked: 'Is it hot in Brighton in August?' because you were planning a holiday, you would be happy to hear that it 'averaged 78°F': you would waste time and effort poring over a sheet of daily temperature readings for the last five years.

(c) *inspire the user's confidence.* Information should not give the user reason to mistrust, disbelieve or ignore it, eg because it is out-of-date, badly presented or from an unreliable source. It should be *verifiable* by reference, or by application (which risks finding out the hard way, if the information is incorrect).

(d) *be timely.* Information must be readily available within the time period which makes it useful: ie it must be in the right place at the right time. A beautifully researched and presented report will be of no value if it arrives on a manager's desk too late to influence his decision on the matter in hand. A report or return to an outside agency which misses the specified date for submission may be valueless, or may incur sanctions or penalties.

(e) *be appropriately communicated.* Information will lose its value if it is not clearly communicated to the user in a suitable format and through a suitable medium. For example, your words and symbols should be familiar or explained to the user; the layout of text, tables and graphics should be easy to read; a telephone call may not be appropriate for complex or confidential matters, or those requiring written records (eg legal documents).

(f) *be cost-effective.* Good information should not cost more than it is worth. Gathering, storing, retrieving and communicating an item of information may require expense of time, energy and resources: if the expense is greater than the potential value of the item, re-consider whether the information is necessary to such a degree of accuracy, completeness etc or even necessary at all.

1.12 Information is the life blood of an organisation, flowing through it and prompting actions and decisions: without information, no-one in an organisation could take a single effective action. As a simple example, giving an order to a subordinate is a flow of information: the manager or supervisor gathers data about a problem, 'processes' it to decide what needs to be done and then communicates his or her decision as an order to a subordinate.

Business information

1.13 *Business information* is any information which relates to the organisation and activities of one or more businesses. This definition includes:

(a) information about 'business' in general. This is based on analysis of the nature and philosophy of businesses, their organisation and activities;

(b) information generated by and about each organisation.

Demand for information

1.14 There is a constant demand for information within the organisation, and also from outside. *Internal* demand comes from every member of the organisation, and management in particular, for:

(a) records of past and current transactions to be stored for confirmation, later analysis etc;

(b) routine information on which to base current operations and decisions (for example, the information on a customer order dictates how many items, and of what sort, must be supplied from stock, delivery and payment arrangements etc);

(c) information about past trends and current operations on which to base planning and decision-making. For example, the past rate at which raw materials were consumed by a production process would dictate the frequency and amount of stock orders in the future; trends in the market, ie customer demand for a product or service, would indicate the area, level and pricing of an organisation's activity;

(d) information about performance to compare with plans, budgets, forecasts etc for the purposes of *control,* ie checking for and correcting errors and shortcomings.

Types (c) and (d) are the main types of information required in preparing periodic performance reports for management.

1.15 The quantity and quality of financial information provided to managers depend on their level in the organisation's structure.

(a) *Strategic information* is needed by senior managers who are involved in setting objectives for the organisation as a whole. In an organisation with various branches or subsidiaries, senior managers will need information on the efficiency and profitability of each of them if it is considering, for example, how to reduce the organisation's operations.

(b) *Tactical information* will be needed by middle managers who are looking to ensure that the organisation's existing resources and structure are used efficiently. Middle managers will require financial information on the seven factories in order to decide how to improve performance in all parts of the organisation, for example by introducing new control measures.

(c) *Operational information.* 'Front-line' managers such as works supervisors and foremen require information on the day-to-day operations of the organisation. Financial information will be required on direct and indirect costs, idle time and overtime costs.

1.16 There is also *external* demand for information from various sources.

(a) Firstly, there are others involved in the business's transactions, such as customers, suppliers, or sub-contractors, require instructions or requests eg orders, invoices, acknowledgements etc.

(b) Parties interested in the financial performance of the organisation include the owners (shareholders), investors and creditors (those to whom the firm owes money, such as banks) require information on the financial position of the organisation. Insurers of a business may also require detailed information to be entered on proposal forms (this can include accounting information, to help in assessing claims for loss of revenue).

(c) External information-collecting agencies require information for surveys, or for their own activities. Trade associations conduct voluntary surveys of members (for example, of wages and room occupancy figures in the hotel trade). The Department of Trade and Industry requires company accounts to be filed; returns have to be made to the Inland Revenue for the purposes of assessing tax and National Insurance contributions; value added tax (VAT) is administered by the Excise authorities, and so on.

(d) In many industries, regulatory bodies have powers to require financial or non-financial information from organisations. Non-financial information has to be supplied on working practices to the Health and Safety Executive; information on employees to the Training Commission and its agencies; variations in usage of buildings and new works of any kind have to be notified to local government planning departments; proposed changes in the structure or operation of the company which affect employment activities and prospects will normally be discussed with the appropriate trade unions. In the financial services industry, firms are required to report to the regulatory organisation dealing with their sector of the industry. All of these are regulatory agencies aimed at stopping the company from ruining the environment, being irresponsible towards its employees and creditors and generally behaving in a 'selfish' way.

(e) Grant-awarding agencies require information to support grant applications. Examples of current schemes are the Business Start-Up Scheme available through Training and Enterprise Councils (TECs) and the Loan Guarantee Scheme - not, strictly speaking, a grant scheme - available through banks. Some regional help and help with consultancy costs can also be applied for through the Department of Trade and Industry (see the box below on the Enterprise Initiative).

The main types of external organisations requiring reports and returns are information-collecting agencies, regulatory bodies and grant awarding agencies.

Sources of business information

1.17 *Internal sources*

(a) A lot of data is gathered by an organisation in the course of its business. It will appear on the various documents used by the firm: invoices, orders, delivery notes, job cards etc. This involves formal systems for collecting or measuring data - measuring output, sales, costs, cash receipts and payments, purchases, stock turnover etc. In other words, there must be established procedures for what data is collected, how frequently, by whom, by what methods etc and how it is processed, filed and/or communicated as information.

(b) An organisation will also take advantage of and indeed rely on informal communication between managers and staff (by word-of-mouth, at meetings, by telephone).

1.18 *External sources*

Obtaining information from outside the organisation might be formally delegated to particular individuals, eg the tax or legal expert, the Market Research manager, the secretary who has to make travel arrangements; it might also be 'informal'. Informal gathering of information from outside sources goes on all the time, consciously or unconsciously, because the employees of an organisation learn what is going on in the world around them - from newspapers, television, experience or other people.

The Enterprise Initiative

The Enterprise Initiative is a package of measures offered by the Department of Trade and Industry (DTI) to businesses in the UK. It includes regional selective grant assistance. Application for help is normally made by contacting the nearest DTI Regional Office, the Scottish Office or the Welsh Office.

The Regional initiative

- *Regional Selective Assistance*
  Selective assistance is available for investment projects undertaken by firms in 'Assisted Areas'.

  The project must be commercially viable, create or safeguard employment, demonstrate a need for assistance and offer a distinct regional and national benefit.

  The amount of grant will be negotiated as the minimum necessary to ensure the project goes ahead.

- *Regional Enterprise Grants*
  If you are a small firm employing fewer than 25 in one of the Development Areas, there is a scheme specially geared to helping you expand and diversify. Regional enterprise grants can help finance viable projects for:

  - investment - grants of 15% of the cost of fixed assets up to a maximum of £15,000 are available

  - innovation - grants of 50% of the agreed project cost up to a maximum grant of £25,000 are available.

Support services

Support services available through the DTI include the following.

- Business information, including banks of data on products, industries and overseas market. *Business monitors* are available (for a small charge), including production, sales, trade and other industrial statistics for each sector of British industry.

- The Small Firms Service (funded by the TECs), providing free advice and information throughout the country on a variety of business problems.

1.19 An organisation can 'tap into' data banks compiled by other organisations: the Central Statistical Office is one example. The DTI is another. Various publications - specific trade journals or more general magazines such as *Management Today* - can also be helpful in judging trends and setting standards. A business can also employ a research organisation such as MORI or Gallup to carry out an investigation into market trends or other matters of interest.

2. Accountants as information providers

2.1 The functions of the financial accountant include communicating information. Although financial accounting is also concerned with operational matters, such as receiving and paying cash, borrowing and repaying loans, granting credit to customers and chasing late payers in the debt collection process, it is largely a process of keeping data records and providing information.

(a) The annual profit and loss account and balance sheet contains information for shareholders, management, the investing public, government, employees and creditors etc.

(b) The accounting records provide the basic data from which the financial accounts are prepared. They also provide information to allow the financial accounting function to operate - eg information about which creditors need paying, which debts are overdue, how much unused credit a customer has etc.

(c) Accountants also try and make the numbers they present meaningful to the recipient.

Financial accounting therefore consists of a mixture of 'line operations', keeping data records and providing information.

2.2 *Cost and management accounting* on the other hand is concerned entirely with providing information in the form of periodic performance reports or special 'one-off' reports, for example:

(a) information about product costs and profitability;

(b) information about departmental costs and profitability;

(c) cost information to help with pricing decisions;

(d) budgets and standard costs;

(e) actual performance measured in accounting terms, and variances between actual and budget;

(f) information to help with the evaluation of one-off decisions, such as capital expenditure decisions.

2.3 With whom do accountants communicate? Management accountants communicate mainly with other managers. Financial accountants provide information about the organisation to the 'outside world'. Users of accounting information who are outside the organisation's management were identified in *The Corporate Report* (1975) of the Accounting Standards Steering Committee as:

(a) equity investors (ie shareholders);

(b) loan creditors (such as debenture holders, banks);

(c) employees;

(d) financial analysts and advisers including journalists, economists, statisticians, trade unions, stockbrokers and credit rating agencies;

(e) business contacts - notably customers and trade creditors and suppliers;

(f) the government;

(g) the general public.

3. Management information systems

Users of accounting information

3.1 For accountants and cost and management accountants in particular, among the users of information are other managers, who need information to help them plan and control the resources of the organisation in the most effective and efficient way, so as to enable the organisation to achieve its objectives.

Information systems in an organisation

3.2 A management information system (MIS) has been defined as 'an information system designed to supply managers with the information needed to plan, organise, direct staff and control the operations of the organisation'. (*Accounting Information and Data Processing Systems*, Bhaskar and Housden).

3.3 It is the task of the accountant to provide information to others, in reports and statements etc, and communication, of course, is the process of providing information to others. It has been suggested that there are several large and fairly distinct management information systems within an organisation (although they do overlap and are interrelated). These are:

(a) the financial information system, with which we are mainly concerned in this Tutorial Text;

(b) the logistics information system (concerned with the physical flow of goods through production and to the customer, or the physical provision of services to the customer);

(c) the personnel information system (concerned with employees and employee records).

3.4 There might also be a distinct research and development information system, and a marketing information system and so on. However, the financial information system is essential to help managers to plan and control the activities of their organisation, because either:

(a) the objectives of the organisation will be financial ones (perhaps to maximise profits or return on investment); or

(b) the objectives of the organisation will be subject to financial constraints (for example a hospital service aims to provide patient care, subject to the restrictions of what it can afford within its budget allowance).

3.5 As you should appreciate, accounting information is used by managers throughout an organisation, and accountants are important providers of management information. It has been suggested that an organisation's accounting systems are at the core of its MIS.

In what form might accounting information be communicated?

3.6 Information can be communicated in a variety of ways, including visually, verbally and electronically (by computer system).

3.7 It may be helpful to think of a formal accounting information system as taking the form of a series of reports and accounting statements. In cost and management accounting, these would include (some of which are used in later examples provided in this Tutorial Text):

(a) cost statements;
(b) product profit statements;
(c) budgets;
(d) standard cost statements;
(e) operating statements, comparing actual results against budget;
(f) forecast profit and cost statements;
(g) breakeven statements and contribution statements;
(h) investment appraisal and payback forecasts for capital expenditure decision-making;
(i) job cost estimates.

3.8 Financial accounting information is extracted from the financial accounting records, and results (for companies) in the annual report and accounts, which is produced for shareholders. In the case of large companies, a copy of the report and accounts must be filed with the Registrar of Companies, and so the financial accounting information is made available to a wider public.

3.9 Some external information user groups have access to more detailed information about business organisations than that provided in the annual report and accounts prepared by the financial accountant.

(a) The government's tax officials have a right to certain information for the purpose of assessing the tax payable.

(b) A bank can usually insist on information from a business, such as a cash budget, before agreeing to lend it money or grant an overdraft facility. A bank will also have its own records of the cash receipts and payments and current bank balance of its business customers.

3.10 Some companies provide reports for the benefit of employees. These *employee reports* are often a simplified version of the annual report and accounts, expressed in terms that non-management as well as management employees can understand. They are designed to show employees how the organisation has been performing, and to indicate what consequences the good or bad performance has for employees and employment prospects.

The major significance of employee reports is that companies which produce them recognise their moral obligation to provide financial information to their employees, and that employees, not just shareholders, have an interest in the well-being of their organisation.

4. The qualities of accounting information

The purpose of information

4.1 As we have already seen, information needs to have a purpose.

(a) Financial accounting information helps external users to assess management performance and the prospects of the organisation. (Management must give account of itself to the organisation's owners, hence the principal need for the annual report and accounts).

(b) Management accounting information must also have a purpose, and accounting reports should be produced with this end in view.

4.2 Communication has the general purpose of stimulating change, or enabling inter-group activities to take place. If you think about it, any communication that does not do one of these two things would be useless and purposeless.

4.3 Communication that stimulates change involves giving someone an item of information that makes him or her take a decision, for example a planning decision or a control decision, a decision about what to do next or how to deal with someone.

4.4 Communication that enables inter-group activities to take place involves work that is done by two or more people in conjunction. One must let the other know what he or she is doing or wants to be done. At a simple level, for example, the marketing department might set itself a target of selling 10,000 units of product X: to achieve this target, it must let the production department know what it wants to sell, to ensure that 10,000 units will be made available from the production line.

The quality of information

4.5 For accounting reports to have value, they must act as a spur to management. Managers should take planning or control decisions to earn favourable reports (or avoid bad ones), and when significant adverse reports occur, managers must investigate them with a view to taking control action.

Reports will not provide an impetus for management action unless the information contained in them possesses certain qualities. We discussed qualities of information in general earlier in this chapter. These qualities or attributes are explained with particular reference to accounting information in the following paragraphs.

4.6 The quality of communication is important because:

(a) people need to know what is expected of them - ie they need a goal or target, such as a budget target or a performance standard to reach;

(b) they also need to know how they are doing - ie how their actual performance is measuring up to their target.

Good quality information about targets and plans, and reliable feedback of actual results, are essential for this planning and control cycle to work properly.

4.7 *The Corporate Report*, a publication which argued that companies do not provide enough information about themselves, listed the desirable characteristics of accounting reports. Such reports must be:

(a) relevant
(b) understandable
(c) reliable
(d) complete
(e) objective
(f) timely
(g) comparable

These qualities are appropriate both to information for management and information for 'external groups'.

4.8 *Objectivity*. Accounting reports ought as far as possible to be objective. Any subjective opinions that are formulated should be made by the information users, not the information providers. For example, a variance statement will indicate differences between actual costs and budgeted costs, and any variances that exceed a certain amount (eg 10% of budget): however, managers responsible for planning or control decisions must decide whether these reported variances are too high or not.

4.9 *Comparability*. Accounting information, especially information about return on investment, costs and profits, should enable users to make suitable comparisons. For example:

(a) comparing actual costs against budget;

(b) comparing actual return on capital employed (ROCE) against target, or last year's ROCE;

(c) comparing the forecast return from an investment against the target or cut- off rate;

(d) comparing one company's profits, dividends and earnings per share against another's.

For information to provide comparability, it ought to be prepared on a consistent basis. (This is one of the reasons for having Accounting Standards). Return on capital employed (ROCE) is a performance measure to which we shall return to in a later chapter.

Possible conflicts

4.10 An accounting report is not an end in itself; it is a means towards the end of effective management action. Unfortunately, many of the desirable attributes listed above can be in conflict with each other.

(a) Information should be accurate, but it should also be provided in time for managers to make decisions. A report which is produced in haste to meet a deadline might be so inaccurate that it ceases to be sufficiently reliable.

(b) Reports should be clear and comprehensible to their users, but they must also be comprehensive. If the information in a report covers complex topics it would be inadvisable to 'keep it simple'. Managers should be educated to understand the information they receive, and information should not necessarily be downgraded to the assumed level of comprehension of its users.

(c) Accuracy, comprehensiveness, timeliness (eg using computers) are desirable attributes of information which involve costs. The need to control costs, and ensure that benefits exceed costs incurred, conflicts with all these aspects.

4.11 The attitude of non-accounting managers to accounting reports is often hostile. Accountants might be regarded as interfering busybodies, or even as a group whose purpose is to create more work and find fault with others.

(a) Budget preparation might be regarded as a pointless, time-consuming exercise that the accountants and senior managers impose on other managers.

(b) Budgetary control reports and other performance reports can show how badly a manager is doing, and so be a weapon which senior managers use in getting their subordinates to try harder.

4.12 The response of people to the information they are given depends both on how the information is communicated to them, and how good the information is.

(a) It is much better to communicate directly with the person who will use the information. For example, regular information about the labour productivity in Section X should be sent direct to the supervisor of Section X: the supervisor might resent receiving the information through his boss or his boss's boss.

(b) Regular reports will enable any control action to be taken before the situation gets out of hand, but reports that are too frequent can be irritating as well as unnecessary. Information to help with planning decisions obviously needs to be received in time for the decisions to be taken.

(c) Information should contain all the qualities referred to earlier. Accountants should be wary in particular of making information unclear or misleading.

(d) Information should be given without the suggestion of a threat. This is important in the case of control reports. Reports on actual performance compared with target will provoke defensive and hostile reactions from the managers receiving them if they believe that poor results will be automatically blamed on them. Getting blamed is all too easily associated with loss of promotion prospects or loss of bonuses.

Key points in this chapter

- The demand for business information comes from within the organisation, from external organisations and from individuals on a personal level.
- In a business environment, reports and returns may need to be presented to other parts of the organisation or to external organisations. We need to identify, collate and present the information in a way which best fits the purpose of the report or return. Often, an internal report or return will be needed to help in making business decisions. In reports or returns to external organisations, compliance with laws, regulations or requirements is often what is most important.
- Sources of business information comprise internal sources and external sources, including data banks compiled specifically to meet business information needs.
- Good information is relevant to a user's needs, accurate within the user's needs, well presented, timely, appropriate in style and layout, and cost-effective.
- Data of various kinds provide the raw material for the process of publishing information. Collecting quantitative data and presenting them in a useful form is aided by various techniques in statistics, to which we turn in the next chapter.
- Much accounting work involves communicating information for others to use and consequently accountants need to develop (or be taught) communication skills.
- Information handling and communication skills include:
  - an ability to make full use of computer systems where appropriate to obtain or provide useful information;
  - an ability to recognise that communication is a two-way process, and that it is not simply a matter of handing out information to others;
  - an ability to collect data accurately and to communicate information in a clear and intelligible form.

For practice on the points covered in this chapter you should now attempt the Exercises in Session 2 of the Cost Accounting II Workbook

3. Statistical information

1. **Using statistics**

2. **Populations and types of data**

3. **Sources of statistical data**

1. Using statistics

The meaning of 'statistics'

1.1 Data in the form of figures may be called quantitative data or 'statistics'. In a business environment, all sorts of quantitative data may be available to a manager or supervisor, for example on production levels, costs or sales. On their own, the numbers are unlikely to mean very much. How can a manager make sense of the numbers? This depends partly on the purpose for which the information is needed.

1.2 Note that the word 'statistics' has three meanings.

(a) Firstly, it is used to describe a group of figures. For example, figures relating to a country's imports and exports are often referred to as 'trade statistics' and the figures kept by cricket commentators on past matches are called 'statistics'.

(b) Secondly, it is used as an abbreviation for 'statistical method' which means the methods by which data (that is, *numbers* obtained as a result of counting or measuring something) are presented. The importance of statistical method is that it enables a large mass of meaningless data to be condensed into a more readily understandable form.

(c) Thirdly, it has come to mean the way in which the data are interpreted, once they have been presented in a satisfactory form.

1.3 'Statistics' therefore covers collecting data, presenting them in a useful form and interpreting the data. Knowledge of statistical techniques is important to you not just because you can use these techniques to present information in reports and returns. It is also important because you will often need to interpret information which uses statistical techniques.

The use and abuse of statistics

1.4 Statistics should be compiled only if they have a purpose. If they are not going to be used for anything, then there is no point in having them.

(a) The purpose of having particular statistics ought to be established.
(b) A statistical measure should be selected which achieves this purpose.

1.5 There is a danger that:

(a) statistical data will be collected and analysed in a confusing and unclear way;

(b) the statistical measures that are selected will not be suitable for the purpose for which they are being used; and so

(c) statistics will be interpreted incorrectly, and used to draw incorrect conclusions.

The incorrect use and interpretation of statistics is an abuse of statistics, which you should learn to recognise and to avoid.

Example: using statistics

1.6 Study the following statements, and set out the errors in them.

(a) 30% of students taking accountancy examinations pass. 60% of law students pass solicitors' examinations. Clearly, there are more qualified solicitors than qualified accountants.

(b) 30,000 French citizens can speak Russian, and 60,000 Russians can speak French. Clearly, French is more widely spoken in Russia than Russian in France.

Solution

1.7 Statement (a) shows how percentages without actual total figures can be misleading. If 10,000 accountancy students take examinations each year and just 2,000 law students take solicitors' examinations, the actual numbers becoming qualified each year would be 3,000 accountants and 1,200 lawyers: more accountants than lawyers, not the other way round.

Statement (b) shows how total figures without averages or percentages can be misleading. If the 30,000 French citizens speaking Russian come from a population of 50,000,000, whereas the 60,000 Russians speaking French come from a population of 200,000,000 we could argue that since a *larger proportion* of French citizens speak Russian than Russians speak French, Russian is more widely spoken in France than French in Russia.

2. Populations and types of data

Defining the population

2.1 A statistical survey involves collecting statistics to help answer a question. For example, a cat food manufacturer might want to find out what proportion of cat owners use his particular brand. You might think that the first step to take in conducting such a survey is to collect data: that is, to ask people what they feed their cats. But in fact there are quite a few things to think about first, otherwise a survey can go wrong from the start. If a survey does start off on the wrong track, the data subsequently collected and the conclusions subsequently drawn will be useless.

2.2 A famous example of this occurred years ago in the United States, when somebody was asked to conduct an opinion poll (which is a form of statistical survey) on whether the next president was likely to be Democrat or Republican. The survey was carried out, but in a wrong way. The surveyor *telephoned* people, and far more Republicans than Democrats had telephones. The survey was useless, because it had not been planned properly.

2.3 The reason why the opinion poll turned out so badly, was that the *population* for the survey had not been defined properly. In statistics, the word 'population' refers to the entire collection of items being considered. The opinion poll should have used the population 'all Americans of voting age', whereas it actually used the population 'all Americans with a telephone'.

Attributes and variables

2.4 The data gathered for a particular purpose may be of several types. The first major distinction is between *attributes* and *variables*.

(a) An attribute is something an object has either got or not got. It cannot be measured. For example, an individual is either male or female. There is no measure of *how* male or *how* female somebody is: the sex of a person is an attribute.

(b) A variable is something which can be measured. For example, the height of a person can be measured according to some scale (such as centimetres).

2.5 Variables can be further classified as discrete or continuous.

(a) *Discrete* variables can only take specific values. The range of possible values is split into a series of steps. For example, the number of goals scored by a football team may be 0, 1, 2 or 3 but it cannot be 1.2 or 2.1.

(b) *Continuous* variables may take on any value. They are measured rather than counted. For example, it may be considered sufficient to measure the heights of a number of people to the nearest cm but there is no reason why the measurements should not be made to the nearest 1/1,000 cm. Two people who are found to have the same height to the nearest cm could almost certainly be distinguished if more precise measurements were taken.

Primary data and secondary data

2.6 The data used in a statistical survey, whether variables or attributes, can be either primary data or secondary data.

(a) Primary data are data collected especially for the purpose of whatever survey is being conducted. *Raw data* are primary data which have not been processed at all, but are still just (for example) a list of numbers.

(b) Secondary data are data which have already been collected elsewhere, for some other purpose, but which can be used or adapted for the survey being conducted.

2.7 An advantage of using primary data is that the investigator knows where the data came from, the circumstances under which they were collected, and any limitations or inadequacies in the data.

2.8 In contrast, with secondary data:

(a) any limitations in the data might not be known to the investigator, because he or she did not collect them;

(b) the data might not be entirely suitable for the purpose they are being used for.

2.9 Secondary data are sometimes used despite their inadequacies, simply because they are available cheaply whereas the extra cost of collecting primary data would far outweigh their extra value.

3. Sources of statistical data

Primary data

3.1 Primary data have to be gathered from a source. Methods of collecting primary data include:

(a) personal investigation;
(b) teams of investigators;
(c) questionnaires.

Personal investigation

3.2 Personal investigation involves the investigator collecting all the data himself, for example by interviewing people, or by looking through historical records.

3.3 This method of collecting data is time consuming, expensive and limited to the amount of data a single person can collect. On the other hand, personal investigation has the advantage that the data collected are likely to be accurate and complete, because the investigator knows exactly what he wants and how to get it. He is not relying on other people to do the survey work.

Teams of investigators

3.4 A survey could be carried out by a team of investigators who collect data separately and then pool their results.

3.5 A team of investigators can cover a larger field than personal investigation but will still be expensive. The members of the team must be carefully briefed to ensure that the data they collect are satisfactory. This method is sometimes called delegated personal investigation.

Questionnaires

3.6 With a questionnaire, the questions which need to be answered for the survey are listed and are either sent to a number of people (so that they can fill in their answers and send the questionnaires back) or used by investigators to interview people (perhaps by approaching people in the street and asking them the questions).

3.7 Questionnaires can provide a quick and cheap method of conducting a survey but suffer from several defects which may lead to biased results.

(a) The people completing the forms (the respondents) may place different interpretations on the questions. This problem will be aggravated if the questions are badly phrased.

(b) Large numbers of forms may not be returned or may only be returned partly completed. This may well lead to biased results as the people replying are likely to be those most interested in the survey.

(c) Respondents may give false or misleading information if, for example, they have forgotten material facts or want to give a favourable impression.

In addition, if the questionnaire is being used by an interviewer (on the telephone or in the street), then the following problems could arise.

(d) The interviewer may not really understand the questions.

(e) The interviewer may not understand the replies, or may note down replies wrongly because of personal bias.

Secondary data

3.8 Secondary data are data that were originally collected as primary data for one purpose, or for general use, but are now being used for another purpose. The government, for example, collects data to help with making decisions about running the country, and makes these data available to the public.

Examples of secondary data are:

(a) *published statistics*. For example, the UK Government publishes statistics through the Central Statistical Office (CSO). The European Union and the United Nations also publish statistics. So do various newspapers and accountancy bodies;

(b) *historical records*. The type of historical record used for a survey obviously depends on what survey is being carried out. An accountant producing an estimate of future company sales might use historical records of past sales.

Sources of published statistics

3.9 The range of published economic, business and accounting data is very wide, and a comprehensive knowledge of sources is impracticable. However, the main sources of government statistics form a part of the knowledge and understanding which you are expected to have for Unit 7: *Preparing reports and returns.*

3.10 All published statistics are a source of *secondary data*. Great care must be taken in using them, since the data may not be obtained or classified in precisely the same way as primary data collected *specifically* for the purpose of the current statistical analysis would be.

3.11 Despite the general shortcomings of secondary data there are many circumstances in which published statistics can be of great value. Many government statistics are compiled at least partly for the purpose of being used in further analysis and explanatory notes are given so that the user of the data knows to what extent they are relevant to his needs and what level of confidence he can have in the results of his analysis.

The Central Statistical Office and other bodies

3.12 The Central Statistical Office (CSO) publishes:

(a) the *Monthly Digest of Statistics* (which gives data for the recent past);
(b) the *Annual Abstract of Statistics* (which gives data over a much longer period);
(c) *Economic Trends* (published monthly);
(d) *Financial Statistics* (published monthly).

3.13 The European Union (formerly called the European Community) has a Statistical Office which gathers statistics from each of the member countries. This produces several statistical publications, including *Basic Statistics of the Community*.

3.14 The United Nations also publishes some statistics on the world economy (for example the *Statistical Yearbook*), and a *Yearbook of Labour Statistics* is published by the International Labour Organisation.

3.15 In the remainder of this section, we shall concentrate on government statistical publications in the UK. You need to be aware of what publications are available and the general nature of the information they contain.

The Department of Employment Gazette

3.16 The Department of Employment publishes statistics monthly about employment and unemployment, and about retail prices. The statistics which are published monthly in the *Department of Employment Gazette* include, for example, statistics on:

(a) retail prices;
(b) employment;
(c) unemployment;
(d) unfilled job vacancies;
(e) wage rates;
(f) overtime and short time working;
(g) stoppages at work.

3.17 Retail prices are very important to a wide variety of users.

(a) For the government, the Retail Prices Index (RPI) indicates the degree of success there has been in fighting inflation.

(b) For employees, the RPI may give an indication of how much wages need to rise to keep pace with inflation.

(c) For consumers, the RPI indicates the increases to be expected in the prices of goods in shops.

(d) For businesses, the RPI may give a broad indication of how much costs should have been expected to rise over recent years and months.

The Bank of England Quarterly Bulletin

3.18 The Bank of England issues a quarterly bulletin which includes data on banks in the UK, the money supply and government borrowing and financial transactions.

Population data

3.19 Data on the UK population, such as population numbers in total and by region, births, deaths and marriages, are produced monthly by the Office of Population Censuses and Surveys (OPCS) in a quarterly publication entitled *Population Trends*.

The OPCS also produces an annual statistical review.

Every ten years, there is a full *census* of the whole population, and results of the census are published. The last census was in April 1991.

The Blue Book and the Pink Book

3.20 *The Blue Book on National Income and Expenditure* is published annually by the CSO, giving details of:

(a) gross national product (analysed into sections of the economy such as transport and communication, insurance, banking and finance, public administration and defence);

(b) gross national income (analysed into income from self-employment, income from employment, profits of companies, income from abroad and so on);

(c) gross national expenditure (analysed into expenditure on capital goods, expenditure by consumers and by public authorities, imports and so on).

3.21 This information is augmented by more detailed statistics, also provided in the *Blue Book*. There is also an annual *Pink Book, The UK Balance of Payments* which analyses the UK's external trade, external capital transactions (inflows and outflows of private capital) and official financing.

The Annual Abstract of Statistics

3.22 Most government statistics of economic and business data are brought together into a main reference book, the *Annual Abstract of Statistics*, which is published by the CSO. Notes about the data and definitions of the data provided are contained in the book. If you can, take the opportunity to browse through this publication at your college or public library.

The Monthly Digest of Statistics

3.23 The CSO's *Monthly Digest of Statistics* is an abbreviated version of the *Annual Abstract*, updated and published monthly. A January supplement provides definitions. The information included in the *Monthly Digest* covers a wide area, such as industrial output, production costs, prices and wages, social services, law enforcement, national income, external trade, retailing, transport, construction, agriculture and food.

Financial Statistics

3.24 The CSO publishes a monthly compilation of financial data in *Financial Statistics*. This gives statistics on a variety of financial topics, such as:

(a) government income, expenditure and borrowing;

(b) assets and liabilities of banks and statistics on other financial institutions, such as building societies, unit trusts, investment trusts, insurance companies and pension funds;

(c) companies (profits, sources and uses of capital funds, acquisitions and mergers, share trading and so on);

(d) personal sector finance (loans for home buying, consumer credit, personal income expenditure and saving and so on);

(e) the overseas sector;

(f) the money supply;

(g) issues of capital and Stock Exchange transactions;

(h) exchange rates, interest rates and share prices.

Economic trends

3.25 Like the *Monthly Digest of Statistics* and *Financial Statistics, Economic Trends* is a monthly publication of the CSO. As its name implies, its main purpose is to indicate trends, and the publication includes graphs as well as numerical statistics.

Key points in this chapter

- Statistics involves collecting, presenting and interpreting data. In statistics, data can be classified in different ways. Ways of collecting primary data include investigation, individually or in a team, and questionnaires. Secondary data includes statistics published by government and other organisations.

- UK government statistics are published in various forms. Many of the most useful of the government statistics of economic and business data are collected together in a publication called *Annual Abstract of Statistics.*

For practice on the points covered in this chapter you should now attempt the Exercises in Session 3 of the Cost Accounting II Workbook

4. Presenting data: tables and charts

1. Tables

2. Frequency distributions

3. Charts

1. Tables

1.1 Raw data (for example, the list of results from a survey, or a list of accounting balances) need to be summarised and analysed, to give them meaning. This chapter is concerned with several different ways of presenting data to convey their meaning. We will start with one of the most basic ways, the preparation of a table.

1.2 *Tabulation* means putting data into tables. A table is a matrix of data in rows and columns, with the rows and the columns having titles.

1.3 Since a table is two-dimensional, it can only show two variables. For example, the resources required to produce items in a factory could be tabulated, with one dimension (rows or columns) representing the items produced and the other dimension representing the resources.

Resources for production: all figures in pounds

	Product items				
	A	*B*	*C*	*D*	*Total*
Resources					
Direct material A	X	X	X	X	X
Direct material B	X	X	X	X	X
Direct labour grade 1	X	X	X	X	X
Direct labour grade 2	X	X	X	X	X
Supervision	X	X	X	X	X
Machine time	X	X	X	X	X
Total	X	X	X	X	X

1.4 To tabulate data, you need to recognise what the two dimensions should represent, prepare rows and columns accordingly with suitable titles, and then insert the data into the appropriate places in the table.

Guidelines for tabulation

1.5 The table in paragraph 1.3 illustrates certain guidelines which you should apply when presenting data in tabular form. These are as follows.

(a) The table should be given a clear title.

(b) All columns should be clearly labelled.

(c) Where appropriate, there should be clear sub-totals.

(d) A total column may be presented; this would usually be the right-hand column.

(e) A total figure is often advisable at the bottom of each column of figures.

(f) Tables should not be packed with too much data so that the information presented is difficult to read.

Example: tables

1.6 The total number of employees in a certain trading company is 1,000. They are employed in three departments: production, administration and sales. 600 people are employed in the production department and 300 in administration. There are 110 male juveniles in employment, 110 female juveniles, and 290 adult females. The remaining employees are adult males.

In the production department there are 350 adult males, 150 adult females and 50 male juveniles, whilst in the administration department there are 100 adult males, 110 adult females and 50 juvenile males.

Draw up a table to show all the details of employment in the company and its departments and provide suitable secondary statistics to describe the distribution of people in departments.

Solution

1.7 The basic table required has as its two dimensions:

(a) departments;
(b) age/sex analysis.

1.8 Secondary statistics (not the same thing as secondary data) are supporting figures that are supplementary to the main items of data, and which clarify or amplify the main data. A major example of secondary statistics is percentages. In this example, we could show either:

(a) the percentage of the total work force in each department belonging to each age/sex group, or

(b) the percentage of the total of each age/sex group employed in each department.

In this example, (a) has been selected but you might consider that (b) would be more suitable. Either could be suitable, depending of course on what purposes the data are being collected and presented for.

1.9 *Analysis of employees*

	Department							
	Production		*Administration*		*Sales*		*Total*	
	No	%	No	%	No	%	No	%
Adult males	350	58.4	100	33.3	40	** 40.0	490	* 49.0
Adult females	150	25.0	110	36.7	30	** 30.0	290	29.0
Male juveniles	50	8.3	50	16.7	10	** 10.0	110	11.0
Female juveniles	50	* 8.3	40	* 13.3	20	** 20.0	110	11.0
Total	600	100.0	300	100.0	100	100.0	1,000	100.0

* Balancing figure to make up the column total
** Balancing figure then needed to make up the row total

Rounding errors

1.10 Rounding errors may become apparent when, for example, a percentages column does not add up to 100%. When figures in a table are rounded and then added up, the effect of rounding will depend on the method of rounding used.

(a) With *rounding to the nearest unit,* errors tend to cancel out giving *unbiased* approximation. We may therefore refer to *compensating errors* when figures are rounded to the nearest unit.

(b) With *rounding up,* errors will add together giving *biased* approximation. We may therefore refer to *cumulative errors* when figures are rounded up.

(c) With *rounding down,* as with rounding up, errors will add together giving *biased* approximation and are *cumulative* errors.

To avoid bias, any rounding should be to the nearest unit and the potential size of errors should be kept to a tolerable level by rounding to a small enough unit (for example to the nearest £10, rather than to the nearest £1,000).

Tally marks

1.11 Tally marks are another simple way of presenting data. If we measured the number of jobs completed by each employee during one week, the data could be collected and presented as follows.

Employee	*Jobs completed*	
A	~~////~~ ////	= 9
B	~~////~~ ~~////~~ ////	= 14
C	~~////~~ //	= 7
D	///	= 3

2. Frequency distributions

2.1 If a large number of measurements of a particular variable is taken (for example the number of units produced per employee per week) some values may occur more than once. A *frequency distribution* is obtained by recording the number of times each value occurs.

Example: frequency distribution

2.2 The output in units of 20 employees during one week was as follows.

65	69	70	71	70	68	69	67	70	68
72	71	69	74	70	73	71	67	69	70

2.3 If the number of occurrences is placed against each output quantity, a frequency distribution is produced.

Output of employees in one week in units

Output Units	*Number of employees (frequency)*
65	1
66	0
67	2
68	2
69	4
70	5
71	3
72	1
73	1
74	1
	20

2.4 The number of employees corresponding to a particular volume of output is called a *frequency*. When the data are arranged in this way it is immediately obvious that 69 and 70 units are the most common volumes of output per employee per week.

Grouped frequency distributions

2.5 It is often convenient to group frequencies together into bands or classes. For example, suppose that the output produced by each of 20 employees during one week was as follows, in units.

1,087	850	1,084	792
924	1,226	1,012	1,205
1,265	1,028	1,230	1,182
1,086	1,130	989	1,155
1,134	1,166	1,129	1,160

2.6 An ungrouped frequency distribution would not be a helpful way of presenting the data, because each employee has produced a different number of units in the week.

2.7 The range of output from the lowest to the highest producer is 792 to 1,265, a range of 473 units. This range could be divided into classes of say, 100 units (the *class width* or *class interval*), and the number of employees producing output within each class could then be grouped into a single frequency, as follows.

Output Units	*Number of employees (frequency)*
700 - 799	1
800 - 899	1
900 - 999	2
1,000 - 1,099	5
1,100 - 1,199	7
1,200 - 1,299	4
	20

Grouped frequency distributions of continuous variables

2.8 Grouped frequency distributions can be used to present data for continuous variables. To prepare a grouped frequency distribution, a decision must be made about how wide each class should be.

(a) The size of each class should be appropriate to the nature of the data being recorded, and the most appropriate class interval varies according to circumstances.

(b) The upper and lower limits of each class interval should be suitable 'round' numbers, for class intervals which are in multiples of 5, 10, 100, 1,000 and so on. For example, if the class interval is 10, and data items range in value from 23 to 62 (discrete values) the class intervals should be 20-29, 30-39, 40-49, 50-59 and 60-69, rather than 23-32, 33-42, 43-52 and 53-62.

(c) With continuous variables, either:

(i) the upper limit of a class should be 'up to and including ...' and the lower limit of the next class should be 'over ...'; or

(ii) the upper limit of a class should be 'less than ...', and the lower limit of the next class should be 'at least ...'.

Cumulative frequency distributions

2.9 A cumulative frequency distribution can be used to show the total number of times that a value above or below a certain amount occurs (see the example below).

Example: grouped frequency distribution

2.10 The volume of output produced in one day by each of 20 employees is as follows, in units.

18	29	22	17
30	12	27	24
26	32	24	29
28	46	31	27
19	18	32	25

2.11 We could present a grouped frequency distribution as follows.

Output Units	*Number of employees (frequency)*
Under 15	1
15 or more, under 20	4
20 or more, under 25	3
25 or more, under 30	7
30 or more, under 35	4
35 or more	1
	20

2.12 The two possible cumulative frequency distributions for the same data are as follows.

	Cumulative frequency
⩾ 0	20
⩾ 15	19
⩾ 20	15
⩾ 25	12
⩾ 30	5
⩾ 35	1

	Cumulative frequency
<15	1
<20	5
<25	8
<30	15
<35	19
<47	20

Notes

(a) The symbol > means 'greater than' and ⩾ means 'greater than, or equal to'. The symbol < means 'less than' and ⩽ means 'less than or equal to'.

These symbols provide a convenient method of stating classes.

(b) The first cumulative frequency distribution shows that of the total of 20 employees:

(i) 19 produced 15 units or more;
(ii) 15 produced 20 units or more;
(iii) 12 produced 25 units or more;
and so on.

(c) The second cumulative frequency distribution shows that of the total of 20 employees:

(i) one produced under 15 units;
(ii) five produced under 20 units;
(iii) eight produced under 25 units;
and so on.

3. Charts

3.1 Instead of presenting data in a table, it might be preferable to give a visual display in the form of a chart.

3.2 The purpose of a chart is to convey the data in a way that will demonstrate its meaning or significance more clearly than a table of data would. Charts are not always more appropriate than tables, and the most suitable way of presenting data will depend on:

(a) what the data are intended to show. Visual displays usually make one or two points quite forcefully, whereas tables usually give more detailed information;

(b) who is going to use the data. Some individuals might understand visual displays more readily than tabulated data.

3.3 Types of chart that might be used to present data include:

(a) pictograms;
(b) pie charts;
(c) bar charts.

We shall look at each of these in turn.

Pictograms

3.4 A pictogram is a statistical diagram in which quantities are represented by pictures or symbols.

Example: pictogram

3.5 (a) A pictogram showing the volume of sales of cars would represent the quantities of cars using pictures of cars.

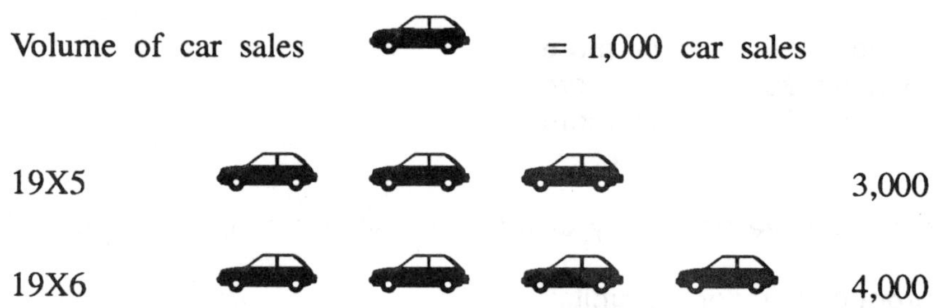

(b) A pictogram showing the number of employees at a factory would represent the quantities of employees using pictures of people.

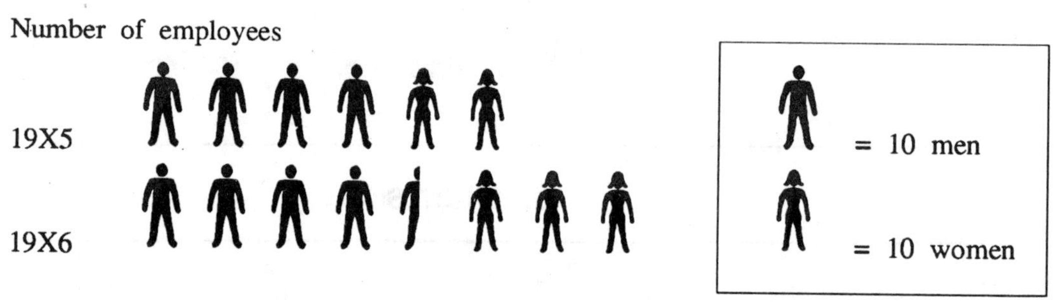

In this example, each picture represents ten employees, and to represent a smaller quantity, a part-picture can be drawn. Here, there were 45 men employed in 19X6.

3.6 The guidelines for drawing a pictogram are as follows.

(a) The symbols should be clear and simple.

(b) The quantity that each symbol represents should be clearly shown in a key to the pictogram.

(c) Bigger quantities ought to be shown by more symbols, not by bigger symbols. For example, if sales of boxes of dishwasher powder double between 19X5 and 19X6, a pictogram should look as follows.

19X5

19X6

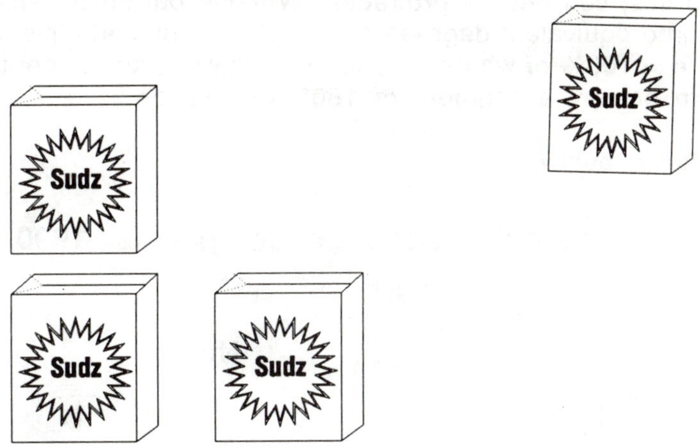

= 10,000 boxes sold

It should *not* show:

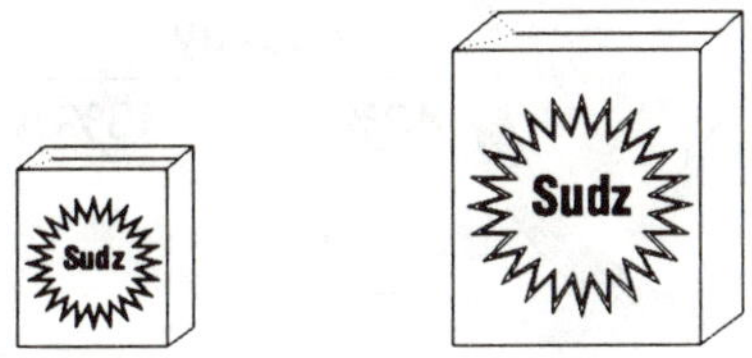

19X5 19X6

In this pictogram, the bigger symbol does not give a true impression of sales growth.

3.7 The advantage of pictograms is that they present data in a simple, readily understood way. Pictograms convey their message to the reader at a glance, and are consequently often used on television and in advertisements.

3.8 The disadvantages of pictograms are that they can only convey a limited amount of information, and that they lack precision. Each symbol must represent quite a large number of items, otherwise a pictogram would contain too many symbols. Using portions of a symbol to represent smaller quantities gives some extra precision, but not much. For example, if

 represents 1,000 men then

 represents less than 1,000 men, but how many exactly? 400? 500? 600?

Pie charts

3.9 A pie chart is used to show pictorially the relative size of component elements of a total. It is called a pie chart because it is circular, and so has the shape of a pie in a round pie dish and because the 'pie' is then cut into slices. Each slice represents a part of the total.

3.10 Pie charts have sectors of varying sizes, and you need to be able to draw sectors fairly accurately. To do this, you need a protractor. Working out sector sizes involves converting parts of the total into equivalent degrees of a circle. A complete 'pie' = 360°: the number of degrees in a circle = 100% of whatever you are showing. An element which is 50% of your total will therefore occupy a segment of 180°, and so on.

A pie chart is shown below.

Breakdown of air and noise pollution complaints, 1990

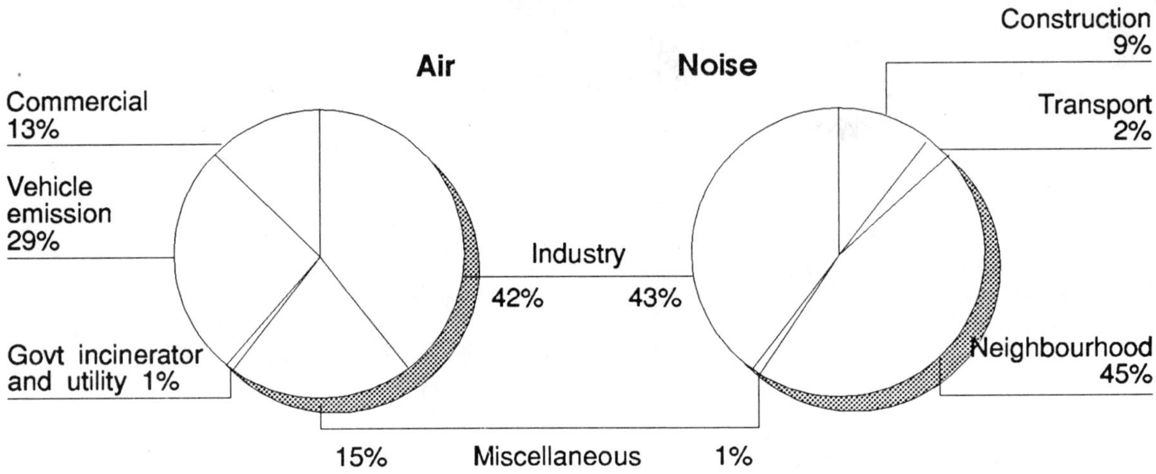

Source: Environmental Protection Department

Example: pie charts

3.11 The costs of production at Factory A and Factory B during March 19X2 were as follows.

	Factory A		*Factory B*	
	£'000	%	£'000	%
Direct materials	70	35	50	20
Direct labour	30	15	125	50
Production overhead	90	45	50	20
Office costs	10	5	25	10
	200	100	250	100

Show the costs for the factories in pie charts.

Solution

3.12 To convert the components into degrees of a circle, we can use either the percentage figures or the actual cost figures.

(a) Using the percentage figures, the total percentage is 100%, and the total number of degrees in a circle is 360°. To convert from one to the other, we multiply each percentage value by 360°/100% = 3.6.

	Factory A		Factory B	
	%	Degrees	%	Degrees
Direct materials	35	126	20	72
Direct labour	15	54	50	180
Production overhead	45	162	20	72
Office costs	5	18	10	36
	100	360	100	360

(b) Using the actual cost figures, we would multiply each cost by

$\frac{\text{Number of degrees}}{\text{Total cost}}$

Factory A $\frac{360}{200} = 1.8$

Factory B $\frac{360}{250} = 1.44$

	Factory A		Factory B	
	£'000	Degrees	£'000	Degrees
Direct materials	70	126	50	72
Direct labour	30	54	125	180
Production overhead	90	162	50	72
Office costs	10	18	25	36
	200	360	250	360

3.13 A pie chart could be drawn for each factory, as follows. This could be drawn using a computer. If the pie chart is drawn manually, a protractor is used to measure the degrees accurately to obtain the correct sector sizes.

Factory A

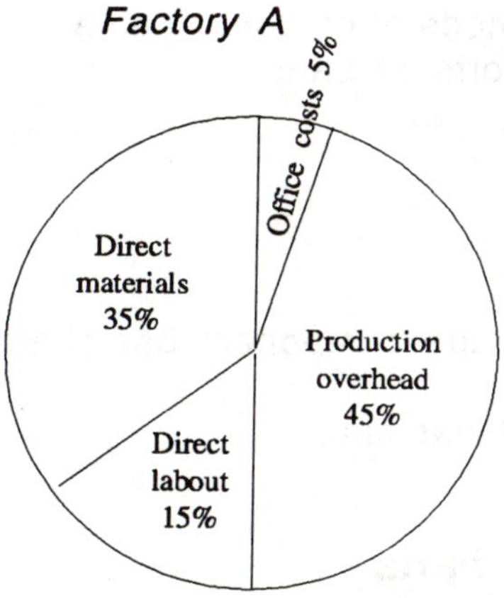

Factory B

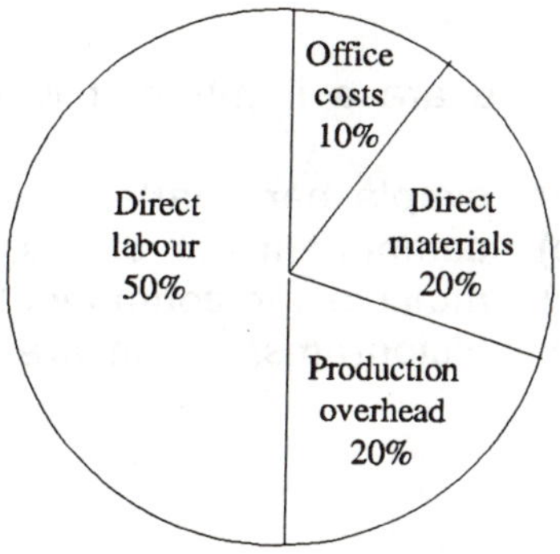

3.14 The advantages of pie charts are as follows.

(a) They give a simple pictorial display of the relative sizes of elements of a total.

(b) They show clearly when one element is much bigger than others.

(c) They can sometimes clearly show differences in the elements of two different totals. In the example above, the pie charts for factories A and B show how factory A's costs mostly consist of production overhead and direct materials, whereas at factory B, direct labour is the largest cost element.

3.15 The disadvantages of pie charts are as follows.

(a) They show only the relative sizes of elements. In the example of the two factories, for instance, the pie charts do not show that costs at Factory B were £50,000 higher in total than at Factory A.

(b) They involve calculating degrees of a circle and drawing sectors accurately, and this can be time consuming.

(c) It is often difficult to compare sector sizes easily. For example, suppose that the following two pie charts are used to show the elements of a company's sales.

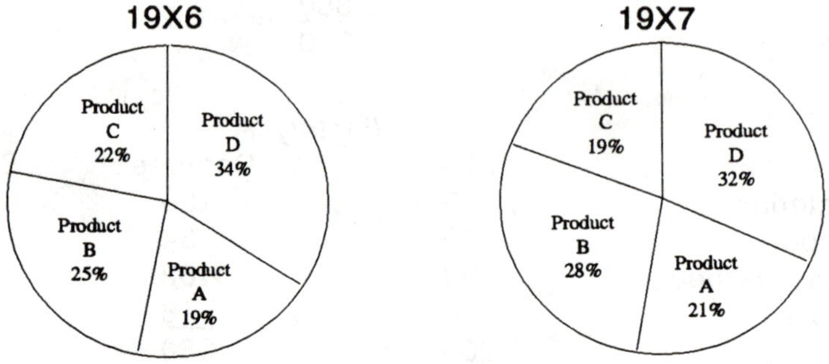

Without the percentage figures, it would not be easy to see how the distribution of sales had changed between 19X6 and 19X7.

Bar charts

3.16 The bar chart is one of the most common methods of presenting data in a visual form. It is a chart in which quantities are shown in the form of bars.

3.17 There are a number of types of bar chart:

(a) simple bar charts;
(b) component bar charts, including percentage component bar charts;
(c) multiple (or compound) bar charts;
(d) histograms, which are a special type of bar chart.

Simple bar charts

3.18 A simple bar chart is a chart consisting of one or more bars, in which the length of each bar indicates the magnitude of the corresponding data item.

Example: simple bar chart

3.19 A company's total sales for the years from 19X1 to 19X6 are as follows.

Year	£'000
19X1	800
19X2	1,200
19X3	1,100
19X4	1,400
19X5	1,600
19X6	1,700

The data could be shown on a simple bar chart as follows.

Company sales

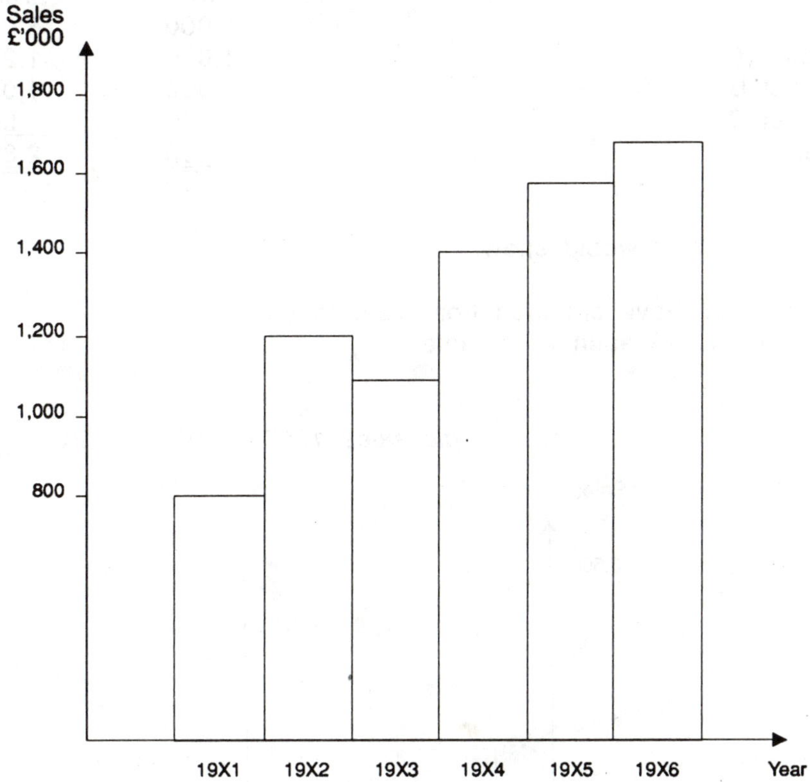

3.20 Each axis of the chart must be clearly labelled, and there must be a scale to indicate the magnitude of the data. Here, the y axis includes a scale for the amount of sales, and so readers of the bar chart can see not only that sales have been rising year by year (with 19X3 being an exception) but also what the actual sales have been each year.

3.21 Simple bar charts serve two purposes.

(a) They show the actual magnitude of each item.

(b) They enable one to compare magnitudes, by comparing the lengths of bars on the chart.

Component bar charts

3.22 A component bar chart is a bar chart that gives a breakdown of each total into its components.

Example: component bar chart (1)

3.23 Charbart plc's sales for the years from 19X7 to 19X9 are as follows.

	19X7	*19X8*	*19X9*
	£'000	£'000	£'000
Product A	1,000	1,200	1,700
Product B	900	1,000	1,000
Product C	500	600	700
Total	2,400	2,800	3,400

3.24 A component bar chart would show:

(a) how total sales have changed from year to year;
(b) the components of each year's total.

Charbart plc sales 19X7 - 19X9

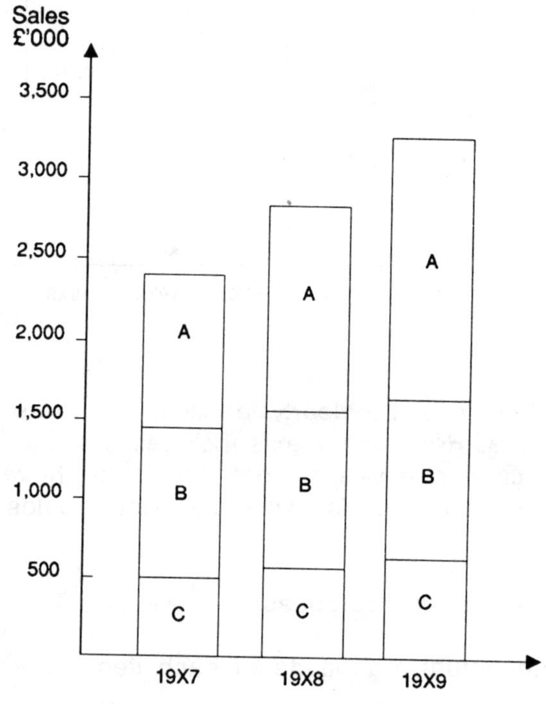

3.25 The bars in a bar chart can either be drawn side by side, with no gap between them, or with gaps between them, as in the diagram here.

3.26 In this diagram the growth in sales is illustrated and the significance of growth in product A sales as the reason for the total sales growth is also fairly clear. The growth in product A sales would have been even clearer if product A had been drawn as the bottom element in each bar instead of the top one.

Example: Component bar chart (2)

3.27 Here is a component bar chart based on one which was published in the Press in 1992.

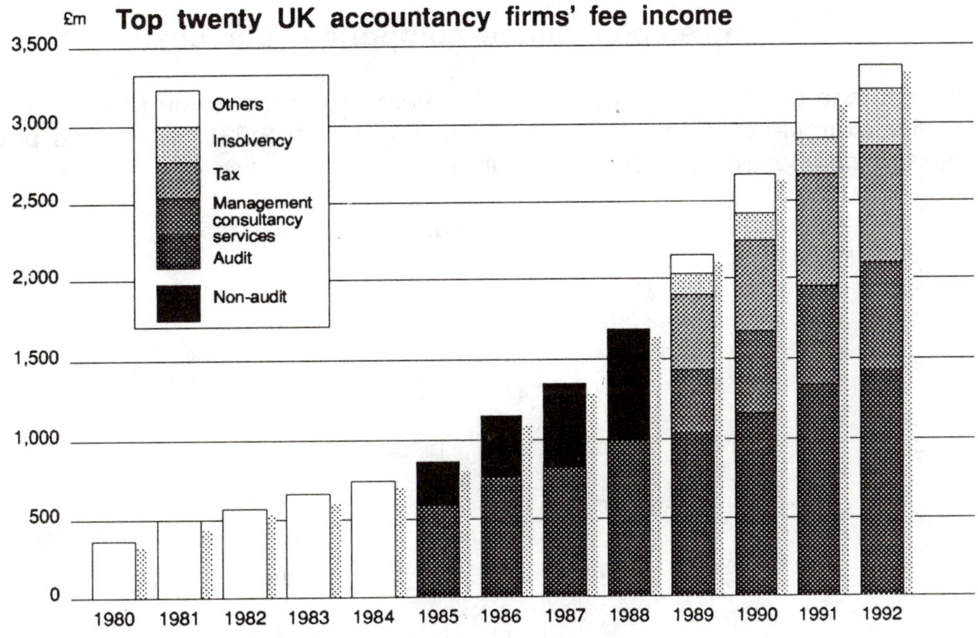

1980-84 figures are total fees; 1985-88 figures are divided into audit & non-audit fees; 1989-92 figures are audit plus non-audit fees sub-divided into four categories

Source: FT annual accountancy tables

3.28 This bar chart needs to be read with care. The bars for 1985–1988 and 1989–1992 are divided up differently, while those for 1980–1984 are not divided up at all. These differences probably occur because whoever compiled the chart does not have the same information available for the three different periods.

3.29 The chart shows the growth in fee income of the top twenty UK accountancy firms over the period 1980 to 1992. It also shows how much of those fees have been for audit work from 1985 onwards and it breaks down non-audit work into four categories for the period 1989 to 1992.

3.30 Did fees for insolvency work increase between 1988 and 1989? The chart does not tell us, as non-audit fees are not split into components for 1988.

3.31 Note also that this chart shows fee income in money terms, without adjusting for inflation. If firms are increasing fee income but by less than the rate of inflation, the amount of business they do is getting less even though their fee income is increasing in money terms. We look at how to adjust data for changing price levels in Chapter 6, but make sure that you understand this point before moving on.

Percentage component bar charts

3.32 The difference between a component bar chart and a percentage component bar chart is that with a component bar chart, the total length of each bar (and the length of each component in it) indicates magnitude. A bigger amount is shown by a longer bar. With a percentage component bar chart, total magnitudes are not shown. If two or more bars are drawn on the chart, the total length of each bar is the same. The only varying lengths in a percentage component bar chart are the lengths of the sections of a bar, which vary according to the relative sizes of the components.

Example: percentage component bar chart

3.33 In a percentage component bar chart, all the bars are of the same height. The information in the earlier example of sales of Charbart plc (paragraph 3.23) could have been shown in a percentage component bar chart as follows.

Charbart plc sales 19X7 - 19X9

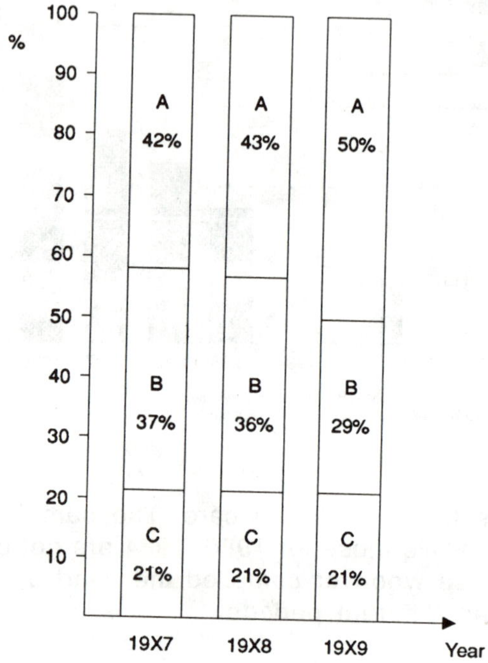

Workings

	19X7		*19X8*		*19X9*	
	£'000	%	£'000	%	£'000	%
Product A	1,000	42	1,200	43	1,700	50
Product B	900	37	1,000	36	1,000	29
Product C	500	21	600	21	700	21
Total	2,400	100	2,800	100	3,400	100

3.34 This chart shows that sales of C have remained a steady proportion of total sales, but the proportion of A in total sales has gone up quite considerably, while the proportion of B has fallen correspondingly.

Multiple bar charts (compound bar charts)

3.35 A multiple bar chart (or compound bar chart) is a bar chart in which two or more separate bars are used to present sub-divisions of data.

Example: multiple bar chart

3.36 The output of Rodd Ltd in the years from 19X6 to 19X8 is as follows.

	19X6	*19X7*	*19X8*
	'000 units	*'000 units*	*'000 units*
Product X	180	130	50
Product Y	90	110	170
Product Z	180	180	125
Total	450	420	345

The data could be shown in a multiple bar chart as follows.

Output of Rodd Ltd

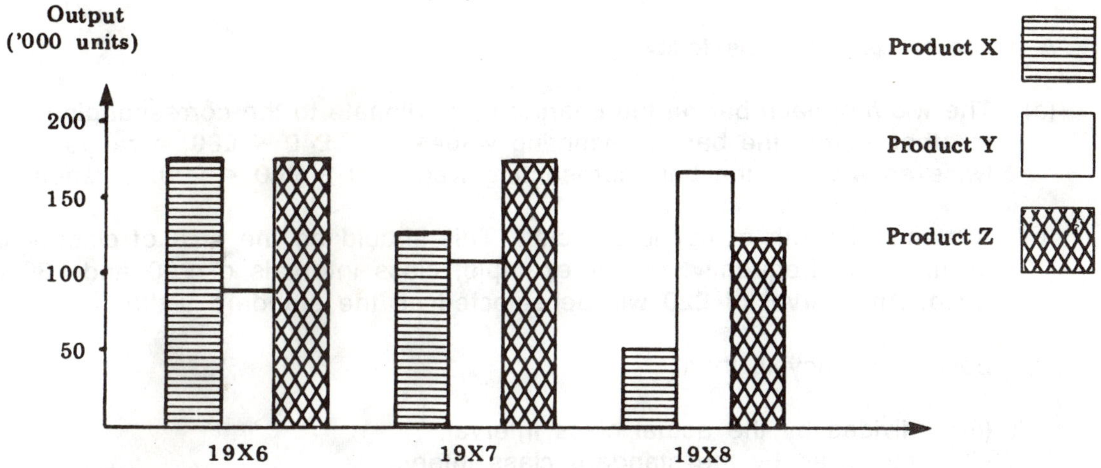

3.37 A multiple bar chart uses several bars for each total. In the above example, the sales in each year are shown as three separate bars, one for each product, X, Y and Z. Multiple bar charts are sometimes drawn with the bars horizontal instead of vertical.

3.38 Multiple bar charts present similar information to component bar charts, except that:

(a) multiple bar charts do not show the grand total (in the above example, the total output each year) whereas component bar charts do;

(b) multiple bar charts illustrate the comparative magnitudes of the components more clearly than component bar charts.

Histograms

3.39 A histogram is a form of bar chart but with important differences. It is used when *grouped data of a continuous variable* are presented. It can also be used for discrete data, by treating the data as continuous so there are no gaps between class intervals: for example with a cricketer's scores in various games, using ⩾ 0 < 10, ⩾ 10 < 20 and so on, instead of 0–9, 10–19 and so on.

3.40 The number of observations in a class is represented by the *area* covered by the bar, rather than by its height.

Example: histograms

3.41 The weekly wages of employees of Salt Lake Ltd are as follows.

Wages per employee	*Number of employees*
> £ 40 ≤ £ 60	4
> £ 60 ≤ £ 80	6
> £ 80 ≤ £ 90	6
> £ 90 ≤ £120	6
> £120 ≤ £150	3

The class intervals for wages per employee are not all the same, and range from £10 to £30.

3.42 A histogram is drawn as follows.

(a) The *width* of each bar on the chart is proportionate to the corresponding class interval. In other words, the bar representing wages of > £40 ≤ £60, a range of £20, will be twice as wide as the bar representing wages of > £80 ≤ £90, a range of only £10.

(b) A standard width of bar is selected. This should be the size of class interval which occurs most frequently. In our example, class intervals of £20 and £30 each occur twice. An interval of £20 will be selected as the standard width.

(c) Each frequency is then:

(i) divided by the actual class interval;
(ii) multiplied by the standard class interval;

to obtain the *height* of the bar in the histogram.

Class interval	*Size of interval*	*Frequency*	*Adjustment*	*Height of bar*
> £ 40 ≤ £ 60	£20	4	× 20/20	4
> £ 60 ≤ £ 80	£20	6	× 20/20	6
> £ 80 ≤ £ 90	£10	6	× 20/10	12
> £ 90 ≤ £120	£30	6	× 20/30	4
> £120 ≤ £150	£30	3	× 20/30	2

3.43 Note the following points.

(a) Because the class intervals of the first two bars are the same as the standard interval (20), the heights of the bars are the same as the class frequencies.

(b) The third bar will be twice as high as the class frequency (6) would suggest, to compensate for the fact that the class interval, £10, is only half the standard size.

(c) The fourth and fifth bars will be two thirds as high as the class frequencies (6 and 3) would suggest, to compensate for the fact that the class interval, £30, is 150% of the standard size.

HISTOGRAM

Weekly earnings: Salt Lake Ltd

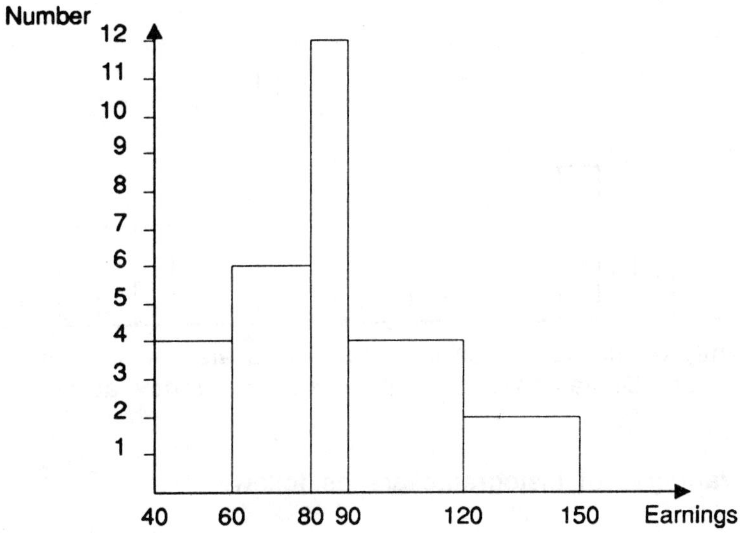

The advantages and disadvantages of histograms

3.44 Histograms are frequently used to display grouped frequency distributions graphically.

(a) They display clearly the comparative frequency of occurrence of data items within classes.

(b) They indicate whether the range of values is wide or narrow, and whether most values occur in the middle of the range or whether the frequencies are more evenly spread.

3.45 Consider these two histograms.

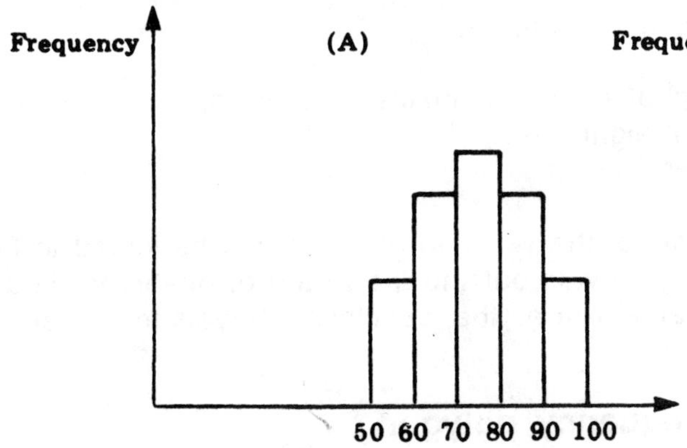

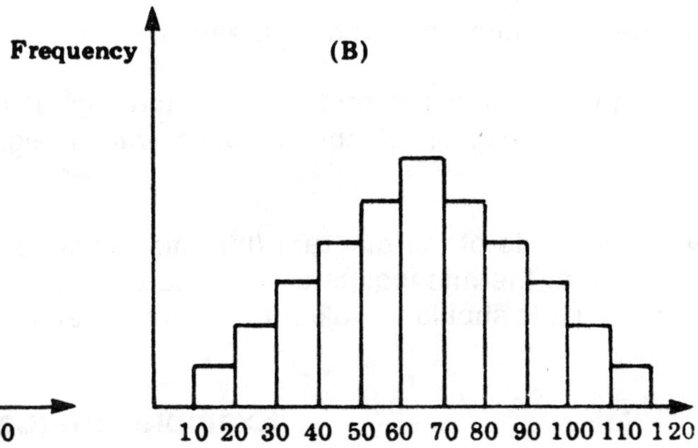

In (A) there is a narrower range of values than in (B). Both have the most frequently occurring value somewhere in the middle of the range (70–80 with A and 60–70 with B).

Now compare these two histograms.

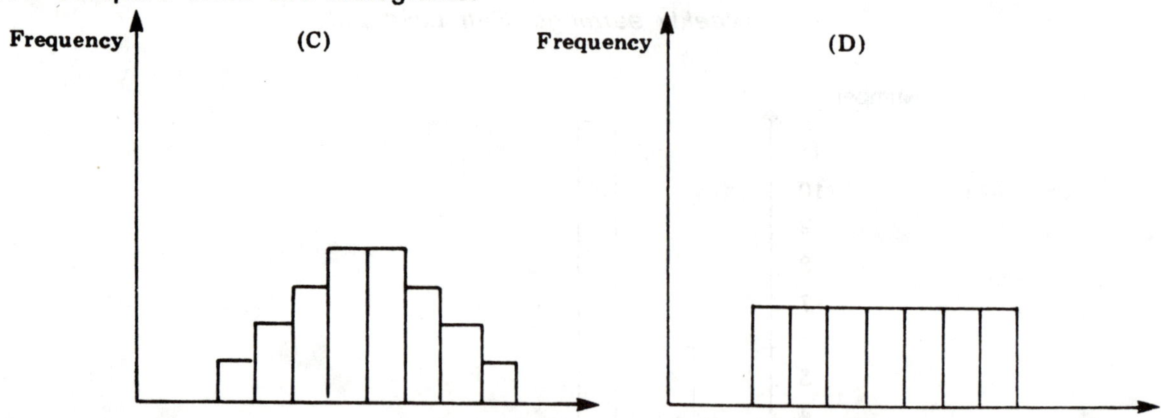

The most frequently occurring values in histogram C are towards the middle of the range, whereas in histogram D, values occur with equal frequency across the entire range.

3.46 The main disadvantages of histograms are as follows.

(a) If a histogram represents sample data, the measurements in the histogram might give a false sense of accuracy. The sample data will not be an *exact* representation of the population as a whole.

(b) If the histogram is showing data about a *continuous* variable, the sharp steps of the histogram bars would be a little misleading.

Frequency polygons

3.47 A histogram can be converted into a *frequency polygon,* which is drawn on the assumption that *within each class interval,* the frequency of occurrence of data items is not evenly spread. There will be more values at the end of each class interval nearer the histogram's peak (if any), and so the flat top on a histogram bar should be converted into a rising or falling line.

3.48 A frequency polygon is drawn from a histogram, by:

(a) marking the mid-point of the top of each bar in the histogram;
(b) joining up all these points with straight lines.

3.49 The ends of the diagram (the mid-points of the two end bars) should be joined to the base line at the mid-points of the next class intervals outside the range of observed data. These intervals should be taken to be of the same size as the last class intervals for observed data.

Example: frequency polygon

3.50 The following grouped frequency distribution relates to the number of occasions during the past 40 weeks that a particular cost has been a given amount.

Cost £	*Number of occasions*
> 800 ⩽ 1,000	4
> 1,000 ⩽ 1,200	10
> 1,200 ⩽ 1,400	12
> 1,400 ⩽ 1,600	10
> 1,600 ⩽ 1,800	4
	40

Prepare a frequency polygon.

Solution

3.51 A histogram is first drawn, in the way described earlier. All classes are of the same width.

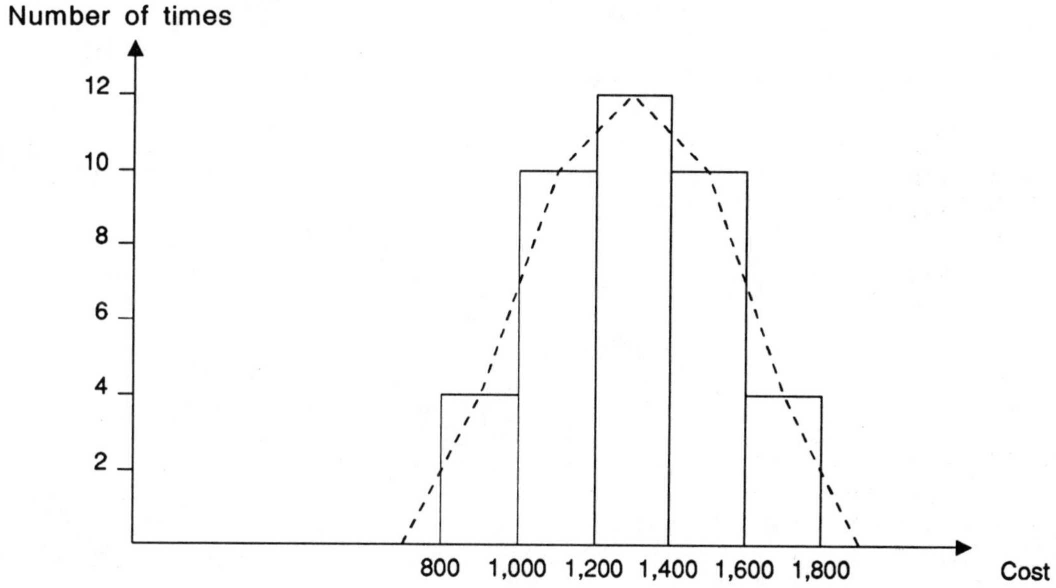

The mid-points of the class intervals outside the range of observed data are 700 and 1,900.

Key points in this chapter

- In this chapter we have looked at a number of different ways of presenting data.
- When you have to select a method, you should ask yourself two questions.
  - What information must be shown? For example, if absolute rather than relative magnitudes are important, pie charts will be of no use.
  - What will the user find most helpful? The presentation should not be unnecessarily complex.

For practice on the points covered in this chapter you should now attempt the Exercises in Session 4 of the Cost Accounting II Workbook

5. Presenting data: graphs

1. **Drawing graphs**
2. **Types of graph**
3. **Graphical presentation of information in public reports**

1. Drawing graphs

1.1 Graphs are a form of visual display. A graph shows, by means of either a straight line or a curve, the relationship between two variables. In particular, it shows how the value of one variable changes given changes in the value of the other variable.

1.2 For example, a graph might be used to show how:

(a) sales turnover changes over time;
(b) a country's population changes over time;
(c) total costs of production vary with the number of units produced.

1.3 The variable whose value is influenced by the value of the other variable is referred to as the *dependent variable.* In the examples above, sales turnover, population and total costs would be the dependent variables in (a), (b) and (c) respectively.

The variable whose value affects the value of the dependent variable is known as the *independent variable.* In the examples above, these are time in (a) and (b) and number of units produced in (c).

1.4 The relationship between variables can often be presented more clearly in graph form than in a table of figures, and this is why graphs are so commonly used.

The rules for drawing graphs

1.5 A graph has a horizontal axis, the x axis, and a vertical axis, the y axis. The x axis is used to represent the independent variable and the y axis is used to represent the dependent variable.

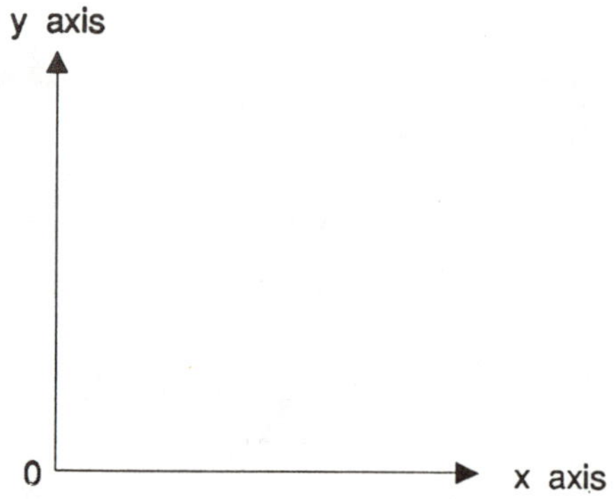

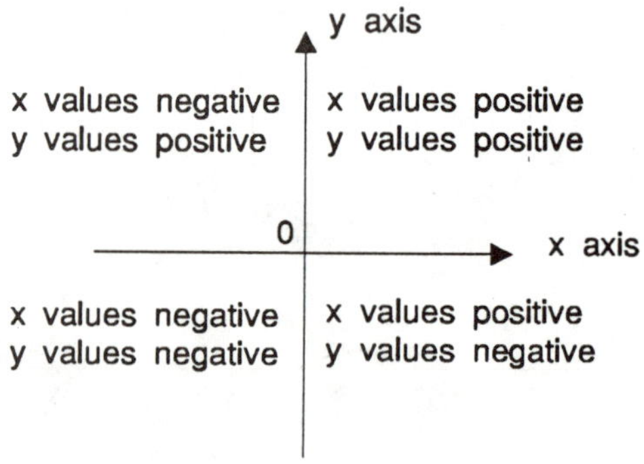

1.6 If time is one variable, it is always treated as the independent variable. When time is represented by the x axis on a graph, we have a *time series.* The analysis of time series is covered in detail in the next chapter of this Tutorial Text.

1.7 (a) If the data to be plotted are derived from calculations, rather than given in the task set, make sure that there is a neat table in your working papers.

(b) The scales on each axis should be selected so as to use as much of the available space as possible. Do not cramp a graph into one corner.

(c) In some cases it is best not to start a scale at zero so as to avoid having a large area of wasted paper. This is perfectly acceptable as long as the scale adopted is clearly shown on the axis. One way of avoiding confusion is to break the axis concerned, as follows.

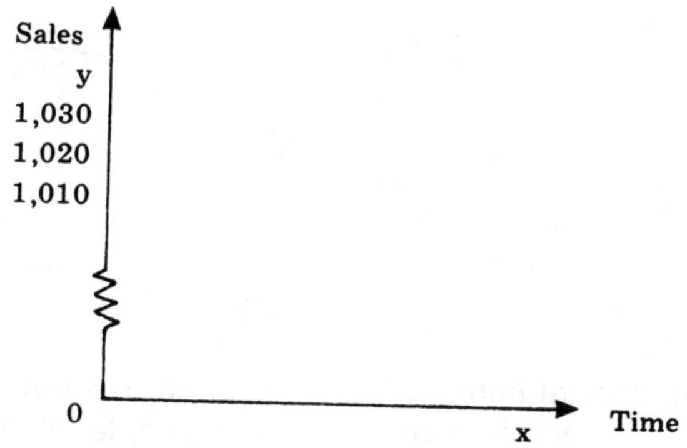

(d) The scales on the x axis and the y axis should be marked. For example, if the y axis relates to amounts of money, the axis should be marked at every £1, or £100 or £1,000 interval or at whatever other interval is appropriate. The axes must be marked with values to give the reader an idea of how big the values on the graph are.

(e) A graph should not be overcrowded with too many lines. Graphs should always give a clear, neat impression.

(f) A graph must always be given a title, and where appropriate, a reference should be made to the source of data.

Using graphs badly

1.8 It might be tempting to put as much information into a single graph as possible, but graphs usually convey their meaning more clearly when they are relatively simple, with very few lines. When drawing graphs, two useful guidelines are as follows.

(a) If necessary, draw several graphs instead of just one, if it helps to keep the information clear. For example, graph A below could be re-drawn as graphs B, C and D.

Graph A

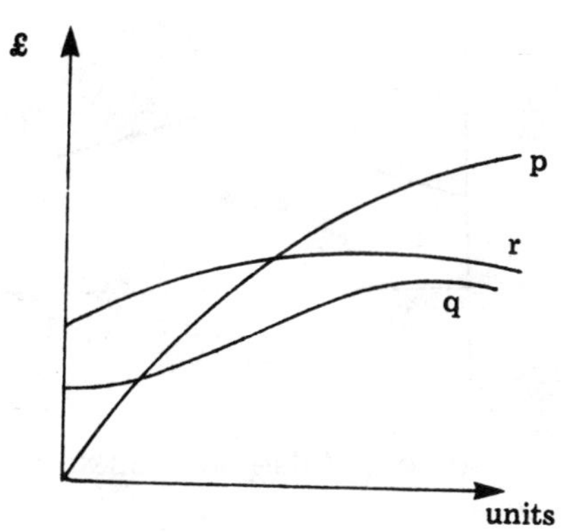

Graphs B, C, D

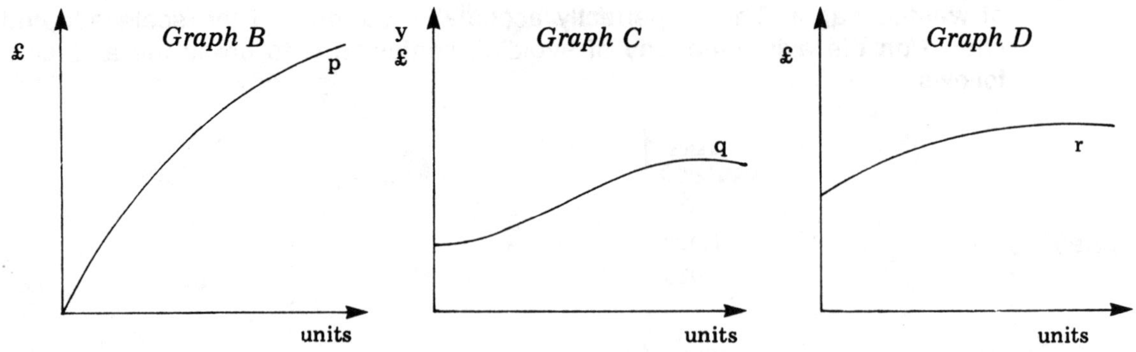

(b) Only show important information on a graph. Do not clutter up a graph with information that is of subsidiary importance. For example, if a graph is intended to show the amount by which sales in region A exceed sales in region B each month, instead of a graph showing sales in A and B as follows:

Regional sales

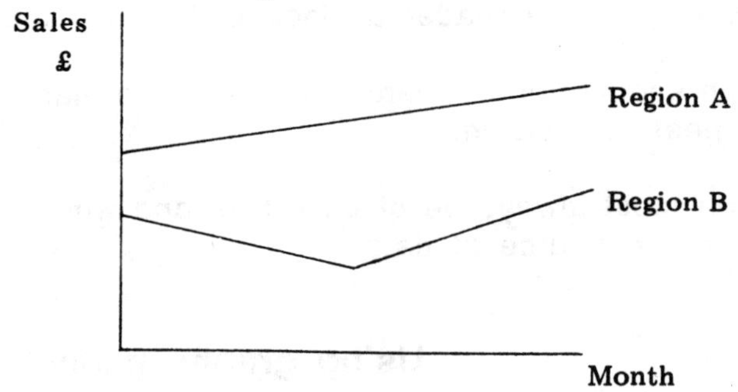

we could draw a graph that simply shows the difference, as follows:

Regional sales:
difference in sales between A and B

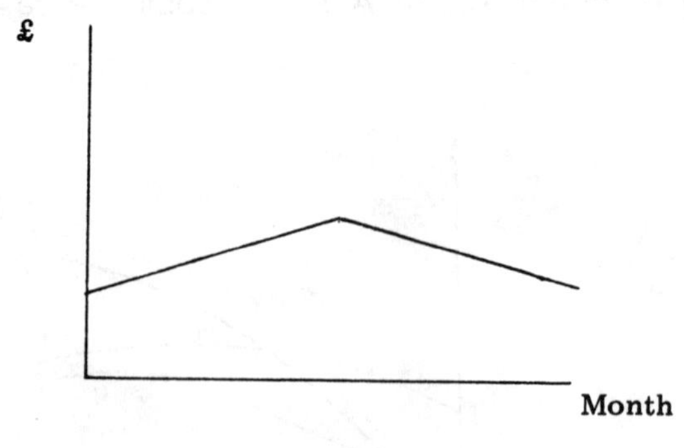

1.9 It is possible to use a graph to give a false impression.

This can be done by selecting wide (or narrow) intervals for the x axis and narrow (or wide) intervals for the y axis. Look at the two graphs below.

A. Growth in sales

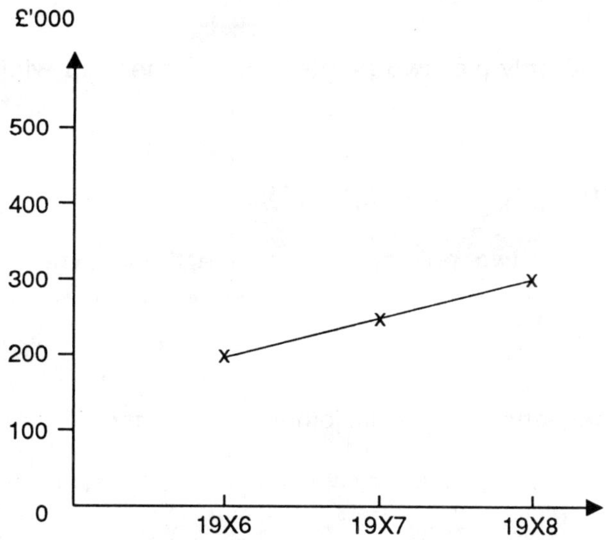

B. Growth in sales

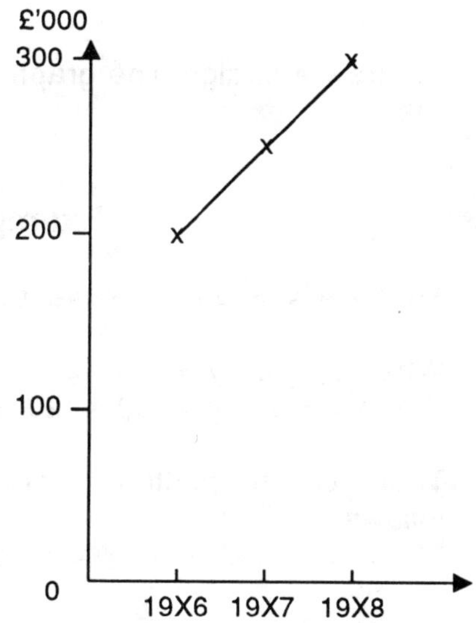

Sales growth looks much more rapid in B than in A, because the graph line rises more steeply. But the two graphs record the same data, with the x axis using wider intervals and the y axis narrower intervals in A than in B.

1.10 Just what is a distortion and what is not will depend on circumstances, but starting the axes of the graph at zero will prevent the sort of distortion shown below. Graph C shows the same data as A and B, but the growth in sales looks even more dramatic because the y axis starts at £200,000 and not at zero.

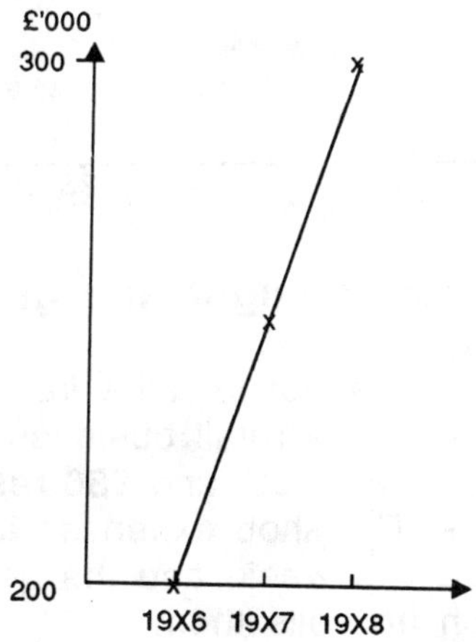

This is why it is important to make a non-zero starting point clear with an axis break, as shown in paragraph 1.7.

Straight line graphs

1.11 A straight line graph is one which can be expressed by a formula y = a + bx where a and b are fixed, constant values. Here are some examples.

$$y = 100 + 3x$$
$$y = 1{,}000 + 0.2x$$
$$y = -60 + 12x$$

There are no x^2, x^3, x^4, $\sqrt{x}$ or $1/x$ terms. If there were, the corresponding graphs would not be straight lines.

1.12 To draw a straight line graph, we need only plot two points and join them up with a straight line.

Example: straight line graph (1)

1.13 To draw $y = 50 + 2x$ we can take any two points, for example these two.

When $x = 0$, $y = 50$
When $x = 10$, $y = 50 + 20 = 70$

These can be plotted on graph paper, and the points joined up and the line extended as follows.

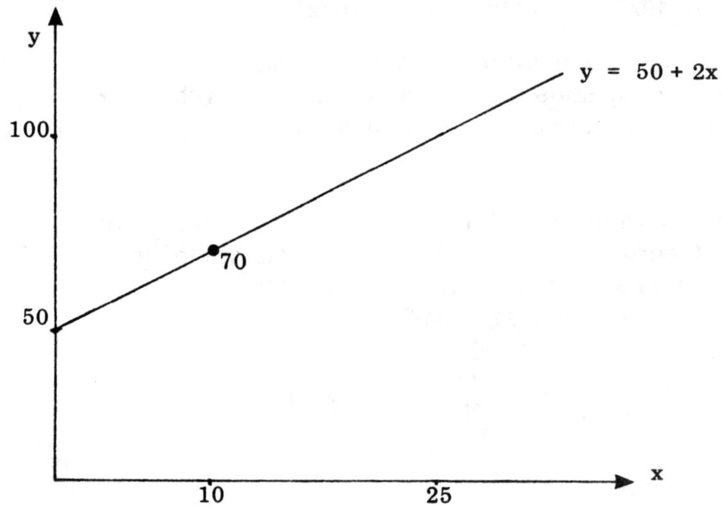

Example: straight line graph (2)

1.14 An accounting technician who is about to retire intends to use his savings and retirement gratuity totalling £52,000 to set up a retail business. He plans to employ three assistants whose weekly salaries will be £120, £96, and £80 respectively, together with a commission of 3% on their individual sales. The shop expenses apart from the assistants' remuneration are expected to amount to £240 a week, and the goods to be sold will be bought at 25% less than the prices at which he sells them.

Tasks

(a) Draw a graph to show total weekly expenses for sales ranging from £1,000 to £5,000 a week.

(b) Draw a graph from which can be read the weekly sales necessary to yield weekly profits from nil to £500.

Solution

1.15 The costs of the business are partly fixed and partly variable. Fixed costs are costs that are a given amount each week, and these are as follows.

	£
Salaries (120 + 96 + 80)	296
Expenses	240
	536

The variable costs are costs that vary with sales. These are as follows.

Commission	3% of sales
Purchase costs	75% of sales
	78% of sales

1.16 Total weekly costs are C = 536 + 0.78 S, where S = weekly sales.

This can be drawn as a straight line on a graph. To draw a straight line, we need only plot two points. Any points can be chosen, but x = 0 is always an easy one to use. Here x = 0 and x = 5,000 have been selected.

Sales		*Costs*
£		£
0	(536 + 0)	536
5,000	(536 + 0.78 × 5,000)	4,436

Costs of the business per week

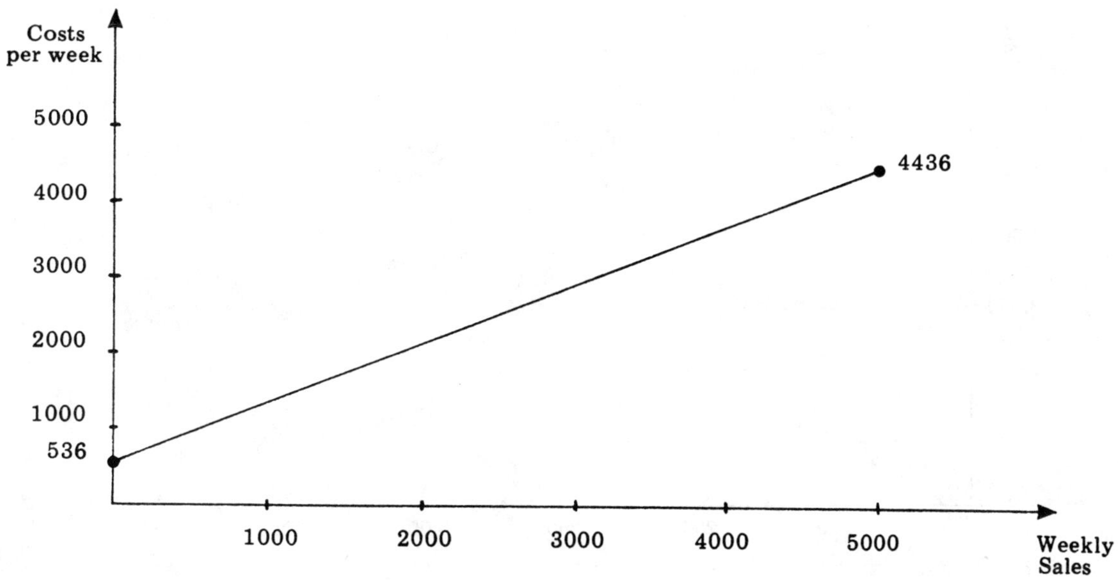

Weekly sales are shown on the x axis and costs on the y axis, because the graph is intended to show how costs vary with sales, or how costs depend on sales volume. The y axis is used to represent the dependent variable, the x axis to represent the independent variable.

1.17 The sales necessary to achieve a profit of a given amount can also be shown as a straight line on a graph, with profit on the x axis and sales on the y axis, because the graph will show what sales must be to achieve a given profit figure. Sales are being treated as the dependent variable.

We need to establish two points on the line to construct a graph.

Profit P = S - 0.78S - 536

where S is the weekly sales
0.78S is the variable cost of sales
536 is the weekly fixed expenditure

P = 0.22S - 536

(a) When profit is 0:

0 = 0.22S - 536
0.22S = 536
S = 2,436.4

(b) When profit is 500:

500 = 0.22S - 536
0.22S = 500 + 536 = 1,036
S = 4,709.1

Sales needed to yield a given weekly profit

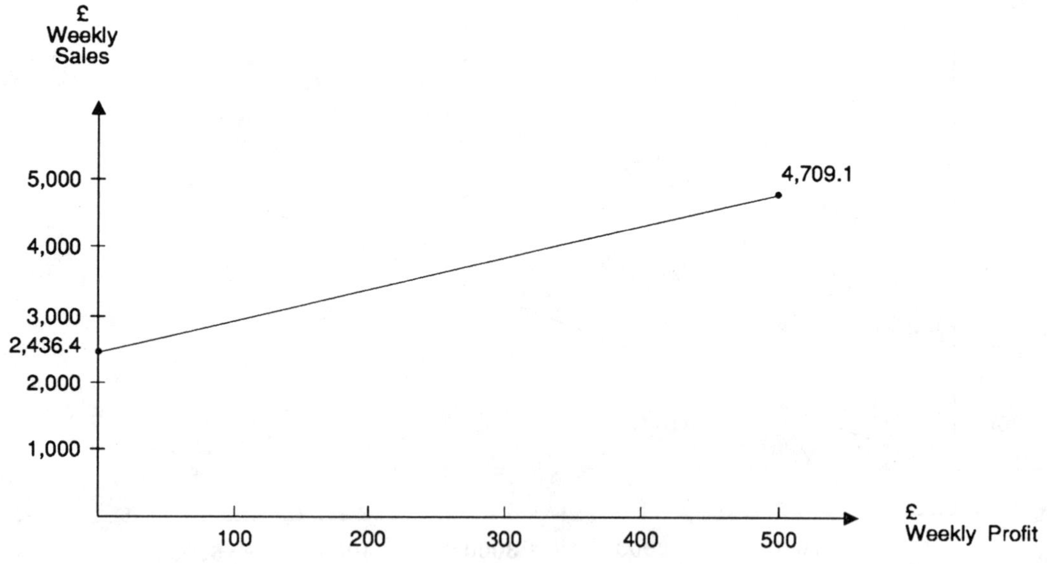

Interpreting graphs

1.18 Graphs can be misleading if they are not read properly, and when you need to interpret the meaning of data in a graph you should:

(a) study what the x axis and y axis represent. The variable on the x axis will be the independent variable and the variable on the y axis will be the dependent variable;

(b) look at the scales on the x axis and y axis. Both of the graphs below show y = 100 + 10x, but with different scales on the x axis.

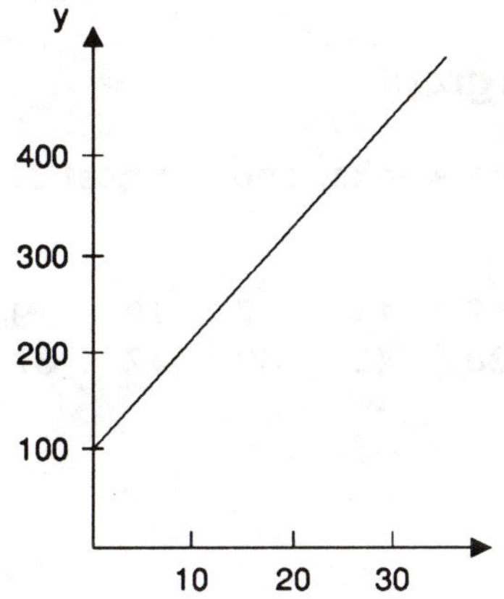

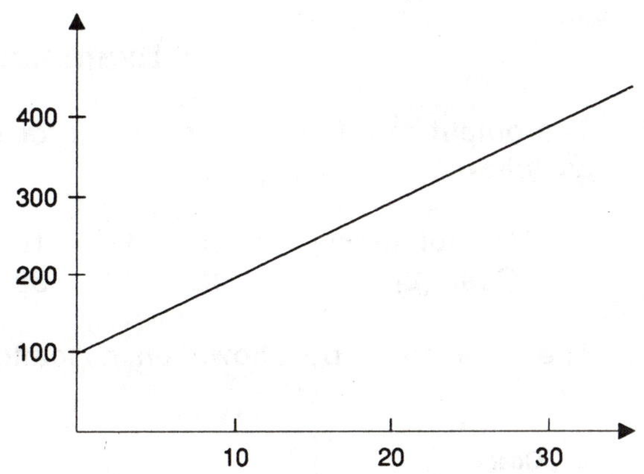

The steeper slope of the left hand graph can be deceptive. This important point has been made before, and you should be ready to comment on it;

(c) consider whether the most suitable dependent variable has been selected for presenting the data. For example, if a graph is presented showing sales over a period of time, it might take units sold as the dependent variable.

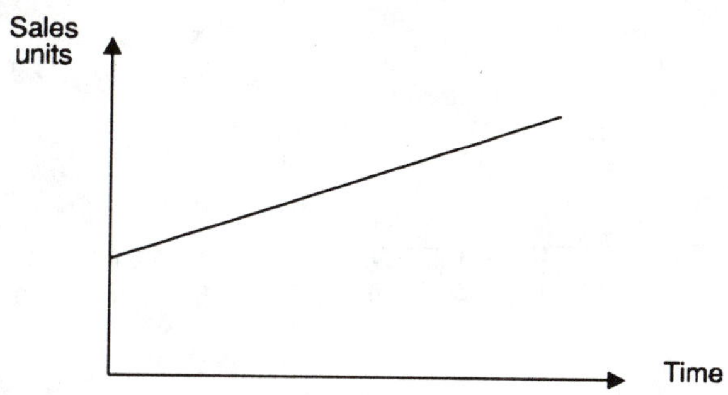

However, if selling *prices* have fallen, the increase in units sold might be explained by the lower prices, and total *turnover* might even have fallen. Turnover might be a more suitable dependent variable for the y axis, depending on the purposes for which the graph is to be used.

Scattergraphs

1.19 Scattergraphs are graphs which are used to exhibit data, rather than equations which produce simple lines or curves, in order to compare the way in which two variables vary with each other. The x axis of the graph is used to represent the independent variable and the y axis represents the dependent variable.

1.20 To construct a scattergraph or scatter diagram, we must have several pairs of data, with each pair showing the value of one variable and the corresponding value of the other variable. Each pair is plotted on a graph. The resulting graph will show a number of pairs, scattered over the graph. The scattered points might or might not appear to follow a trend.

Example: scattergraph

1.21 The output at a factory each week for the last ten weeks, and the cost of that output, were as follows.

Output (units)	10	12	10	8	9	11	7	12	9	14
Cost (£)	42	44	38	34	38	43	30	47	37	50

The data could be shown on a scattergraph.

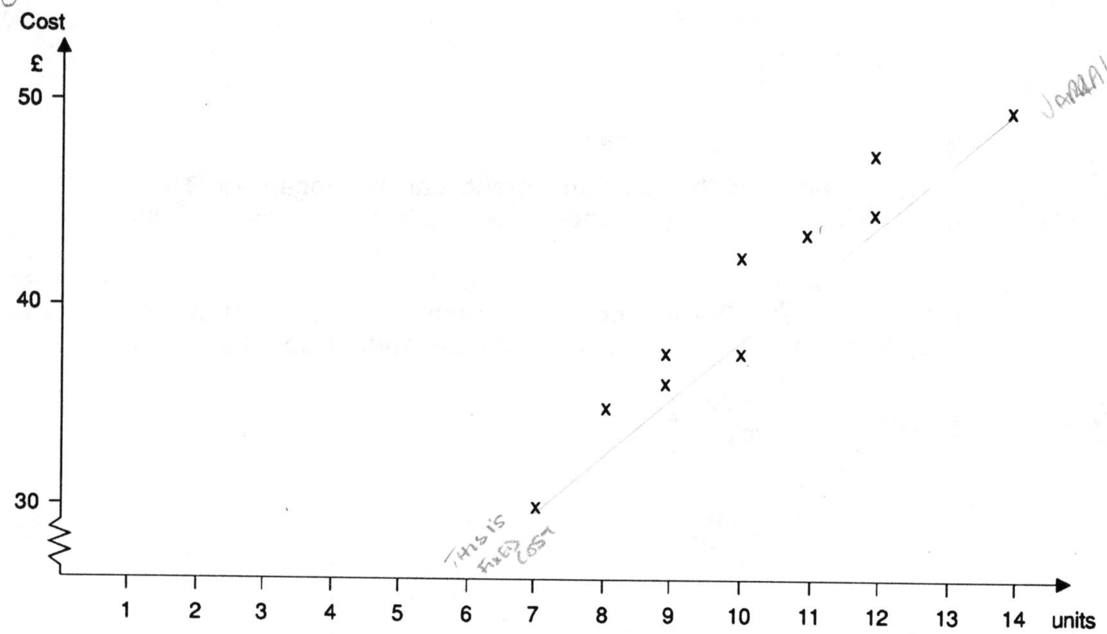

1.22 The cost depends on the volume of output: volume is the independent variable and is shown on the x axis.

1.23 You will notice from the graph that the plotted data, although scattered, lie approximately on a rising trend line, with higher total costs at higher output volumes. (The lower part of the y axis has been omitted, so as not to waste space. The break in the y axis is indicated by the jagged line.)

Curve fitting

1.24 For the most part, scattergraphs are used to try to identify trend lines.

1.25 If a trend can be seen in a scattergraph, the next step is to try to draw a trend line. Fitting a line to scattergraph data is called *curve fitting*.

The reason for wanting to do this is to make predictions.

(a) In the previous example, we could draw a trend line from the scattergraph of output units and production cost. This trend line might turn out to be, say, y = 10 + 3x. We could then use this trend line to establish what we think costs ought to be, approximately, if output were, say, 10 units or 15 units in any week. (These 'expected' costs could subsequently be compared with the actual costs, so that managers could judge whether actual costs were higher or lower than they ought to be.)

(b) If a scattergraph is used to record sales over time, we could draw a trend line, and use this to forecast sales for next year.

1.26 The trend line could be a straight line, or a curved line. The simplest technique for drawing a trend line is to make a visual judgement about what the closest-fitting trend line seems to be.

1.27 Here is an example of a scattergraph with a trend line added.

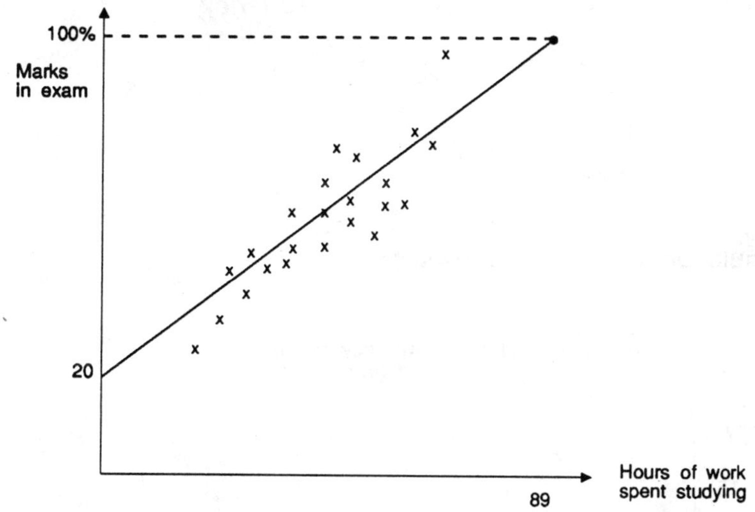

The line passes through the point x = 0, y = 20, so if its equation is y = a + bx, we have a = 20. The line also passes through x = 89, y = 100, so 100 = 20 + b × 89, and b = (100 − 20)/89 = 0.9. The line is y = 20 + 0.9x.

2. Types of graph

2.1 Having considered the rules for constructing graphs, we shall now turn to various ways of presenting statistical data in graphical form.

We shall look at:

(a) ogives;
(b) Lorenz curves;
(c) Z charts;

(d) band curves;
(e) frequency distribution curves;
(f) ratio scale graphs;
(g) break even charts.

Ogives

2.2 An ogive, also known as a cumulative frequency curve, shows the cumulative number of items with a value less than or equal to, or alternatively greater than or equal to, a certain amount.

Example: ogives (1)

2.3 Consider the following frequency distribution.

Number of faulty units rejected on inspection	*Frequency* *f*	*Cumulative frequency*
1	5	5
2	5	10
3	3	13
4	1	14
	14	

An ogive would be drawn as follows.

Cumulative frequency curve of rejected items

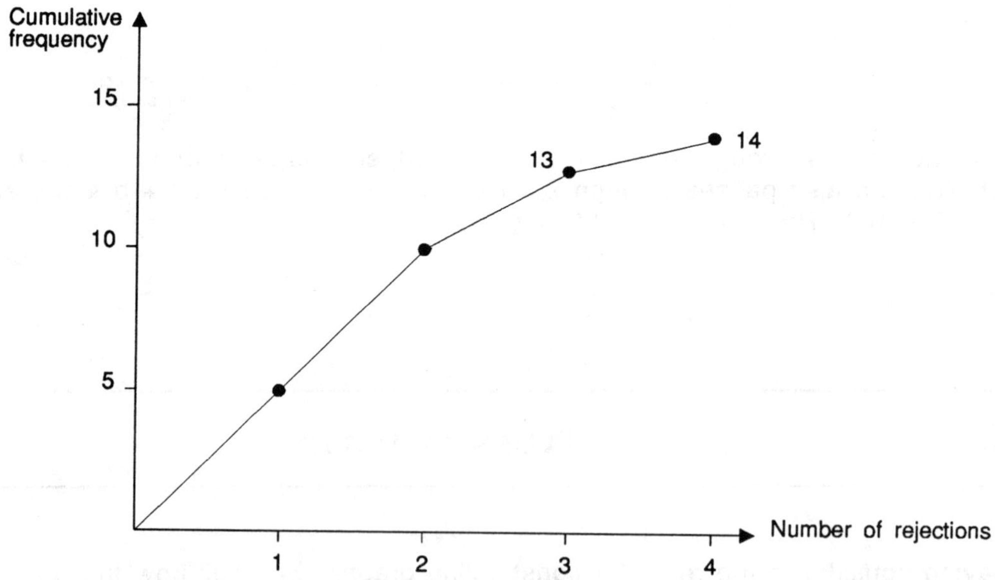

2.4 The ogive is drawn by plotting the cumulative frequencies on the graph, and joining them with straight lines. Although many ogives are more accurately curved lines, you can use straight lines in drawing an ogive in work for an assessment.

2.5 For grouped frequency distributions, where we work up through values of the variable, the cumulative frequencies are plotted against the *upper* limits of the classes. For example:

(a) for the class 'over 200, up to and including 250', the cumulative frequency should be plotted against 250;

(b) for the class 'from 100 up to but not including 150' the cumulative frequency for a continuous variable should be plotted against 150. For a discrete variable, it would be plotted against the highest value less than 150, probably 149.

2.6 We can also draw ogives to show the cumulative number of items with values greater than or equal to some given value.

Example: ogives (2)

2.7 Output at a factory over a period of 80 weeks is shown by the following frequency distribution.

Output per week Units	*Number of weeks output achieved*
>0 ≤ 100	10
>100 ≤ 200	20
>200 ≤ 300	25
>300 ≤ 400	15
>400 ≤ 500	10
	80

2.8 If we wished to draw an ogive to show the number of weeks in which output exceeded a certain value, the cumulative total would begin at 80 and drop to 0.

In drawing an ogive when we work down through values of the variable, the descending cumulative frequency should be plotted against the lower limit of each class interval.

Lower limit of interval	*Frequency* f	*Cumulative ('more than') frequency*
0	10	80
100	20	70
200	25	50
300	15	25
400	10	10
500	0	0

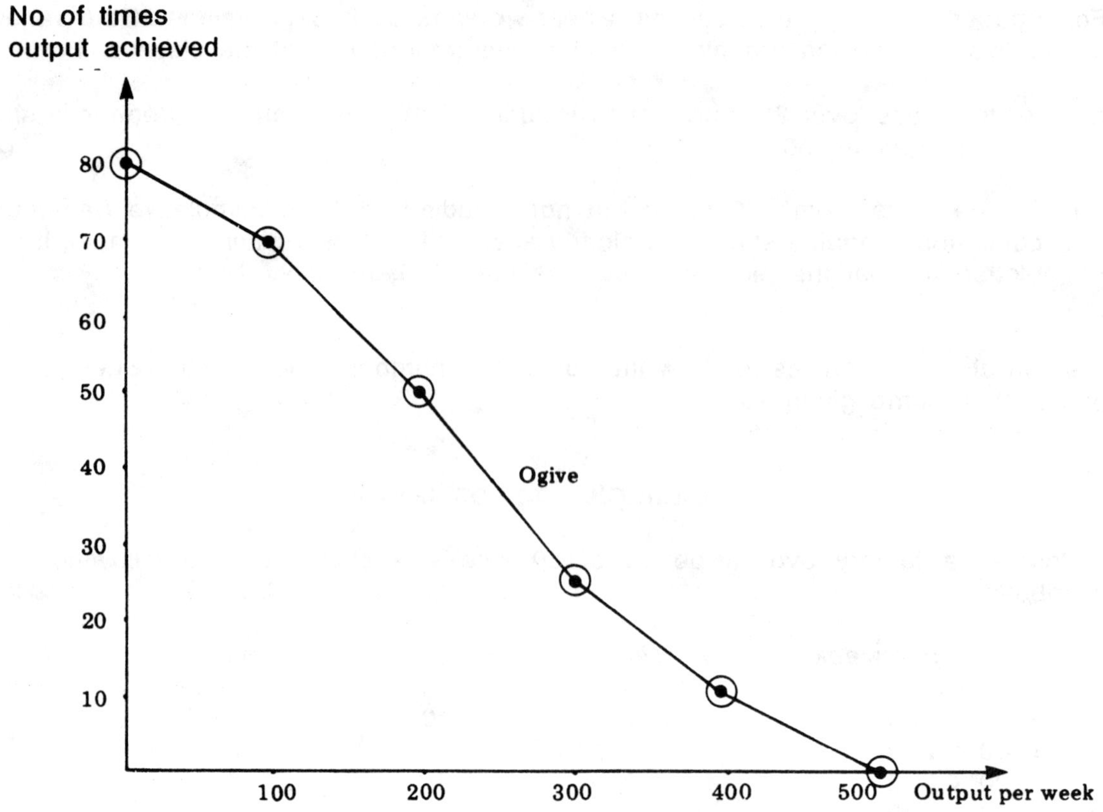

Make sure that you understand what this curve shows.

For example, 350 on the x axis corresponds with about 18 on the y axis. This means that output of 350 units *or more* was achieved 18 times out of the 80 weeks.

What information does an ogive provide?

2.9 An ogive represents a cumulative frequency distribution and it can be used to show what range of values contain given proportions of the total population. For example, it can be used to find:

(a) the range of values of the first 50% of the population;
(b) within what range of values the middle 50% of the population falls.

2.10 These particular pieces of information can be obtained by finding from the ogive:

(a) the value of the middle item in the range, corresponding to a cumulative frequency of 50% of the *total*. For example, if there are 11 data items, the middle item would be the sixth. If there are ten data items, we would take the fifth item.

The middle item of n data items is the [(n + 1)/2]th where n is an odd number and the (n/2)th where n is an even number (it is not usually worth worrying about the fact that when n is even, there are two items which are equally 'in the middle').

The value of the middle item is called the *median* value;

(b) the value of the item which is a quarter (25%) of the way through the cumulative frequencies (running from low values up to high values). For example, if there are 11 data items, this would be the third item. If there are ten data items, it would be taken as the mid-way point between the second and third items: the '2½th' item. However, one might decide to approximate and take the third item.

This quarter-way-through item is called the *lower quartile* or the *first quartile*;

(c) the value of the item which is three quarters (75%) of the way through the cumulative frequencies. For example, if there are 11 data items, this would be the value of the ninth item.

This three-quarters-way-through value is called the *upper quartile* or the *third quartile*. (The second quartile is the median.)

Example: ogives (3)

2.11 The production of each manufacturing department of your company is monitored weekly to establish productivity bonuses to be paid to the members of that department.

250 items have to be produced each week before a bonus will be paid. The production in one department over a 40 week period is shown below.

382	367	364	365	371	370	372	364	355	347
354	359	359	360	357	362	364	365	371	365
361	380	382	394	396	398	402	406	437	456
469	466	459	454	460	457	452	451	445	446

Tasks

(a) Form a frequency distribution of five groups for the number of items produced each week.

(b) Construct the ogive for the frequency distribution established in (a).

(c) Establish the value of the median from the ogive.

(d) Establish the values of the upper and lower quartiles.

(e) Interpret the results that you obtain in (c) and (d).

Solution

2.12 The first step is to decide on the size of class intervals for a grouped frequency distribution, given that the requirement here is for five classes.

Highest value amongst the data	469
Less lowest value amongst the data	347
Range of values	122

This gives a minimum average class interval of $\frac{122}{5}$ = 24.4, say 25.

However, it is not obvious what the lowest and highest values of each class would be, and it might be easier to make the class intervals 30. This would give a range of values of 30 × 5 = 150, which is 28 more than the range of 122 that we need. By sharing the 'excess' between the low and high ends of the range and also looking for suitable lower and upper limits to each class, we arrive at classes from 341 - 370 to 461 - 490.

Class	*Frequency* *f*	*Cumulative frequency*
341 - 370	17	17
371 - 400	9	26
401 - 430	2	28
431 - 460	10	38
461 - 490	2	40
	40	

2.13 The ogive is now constructed by marking units along the x axis and cumulative frequency along the y axis. The first class interval is 341 - 370, and so the x axis starts at 340.

Ogive of weekly production

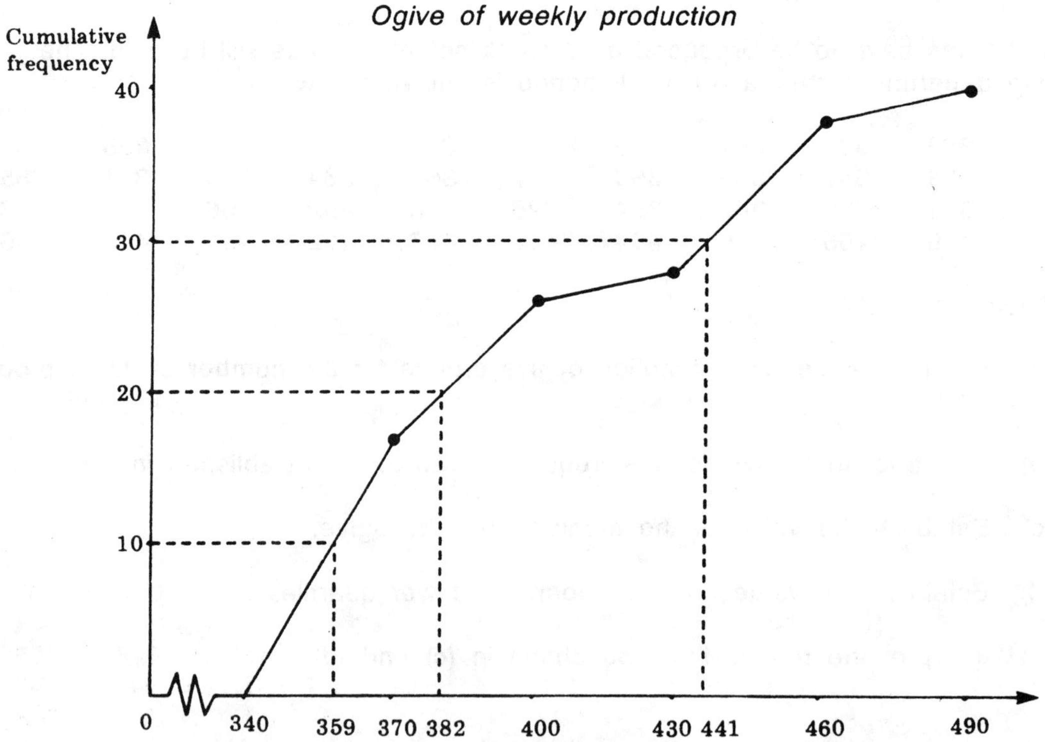

2.14 The median is the $\frac{1}{2} \times 40 = 20$th value. Reading off from the ogive, this value is 382 units per week.

The upper quartile is the $\frac{3}{4} \times 40 = 30$th value. The lower quartile is the $\frac{1}{4} \times 40 = 10$th value. Reading off from the ogive, these values are 441 units and 359 units respectively.

2.15 These values show that in half of the weeks production was in the range 359 to 441 units, with the middle-of-the-range value (the median) being 382, which is closer to the lower quartile than to the upper quartile.

Lorenz curves

2.16 A Lorenz curve is a form of cumulative frequency curve, which measures one cumulative amount against another. It is normal, though not essential, for both the x axis and the y axis to be shown in terms of percentages (each up to 100%).

Example: Lorenz curve

2.17 The following table shows the distribution of the levels of turnover of the companies in a certain industry.

Turnover £'000	*Number of companies*
over 500 - 1,000	32
over 1,000 - 1,500	58
over 1,500 - 2,000	41
over 2,000 - 2,500	33
over 2,500 - 3,000	28
over 3,000 - 3,500	16

(a) Construct a Lorenz chart from these data. Use the mid-point of each class as the turnover of each company in the class.

(b) State what this chart shows.

Solution

2.18 *Calculation of figures for Lorenz chart*

Turnover £'000	*Turnover: class midpoint* £'000	*No of cos*	*Total turnover* £'000	*Cumulative turnover* £'000	*Cumulative turnover*	*Cumulative companies*	*Cumulative companies*
	x	f	fx		%		%
over 500 - 1,000	750	32	24,000	**24,000**	**6.46**	**32**	**15.38**
over 1,000 - 1,500	1,250	58	72,500	**96,500**	**25.97**	**90**	**43.26**
over 1,500 - 2,000	1,750	41	71,750	**168,250**	**45.29**	**131**	**62.98**
over 2,000 - 2,500	2,250	33	74,250	**242,500**	**65.28**	**164**	**78.85**
over 2,500 - 3,000	2,750	28	77,000	**319,500**	**86.00**	**192**	**92.30**
over 3,000 - 3,500	3,250	16	52,000	**371,500**	**100.00**	**208**	**100.00**

2.19 The Lorenz curve is now drawn. The number of companies has been recorded on the y axis and turnover on the x axis, but it would be equally suitable to have turnover on the y axis and the number of companies on the x axis.

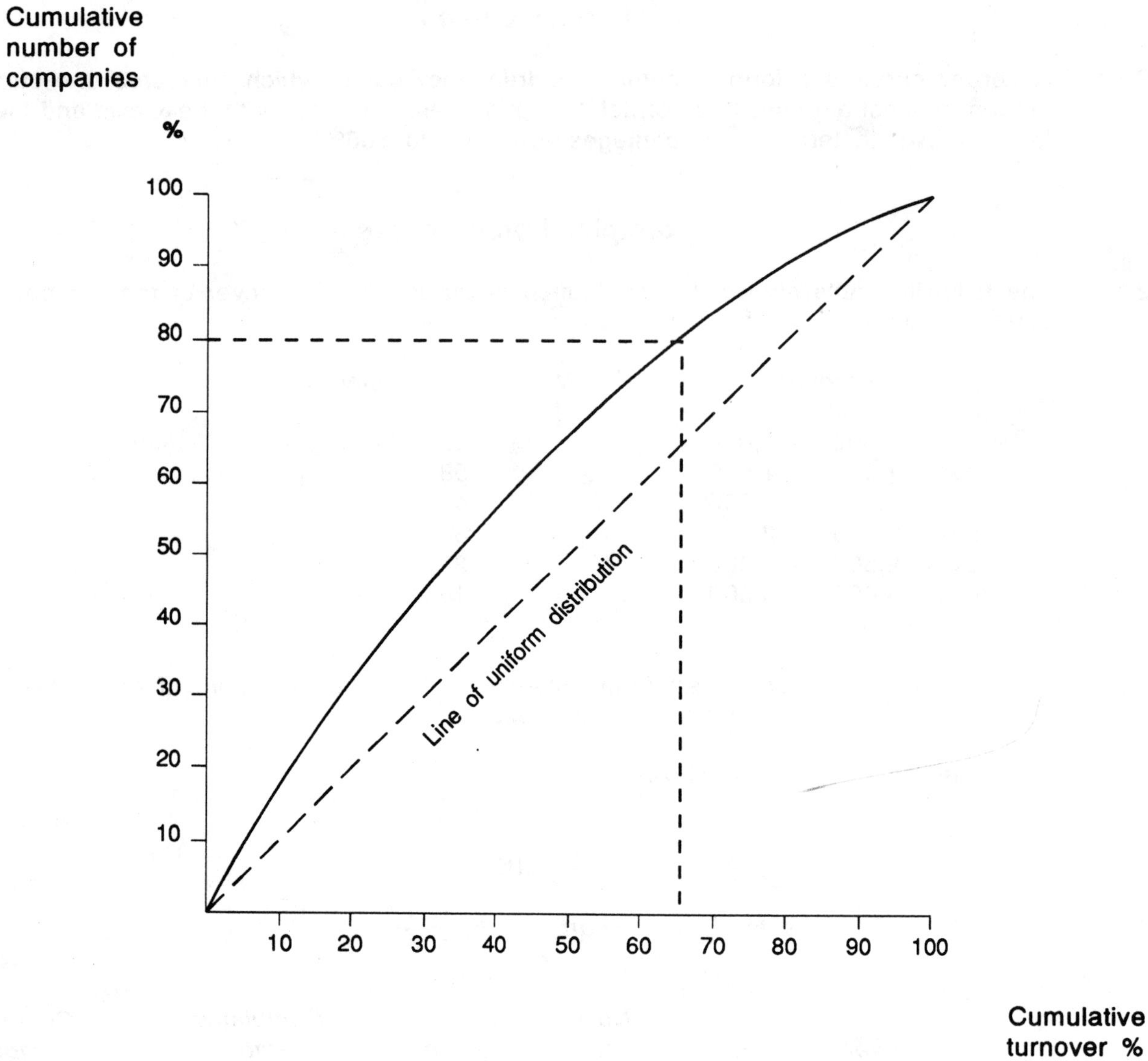

2.20 A Lorenz curve shows degree of concentration. The Lorenz curve in this example shows the degree of concentration of total revenue within the population of companies. The further the curve is away from the diagonal the greater is the degree of concentration of revenue.

In this case it appears that there is a moderate degree of concentration of turnover. Approximately 80% of companies share only about 65% of the total turnover, so the top 20% of companies have 35% of total turnover.

Z charts

2.21 A Z chart is a time series graph which can be very useful for presenting business data. It can show:

(a) how results are changing from period to period;
(b) how results compare with the previous year;
(c) how results compare with the budget for the year to date.

2.22 A Z chart shows:

(a) the value of a variable plotted against time over the year;
(b) the cumulative sum of values for that variable over the year to date;
(c) the annual moving total for that variable.

2.23 The annual moving total is the sum of values of the variable for the 12 month period up to the end of the month under consideration.

A line for the budget for the year to date may be added to a Z chart, for comparison with the cumulative sum of actual values.

Example: Z charts

2.24 The sales figures for a company for 19X2 and 19X3 are as follows.

	19X2 sales	*19X3 sales*
	£m	£m
January	7	8
February	7	8
March	8	8
April	7	9
May	9	8
June	8	8
July	8	7
August	7	8
September	6	9
October	7	6
November	8	9
December	8	9
	90	97

Task

Draw a Z chart to represent these data.

Solution

2.25 The first thing to do is to calculate the cumulative sales for 19X3 and the annual moving total for the year.

	Sales 19X2	*Sales 19X3*	*Cumulative sales 19X3*	*Annual moving total*
	£m	£m	£m	£m
January	7	8	8	91
February	7	8	16	92
March	8	8	24	92
April	7	9	33	94
May	9	8	41	93
June	8	8	49	93
July	8	7	56	92
August	7	8	64	93
September	6	9	73	96
October	7	6	79	95
November	8	9	88	96
December	8	9	97	97

The first figure in the annual moving total is arrived at by taking the sales for the year ended December 19X2, adding those for January 19X3 and subtracting those for January 19X2. This gives the sales for a 12 month period to the end of January 19X3: 90 + 8 - 7 = 91.

A similar approach is used for the rest of the year, by adding on the new 19X3 month and deducting the corresponding 19X2 month.

The Z chart is given on the next page.

2.26 You will notice that while the values of the annual moving total and the cumulative values are plotted on month end positions, the values for the current monthly figures are plotted on mid-month positions. This is because the monthly figures represent achievement over a particular month whereas the annual moving totals and the cumulative values represent achievement up to a particular month end.

The interpretation of Z charts

2.27 The popularity of Z charts in practical applications derives from the wealth of information which they can contain.

(a) *Monthly totals* show the monthly results at a glance together with any seasonal variations.

(b) *Cumulative totals* show the performance to date, and can be easily compared with planned or budgeted performance by superimposing a budget line.

(c) *Annual moving totals* compare the current levels of performance with those of the previous year. If the line is rising then this year's monthly results are better than the results of the corresponding month last year. The opposite applies if the line is falling. The annual moving total line indicates the long term trend in values of the variable, whether rising, falling or steady.

2.28 You should note that Z charts do not have to cover 12 months of a year. They could also be drawn for (for example) four quarters of a year, or seven days of a week. The method would be exactly the same.

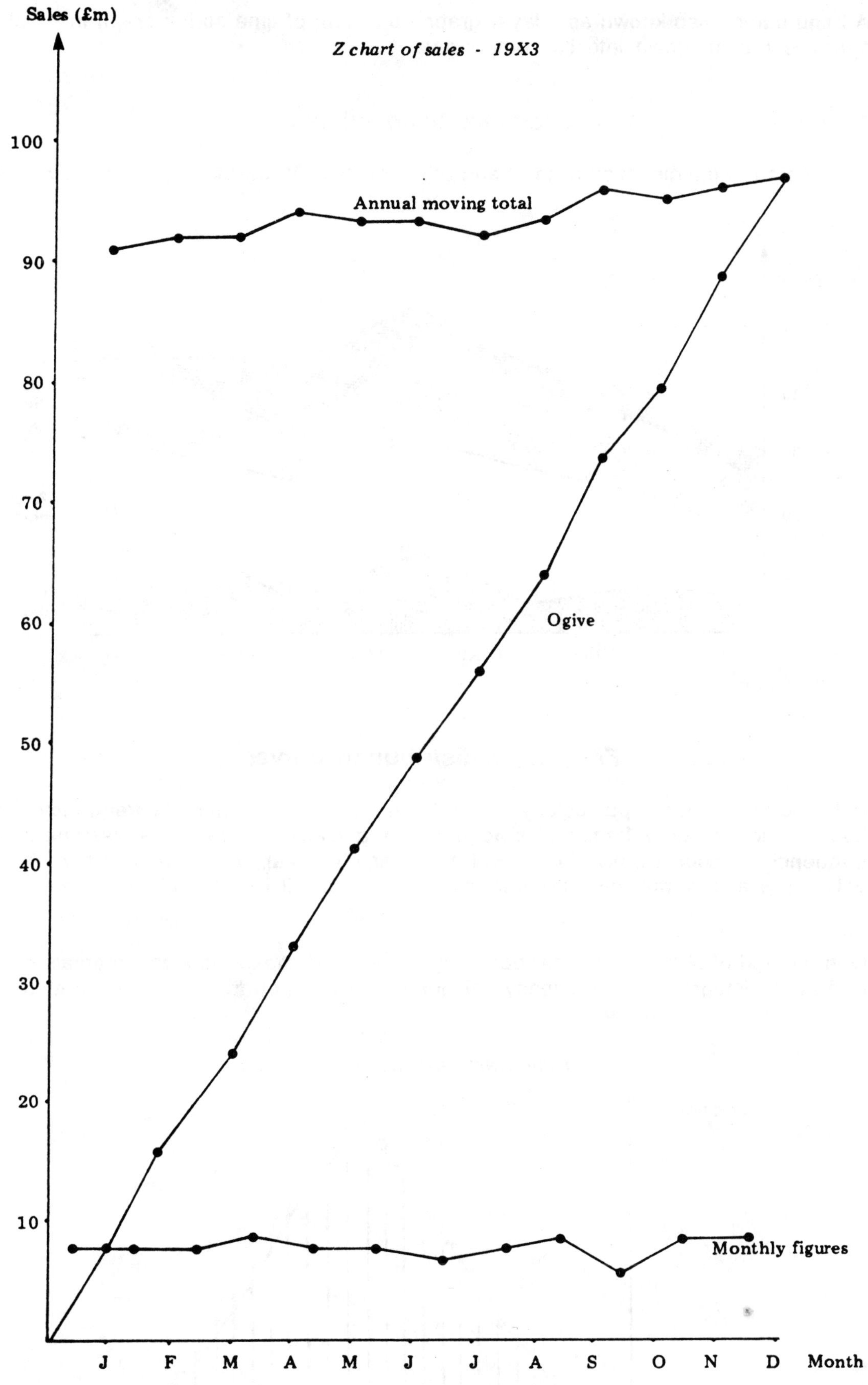
Sales (£m)
Z chart of sales - 19X3
100
90
80
70
60
50
40
30
20
10
Annual moving total
Ogive
Monthly figures
J
F
M
A
M
J
J
A
S
O
N
D
Month

Band curves

2.29 A band curve, also known as a layer graph, is a form of time series graph in which the total figure is broken down into its components.

Example: band curves

2.30 The costs of administration at the head office of Piper Wark Ltd might be shown as follows.

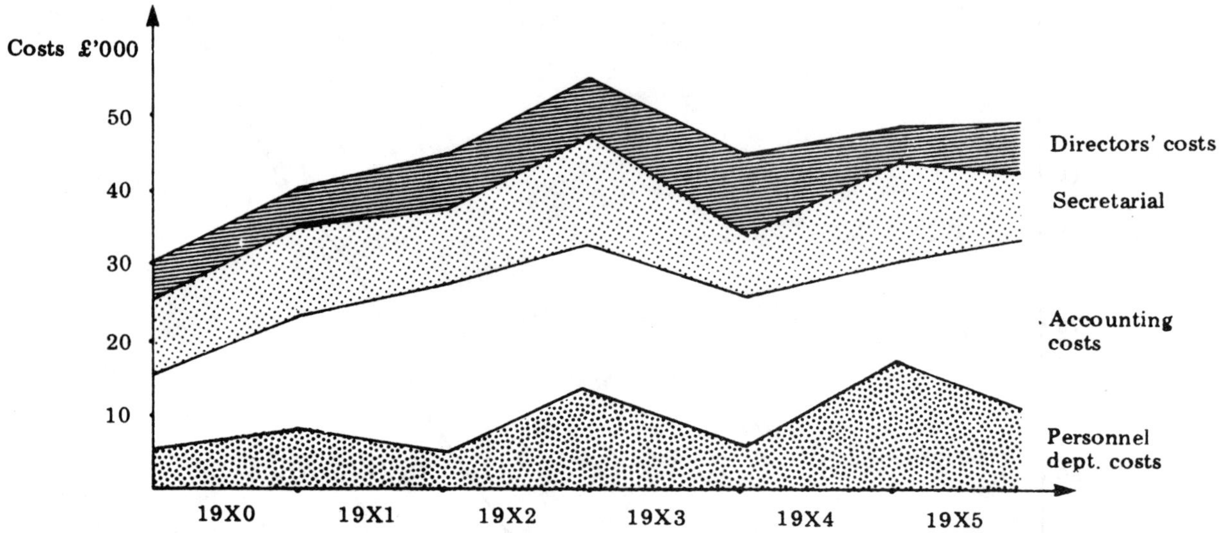

Frequency distribution curves

2.31 A histogram is not a particularly accurate method of presenting a frequency distribution, because in grouping frequencies together in a class interval, it is assumed that these frequencies occur evenly throughout the class interval, which is unlikely. A frequency polygon is also somewhat unrepresentative, because it has straight lines between points.

2.32 One method of obtaining greater accuracy would be to make the class intervals smaller, and to draw a histogram or a frequency polygon of the grouped frequency distribution with these small intervals, as follows.

Histogram and frequency polygon

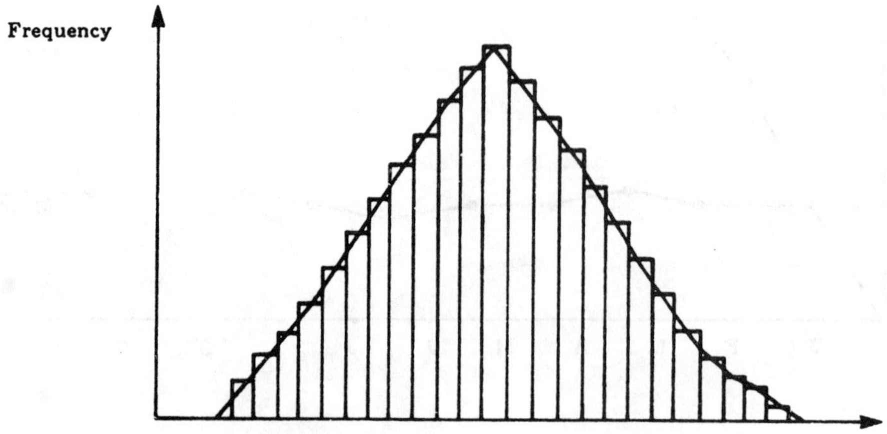

2.33 If the class intervals were made small enough, the frequency polygon would become very smooth. It would become a *curve*. A *frequency distribution curve* from the histogram and polygon above might be as follows.

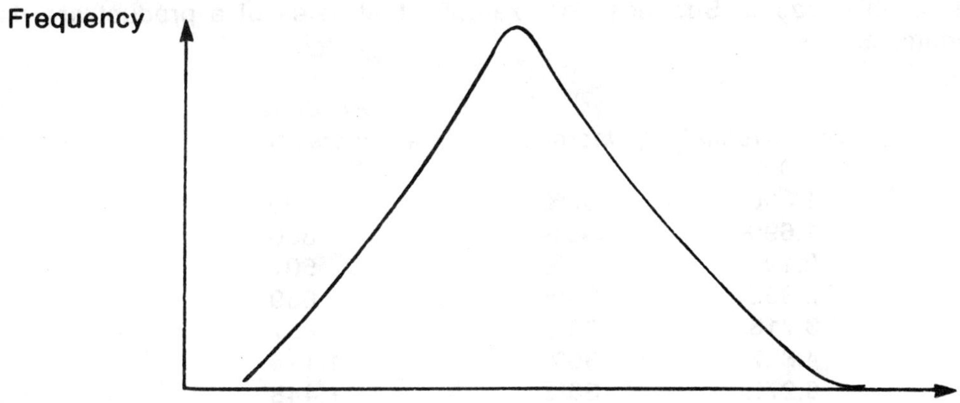

Ratio scale graphs

2.34 A ratio scale or semi-logarithmic graph is one in which the y axis is measured or 'scaled' logarithmically.

2.35 Suppose we wish to plot the values for y = 1,000 to y = 10,000 on a semi-logarithmic graph. The logarithm values of y would range from 3.0 to 4.0. These values would be plotted on the special graph paper as below.

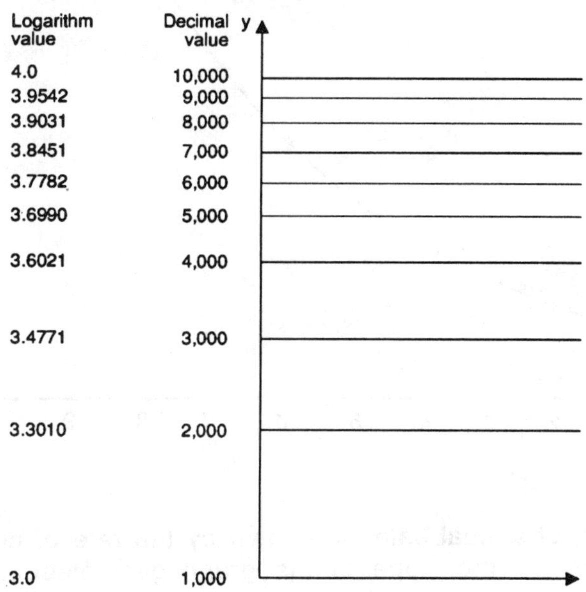

Note that the y axis starts at 1,000, not 0. The graph is to scale in terms of the logarithm values of y, not the 'absolute number' values of y.

Why might a semi-logarithmic graph be useful?

2.36 The value of a semi-logarithmic graph is that it shows *relative* changes, or the *ratio of change* in the value of y more clearly. In fact, semi-logarithmic graphs are also called ratio-scale graphs for this reason. Suppose, for example, that sales of a product are rising by 30% per annum, as follows.

Year	*Sales (units)*	*Increase*	*Absolute increase*
1	1,000		
2	1,300	30%	300
3	1,690	30%	390
4	2,197	30%	507
5	2,856	30%	659
6	3,713	30%	857
7	4,827	30%	1,114
8	6,275	30%	1,448
9	8,157	30%	1,882

2.37 Drawn on an absolute scale graph, the sales growth would look like this.

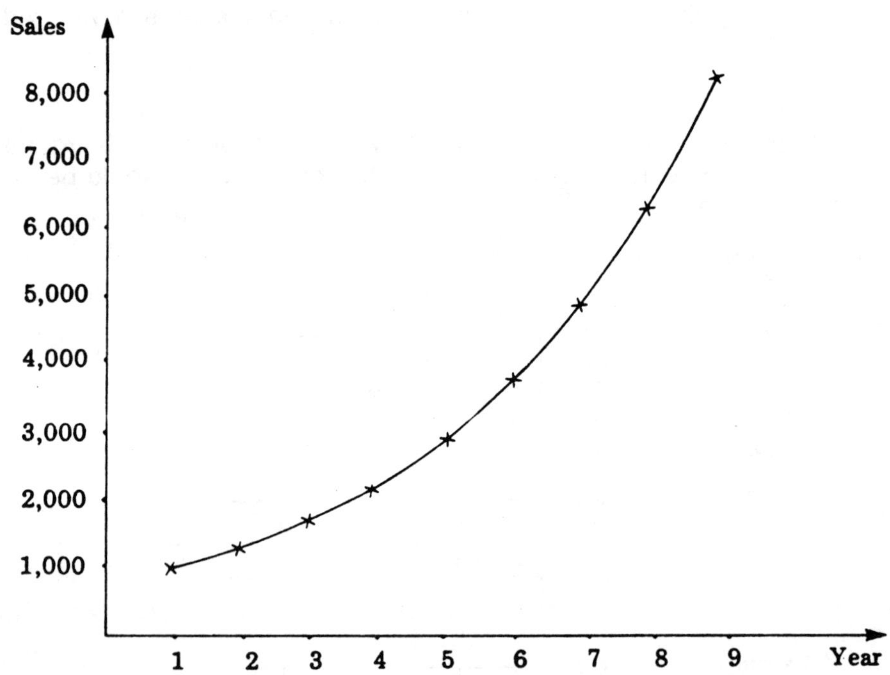

The increasing growth of annual sales is shown by the rate of change in the slope of the graph. In other words, as the slope of the graph gets steeper, then annual sales are growing. But are the sales growing at a constant rate, or are they going up by leaps and bounds? You cannot really tell from an ordinary, absolute scale graph: you need a semi-logarithmic graph.

2.38 The same information drawn on a ratio-scale or semi-logarithmic graph would look like this.

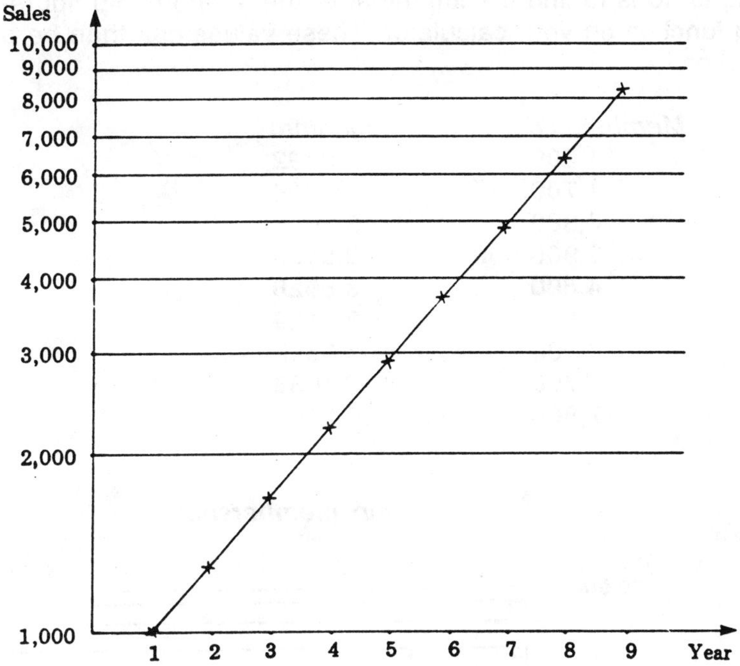

The line of the semi-logarithmic graph is straight, which means that the rate of change of annual sales is constant.

2.39 The reason why the straight line shows a constant ratio or rate of growth may be explained by the mathematics of logarithms. However, such mathematics is outside the elements of competence which you are required to have. What you should remember is that if y is changing by a steady ratio, then a normal graph will represent it as a curve, but a semi-log graph will represent it as a straight line.

Example: semi-logarithmic graph

2.40 The membership of the Union of Widget Turners over the past nine years has been as follows.

Year	*Membership*
1	1,200
2	1,700
3	2,300
4	3,300
5	4,600
6	6,500
7	9,000
8	12,700
9	17,800

Plot the growth in membership on a semi-logarithmic graph and comment on your findings.

Solution

2.41 The first thing to do is to find the logarithm of the membership figures in logarithm tables, or using the log function on your calculator. These values can then be plotted on special semi-log graph paper.

Year	*Membership*	*Logarithm*
1	1,200	3.0792
2	1,700	3.2304
3	2,300	3.3617
4	3,300	3.5185
5	4,600	3.6628
6	6,500	3.8129
7	9,000	3.9542
8	12,700	4.1038
9	17,800	4.2504

2.42

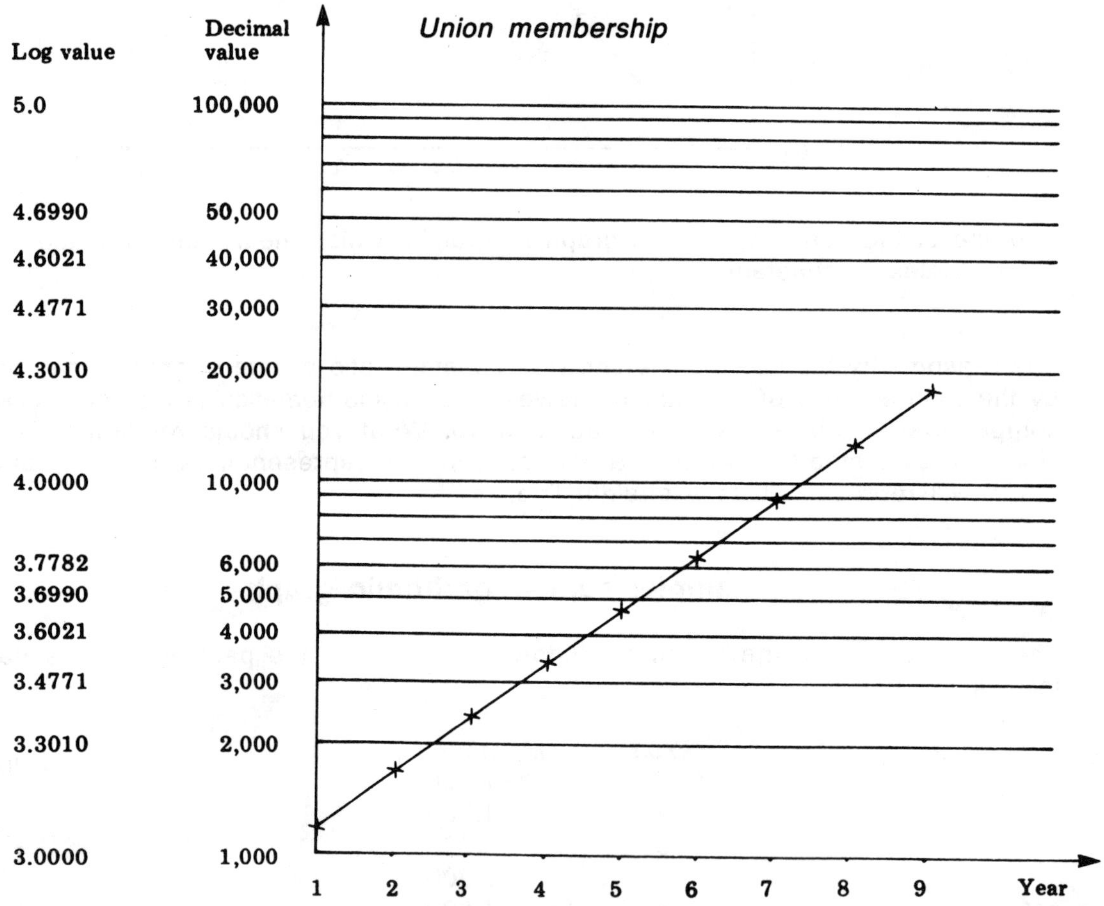

Comment: the rate of growth as a percentage of the previous year's membership has been relatively constant over the entire nine year period, because the membership gives roughly a straight line when plotted on a semi-logarithmic graph.

Breakeven charts: comparing costs and revenues

2.43 A *breakeven chart* is a graph which shows the point at which the costs of a business exactly match its sales revenue. If costs and sales are equal, then the business is not making a profit or a loss - it is breaking even (which is where the chart gets its name from).

2.44 We shall look at breakeven charts briefly below. The topic will be covered in more detail at the AAT Technician Stage (NVQ/SVQ level 4).

2.45 A breakeven chart shows both costs and sales on the same pair of axes, but we will first look at them one at a time so that the explanation is easier to follow. We will therefore start by looking at:

(a) graphs of costs; and
(b) graphs of sales.

Graphs of costs

2.46 When a business makes a product, it incurs costs. These costs are usually broken down into two parts.

(a) *Fixed costs*, ie costs which the business would incur no matter how many items it produces. An example is the rent of a factory. The rent would remain at, say, £5,000, regardless of whether production was 10 items or 10,000 items.

(b) *Variable costs*, ie costs incurred by the business which vary directly with how many items are produced. An example is the materials used in making the product. If production doubles, then the cost of materials used up will also double.

2.47 Total costs therefore equals fixed costs plus variable costs. This relationship can be drawn on a graph as a straight line. How do we know it will be a straight line?

2.48 Remember that the general equation for a straight line is $y = ax + b$. In this instance of production costs:

y = total costs
b = fixed costs
x = no of units produced
a = variable costs per unit

Example: total monthly costs

2.49 The fixed costs in a bed-making factory are £3,000 per month. Variable costs are £100 for material and £150 for labour per bed.

Task

Show total monthly factory costs on a graph.

Solution

2.50 Using the straight line equation $y = ax + b$:

y = total costs
a = variable costs per bed = £250
x = number of beds made
b = £3,000

So the straight line we want is represented by y = 250x + 3,000.

x	*y = 250x + 3,000*
0	3,000
25	9,250
50	15,500

Monthly costs of bed-making factory

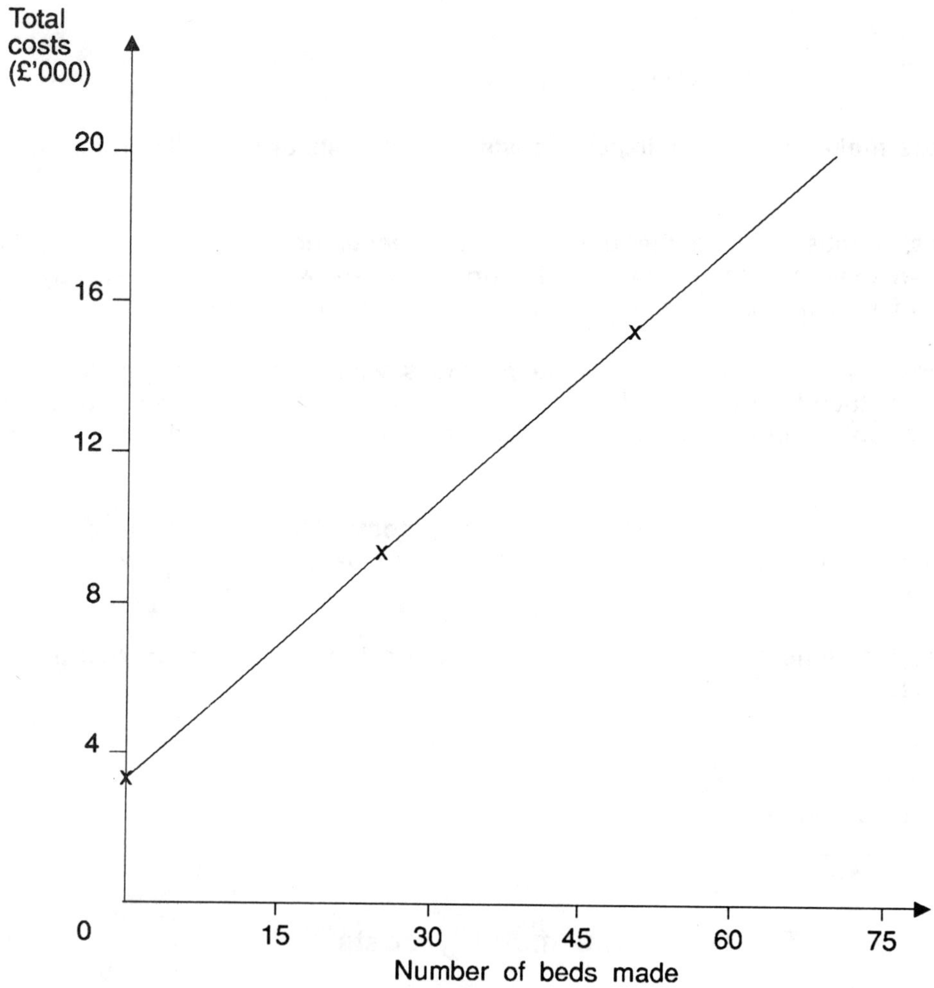

2.51 Notice that the fixed costs are always shown by the point where the line meets the y axis. This is because that particular point represents the case when there is no production (x = 0) and so there are no variable costs. Total costs therefore equal fixed costs, which is exactly what the line shows.

Graph of sales

2.52 Suppose that the business sells its beds for £350 each. Total sales will equal £350 times the number of beds sold. This can be expressed algebraically as follows.

y = 350x; where

y = total sales
x = number of beds sold

2.53 This is just another straight line and we can draw a graph similar to the one we have already drawn for total costs. The x-axis now shows the number of beds sold. The y axis represents £'000s.

x	*y = 350x*
0	0
15	5,250
60	21,000

Sales of bed-making factory

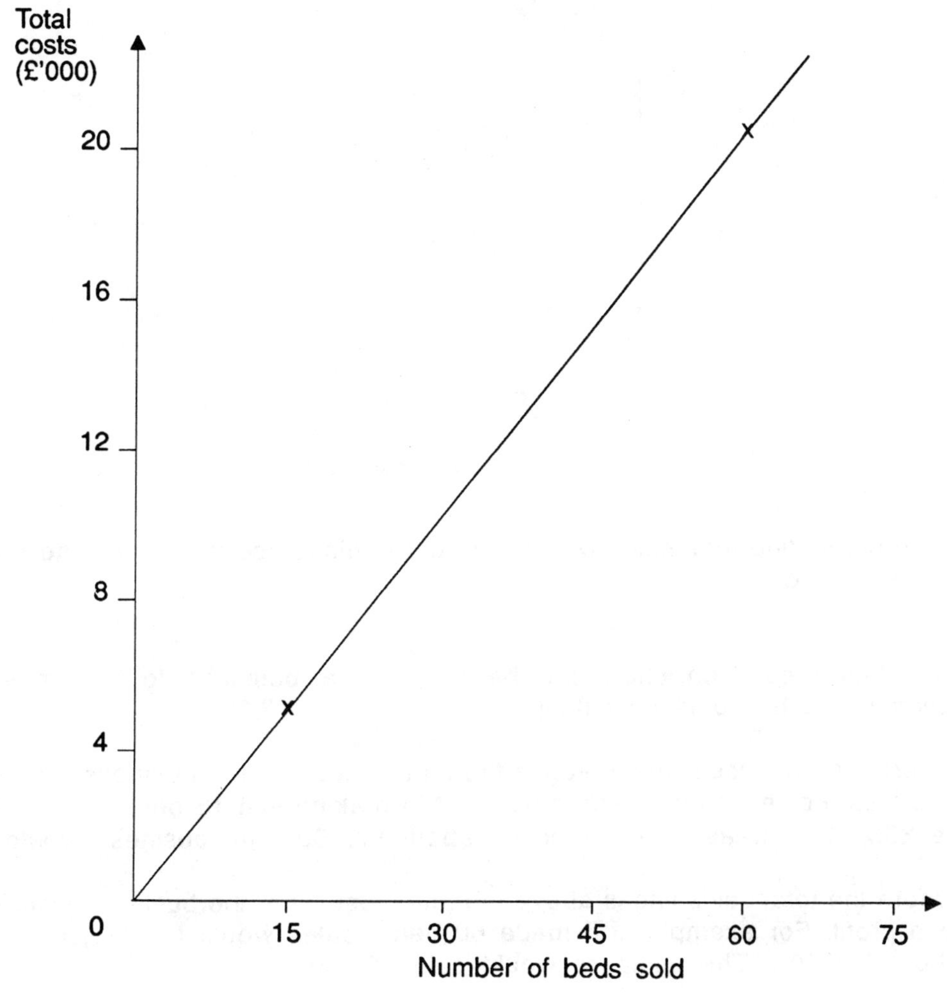

Completing the breakeven chart

2.54 The final step in completing the breakeven chart is to put the sales graph and the costs graph onto the same pair of axes. The x axis now shows either the number of beds *made* or the number of beds *sold*, which are assumed to be equal. The y axis still represents £s.

Breakeven chart for bed manufacture

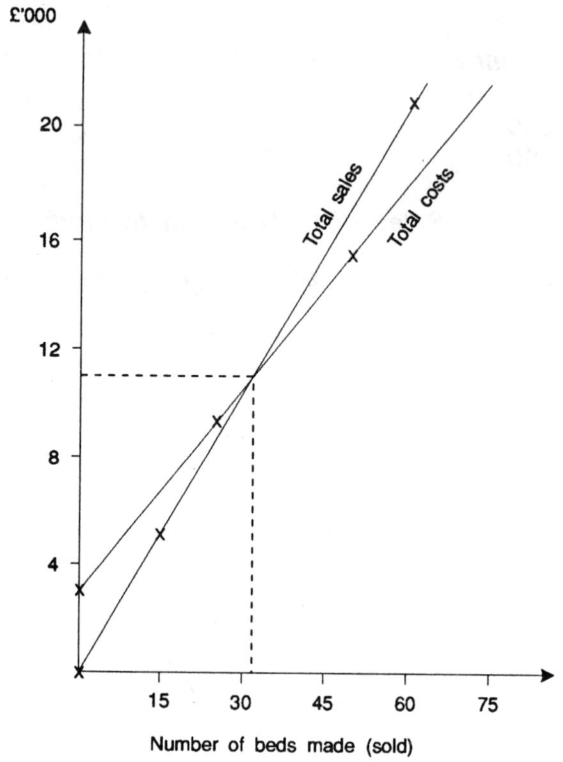

2.55 The line representing total sales will start at the origin, since if there are no beds sold there will be no income.

2.56 The complete breakeven chart can be used by a business to determine the sort of production levels it should be aiming at.

(a) Where the total costs line is above the total sales line, the business would be operating at a loss. For example, there is no point in making just 15 beds, because sales would be £5,250 whereas costs would be about £7,000. The business would lose £1,750.

(b) Where the total sales line is above the total costs line, the business would be operating at a profit. For example, if it made 60 beds, sales would be £21,000 and costs only about £19,000. The business would gain £2,000.

(c) Where the two lines cross, total costs equal total sales, so the business would neither gain nor lose. It would *break even*. In this example, the breakeven point can be read off the chart as being about at (x = 31, y = 10,600) or in other words, if the business made and sold 31 beds, both its costs and its sales would be £10,600.

3. Graphical presentation of information in public reports

3.1 In Unit 7: *Preparing reports and returns* we are mainly concerned with the presentation of information for internal use or for the purposes of an external organisation, and not with information presented to the public. If you go on to study at the AAT Technician stage (NVQ/SVQ level 4) you will learn about the preparation of financial statements, which, in the case of companies, will be available to the general public as well as to shareholders. It is therefore of interest to look a little at the use of graphs in the annual reports of UK companies. It is up to the company whether it includes graphical presentation of information in the reports.

3.2 A 1992 survey reported in *Accounting and business research* found that 79% of large UK companies made use of graphical presentation of information in their annual reports. The average number of graphs (or charts) per report, for those companies using graphs, was 7.5. But was their use objective and unbiased? The survey included some interesting findings.

(a) Graphs of key financial variables are more likely to be included in the annual reports of companies with 'good' rather than 'bad' performance. A significant proportion of the graphs investigated included distortions of rising trends.

(b) We could say that there is 'measurement distortion' if the representation of numbers, as physically measured on the surface of the graph, is not directly proportional to the numerical values of the variable being represented. A common ploy is to use axes which do not start at zero (see the chart below).

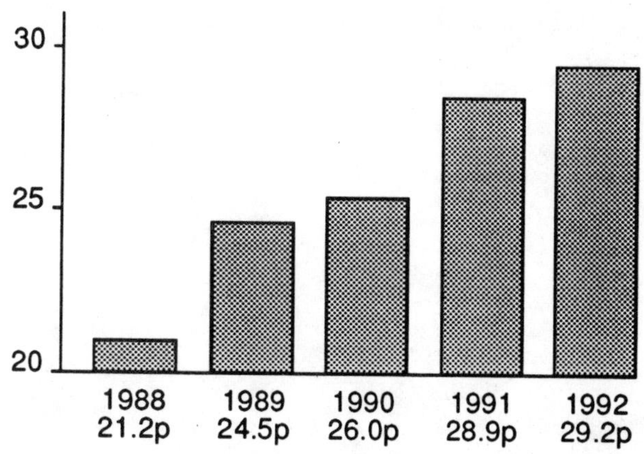

Earnings per share

(c) There was often a lack of proper axes and poor adherence to basic rules of graph construction and design (such as those we have learned about earlier in this Text). This was, perhaps, in some cases, deliberate.

Key points in this chapter

- The first section of this chapter covered the rules for drawing graphs. These rules may seem obvious, but they are still important, and whenever you draw a graph you should check it carefully.
- The second section looked at different types of graph. You should not only ensure that you can draw and interpret different types of graph. You should also think carefully about the different situations in which the various types of graph would be appropriate.
- Finally, we looked briefly at the use (and possible abuse) of the presentation of information using graphs and charts which is made available to the general public. Be prepared to look critically at the way a graph or chart is used to convey information in a particular way.

For practice on the points covered in this chapter you should now attempt the Exercises in Session 5 of the Cost Accounting II Workbook

6. Averages and time series

1. Averages

2. The analysis of time series

3. Finding the trend and seasonal variations

4. Forecasting

1. Averages

1.1 The standards of competence for Unit 7 require you to know and understand time series analysis, which involves statistics recorded over a period of time. Before looking at time series analysis in detail in the next section of this chapter, we need to be clear about the concept of an average.

1.2 An average is a representative figure that is used to give some impression of the size of all the items in a population. The three main types of average used are:

(a) the arithmetic mean;
(b) the mode;
(c) the median.

1.3 An average, whether it is a mean, a mode or a median, is a *measure of central tendency*. By this we mean that while a population may range in values, these values will be distributed around a central point. This central point, or average, is therefore in some way representative of the population as a whole.

The arithmetic mean

1.4 This is the best known type of average. For ungrouped data, it is calculated by the formula

$$\text{Arithmetic mean} = \frac{\text{Sum of values of items}}{\text{Number of items}}$$

Example: arithmetic mean

1.5 The demand for a product on each of 20 days was as follows (in units).

3 12 7 17 3 14 9 6 11 10 1 4 19 7 15 6 9 12 12 8

The arithmetic mean of daily demand is

$$\frac{\text{Sum of demands}}{\text{Number of days}} = \frac{185}{20} = 9.25 \text{ units}$$

1.6 The arithmetic mean of a variable x is shown as $\bar{x}$ ('x bar').

Thus in the above example $\bar{x}$ = 9.25 units.

1.7 In the above example, demand on any one day is never actually 9.25 units. The arithmetic mean is merely an average representation of demand on each of the 20 days.

The arithmetic mean of data in a frequency distribution

1.8 The concept of the frequency distribution was explained earlier. In our previous example, the frequency distribution would be shown as follows.

Daily demand	*Frequency*	*Demand × frequency*
x	*f*	*fx*
1	1	1
3	2	6
4	1	4
6	2	12
7	2	14
8	1	8
9	2	18
10	1	10
11	1	11
12	3	36
14	1	14
15	1	15
17	1	17
19	1	19
	20	185

$$\bar{x} = \frac{185}{20} = 9.25$$

Sigma, Σ

1.9 The statistical notation for the arithmetic mean of a set of data uses the symbol Σ (sigma). Σ means 'the sum of' and is used as shorthand to mean the sum of a set of values.

Thus, in the previous example:

(a) Σ f would mean the sum of all the frequencies, which is 20.

(b) Σ fx would mean the sum of all the values of 'frequency multiplied by daily demand', that is, all 14 values of fx, so Σ fx = 185.

The symbolic formula for the arithmetic mean

1.10 Using the Σ sign, the formula for the arithmetic mean of a frequency distribution is

$$\bar{x} = \frac{\Sigma fx}{n} \quad \text{or} \quad \frac{\Sigma fx}{\Sigma f}$$

where n is the number of values recorded, or the number of items measured.

The arithmetic mean of grouped data in class intervals

1.11 Another common problem is to calculate (or at least approximate) the arithmetic mean of a frequency distribution, where the frequencies are shown in class intervals.

Example: arithmetic mean of grouped data

1.12 Using the example in paragraph 1.6, the frequency distribution might have been shown as follows.

Daily demand	*Frequency*
> 0 ≤ 5	4
> 5 ≤ 10	8
> 10 ≤ 15	6
> 15 ≤ 20	2
	20

1.13 An arithmetic mean is calculated by taking the mid point of each class interval, on the assumption that the frequencies occur evenly over the class interval range. Note that the variable is discrete, so the first class includes 1, 2, 3, 4 and 5, giving a mid point of 3. With a continuous variable (such as quantities of fuel consumed in litres), the mid points would have been 2.5, 7.5 and so on.

Daily demand	*Mid point* *x*	*Frequency* *f*	*fx*
> 0 ≤ 5	3	4	12
> 5 ≤ 10	8	8	64
> 10 ≤ 15	13	6	78
> 15 ≤ 20	18	2	36
		Σf = 20	Σfx = 190

Arithmetic mean $\bar{x} = \frac{\Sigma fx}{\Sigma f} = \frac{190}{20} = 9.5$ units

1.14 Because the assumption that frequencies occurred evenly within each class interval is not quite correct in this example, our approximate mean of 9.5 is not exactly correct, and is in error by 0.25.

As the frequencies become larger, the size of this approximating error should become smaller.

The mode

1.15 The mode is an average which means 'the most frequently occurring value'.

Example: the mode

1.16 The daily demand for stock in a ten day period is as follows.

Demand Units	*Number of days*
6	3
7	6
8	1
	10

The mode is 7 units, because it is the value which occurs most frequently.

The mode in grouped frequency distributions

1.17 In a grouped frequency distribution, the mode can only be estimated approximately.

1.18 The method of making this estimate is as follows.

(a) Establish which is the class with the highest frequency (the modal class).
(b) The mode is taken as

$$L + \frac{(F_1 - F_0) \times c}{2F_1 - F_0 - F_2}$$

where
L = the lower limit of the modal class
F_0 = the frequency of the next class below the modal class
F_1 = the frequency of the modal class
F_2 = the frequency of the next class above the modal class
c = the width of the modal class.

1.19 This formula only works if the modal class, the next class below it and the next class above it all have the same width (class interval).

Example: the mode in grouped frequency distributions

1.20 Calculate the mode of the following frequency distribution.

Value		*Frequency*
At least	*Less than*	
10	25	6
25	40	19
40	55	12
55	70	7
70	85	3

Solution

1.21 The modal class is the class interval with the highest frequency, that is, the class $\geqslant$ 25 and < 40. The class interval is 15. F_1 is 19, the frequency of the modal class. F_0 is the frequency of the class below 25–40, the class 10–25, which is 6. F_2 is the frequency of the class 40–55, which is 12.

The estimated mode is

$$25 + \frac{(19 - 6) \times 15}{(2 \times 19) - 6 - 12}$$

$$= 25 + \frac{(13 \times 15)}{(38 - 18)}$$

$$= 25 + 9.75$$

$$= 34.75$$

The median

1.22 The third type of average is the median. The median is the value of the middle member of a distribution.

1.23 The median of a set of ungrouped data is found by arranging the items in ascending or descending order of value, and selecting the item in the middle of the range. A list of items in order of value is called an *array*.

Example: the median

1.24 The median of the following nine values:

8 6 9 12 15 6 3 20 11

is found by taking the middle item (the fifth one) in the array:

3 6 6 8 9 11 12 15 20

The median is 9.

The median of the following ten values would be the fifth item in the array.

8 6 7 2 1 11 3 2 5 2

1 2 2 2 3 5 6 7 8 11

Median = 3

With an even number of items, we could take the arithmetic mean of the two middle ones (in this example, (3 + 5)/2 = 4), but when there are many items it is not worth doing this.

The median of an ungrouped frequency distribution

1.25 The median of an ungrouped frequency distribution is found in a similar way. Thus the median of the following distribution:

Value	*Frequency*	*Cumulative frequency*
x	*f*	
8	3	3
12	7	10
16	12	22
17	8	30
19	5	35
	35	

would be the (35 + 1)/2 = 18th item. The 18th item has a value of 16, as we can see from the cumulative frequencies in the right hand column of the above table.

The median of a grouped frequency distribution

1.26 The median of a grouped frequency distribution, like the arithmetic mean and the mode, can only be estimated approximately.

1.27 First, we must find the class interval to which the middle item belongs.

1.28 We then use the following formula.

Median = value of lower limit to the class + $(\frac{R}{f} \times c)$

where
- c is the size of the class interval
- f is the frequency of the class
- R is the difference between the middle member ((n + 1)/2 for odd n, n/2 for even n) and the cumulative total of frequencies up to the end of the preceding class.

Example: median of a grouped frequency distribution

1.29 The average monthly earnings of 135 employees of Comedian Ltd have been analysed as a grouped frequency distribution as follows.

Average monthly earnings		*No of employees*	*Cumulative frequency*
More than	*Not more than*		
£	£		
120	140	12	12
140	160	49	61
160	180	25	86
180	200	18	104
200	220	17	121
220	240	14	135
		135	

What are the median monthly earnings of employees of Comedian Ltd?

Solution

1.30 The middle member is the (135 + 1)/2 = 68th item. This occurs in the class £160 - £180.

$$\text{Median} = £160 + (\frac{(68 - 61)}{25} \times £20)$$

$$= £165.60$$

Comparing different types of average

1.31 Above, we have looked at three types of average. Below is a summary of their advantages and disadvantages. Consider how they apply to examples of averages given in newspapers and news broadcasts.

1.32 The advantages of the *arithmetic mean* are as follows.

(a) It is widely understood.
(b) The value of every item is included in the computation of the mean.
(c) It is well suited to further statistical analysis.

The disadvantages of the *arithmetic mean* are as follows.

(a) Its value may not correspond to any actual value. For example, the 'average' family might have 2.3 children, but no family has exactly 2.3 children.

(b) An arithmetic mean might be distorted by extremely high or low values. For example, the mean of 3, 4, 4 and 6 is 4.25, but the mean of 3, 4, 4, 6 and 15 is 6.4. The high value, 15, distorts the average and in some circumstances the mean would be a misleading and inappropriate figure.

1.33 The *mode* will be a more appropriate average to use than the mean in situations where it is useful to know the most common value. For example, if a manufacturer wishes to start production in a new industry, it might be helpful to know what sort of product made by the industry is most in demand with customers. The mode is easy to find and it is uninfluenced by a few extreme values. The main *disadvantage* of the mode is that it ignores dispersion around the modal value, and unlike the mean, does not take every value into account. It is also unsuitable for further statistical analysis.

1.34 The *median* is only of interest where there is a range of values and the middle item is of some significance. Perhaps the most suitable application of the median is in comparing changes in a 'middle of the road' value over time.

The median (like the mode) is unaffected by extremely high or low values. On the other hand, it fails to reflect the full range of values, and is unsuitable for further statistical analysis.

What is a weighted average?

1.35 Suppose you went shopping and spent £16.70 as follows.

Item	*Cost*
	£
Record	6.00
Tape	2.00
Book	2.50
Battery	1.20
Lunch	5.00
	16.70

On average, what was the cost of an item you bought that afternoon?

1.36 The total cost was £16.70, and five items were purchased, so the average unit cost was $\frac{£16.70}{5} = £3.34$.

1.37 But now suppose that instead of just £16.70, you went out and spent a total of £50 as follows.

Item	*Number purchased*	*Cost per item*	*Total cost*
		£	£
Record	3	6.00	18
Tape	5	2.00	10
Book	2	2.50	5
Batteries	10	1.20	12
Lunch	1	5.00	5
	21		50

Now what is the average cost of one of your purchases that afternoon?

1.38 The total cost was £50, and 21 items were purchased, so the average unit cost was

$$\frac{£50}{21} = £2.38$$

1.39 What has happened here? In the first example, average cost was £3.34 but in the second example - even though the same sort of items were being purchased - average cost dropped to £2.38. Why should that be?

1.40 The answer is that in the first example, only one of each item was purchased. So the record, tape, book, battery and lunch were all given equal *weight* when it came to working out the average cost.

1.41 In the second example, different numbers of each item were purchased, so they were given different weights when the average cost was calculated. For instance, twice as many batteries were bought as tapes, so the 'weight' for battery cost was twice that for tape cost. Now you can see why the average cost came down in the second example - more 'weight' was being given to the items which cost less.

Multiplying by the weight

1.42 If somebody had asked us to work out the simple average cost of a book, record, tape, battery and lunch, we would have quickly calculated £3.34 as in paragraph 1.36.

1.43 If somebody had asked us to work out the average of two books, three records, five tapes, ten batteries and a lunch, we would first have to multiply the cost of each item by a weight. In this example, the appropriate weight is just the number of items bought (ie 2, 3, 5, 10 and 1). The result of our calculation is therefore called a *weighted average*.

1.44 The weighted average in the above example happens to be the same as the arithmetic mean of an ungrouped frequency distribution, because all we are doing is multiplying values by their frequency and dividing by the total frequency. In other words, we are working out $\frac{\Sigma fx}{\Sigma f}$, which is the formula for the arithmetic mean of an ungrouped distribution. So for this example, it is not too difficult to see what the weighted average is, and what weights to use. But sometimes it is not so obvious to see what the weight should be.

Example: simple and weighted average

1.45 Peter, Paul and John all invest in a business. Peter invests £10,000 on 1 January 19X6, Paul invests £18,000 on 1 May 19X6 and John invests £8,000 on 1 October 19X6. What was their average investment for 19X6:

(a) ignoring the dates when they made their investments; and
(b) having regard to the dates when they made their investments?

Solution

1.46 If no account is taken of the investment dates, the average investment is simply £12,000.

$$\text{Average investment} = £\frac{10{,}000 + 18{,}000 + 8{,}000}{3}$$

$$= £\ \frac{36{,}000}{3}$$

$$= £12{,}000$$

This is a *simple* average of the three investments.

1.47 However, this is clearly not a very sensible average, because investments made at the start of the year are in the business longer than those investments made at the end of the year. What we have to do is work out a weighted average, and in this example the amounts invested are weighted by the number of months they have been invested.

	Investment £	*No of months invested*	*No of months × investment*
Peter	10,000	12	120,000
Paul	18,000	8	144,000
John	8,000	3	24,000
		23	288,000

So the weighted average investment is $£\ \frac{288{,}000}{23} = £12{,}521.74$

When is a weighted average used?

1.48 A weighted average will be used whenever a simple average fails to give an accurate reflection of the relative importance of the items being averaged.

1.49 We have already seen one use of a weighted average in the accounting field - that of determining the usefulness of investments to a business during a year, when those investments were made at different times. Other uses of the weighted average include calculating the average cost of a product which is made up from different amounts of components which have different prices. This sort of problem is also dealt with by the use of index numbers, which we will look at in the next chapter.

Moving averages

1.50 Moving averages are a special type of average used in connection with *time series* analysis, which we look at in the next section of this chapter.

2. The analysis of time series

2.1 A time series is a series of figures or values recorded over time. Examples of time series are:

(a) output at a factory each day for the last month;
(b) monthly sales over the last two years;
(c) total annual costs for the last ten years;
(d) the Retail Prices Index each month for the last ten years;
(e) the number of people employed by a company each year for the last 20 years.

2.2 A graph of a time series is called a *historigram*. (Note the 'r' and the second 'i'; this is not the same as a histogram.) For example, consider the following time series.

Year	*Sales*
	£'000
19X0	20
19X1	21
19X2	24
19X3	23
19X4	27
19X5	30
19X6	28

The historigram is as follows.

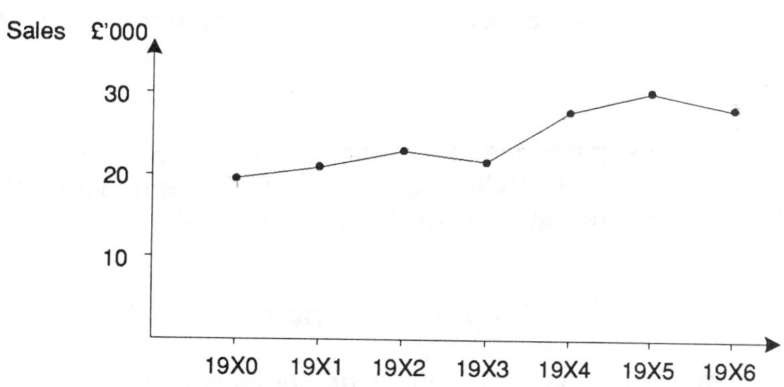

The horizontal axis is always chosen to represent time, and the vertical axis represents the values of the data recorded.

2.3 There are several features of a time series which it may be necessary to identify. These are:

(a) a trend;

(b) seasonal variations or fluctuations;

(c) cycles, or cyclical variations;

(d) non-recurring, random variations; these may be caused by unforeseen circumstances, such as a change in the government of the country, a war, the collapse of a company, technological change or a fire.

The trend

2.4 The trend or 'underlying trend' is the underlying long-term movement over time in the values of the data recorded. In the following examples of time series, there are three types of trend.

	Output per labour hour (units)	*Cost per unit* £	*Number of employees*
19X4	30	1.00	100
19X5	24	1.08	103
19X6	26	1.20	96
19X7	22	1.15	102
19X8	21	1.18	103
19X9	17	1.25	98
	(A)	(B)	(C)

(a) In time series (A) there is a *downward* trend in the output per labour hour. Output per labour hour did not fall every year, because it went up between 19X5 and 19X6, but the long-term movement is clearly a downward one.

(b) In time series (B) there is an *upward* trend in the cost per unit. Although unit costs went down in 19X7 from a higher level in 19X6, the basic movement over time is one of rising costs.

(c) In time series (C) there is no clear movement up or down, and the number of employees remained fairly constant around 100. The trend is therefore a *static,* or level one.

2.5 A trend may be of great significance to a manager who will want to know whether his or her company's results are on an improving or a worsening trend. The difficulty is to isolate a trend from the other factors causing variations in results.

Measuring trends

2.6 Trends are often measured as proportional or percentage changes over time.

For example, if a company's sales are £1,000,000 in 19X8 and £1,200,000 in 19X9, the increase in sales in 19X9 compared with 19X8 is

$$\frac{£200,000}{£1,000,000} \times 100\% = 20\%$$

Example: measuring trends

2.7 You must always interpret trends carefully. Study the following statements carefully to see if you can spot weaknesses in them.

(a) Sales of hods went up by 50% this year, whereas sales of zods went up by only 10%. Hods are a much more successful product than zods.

(b) Accidents at work went up by 200% last year. This is a serious situation and immediate extra safety measures should be taken.

(c) The workforce has consisted of 1,000 full time employees over the past four years. Absentee days from work have been as follows.

	Employee days	*Rate of increase*
		%
19X1	3,000	20
19X2	3,600	20
19X3	4,284	19
19X4	5,055	18

The rate of increase in absenteeism is falling, and so the situation is being brought under control.

Solution

2.8 Statement (a) might be true, but it might not be. It all depends on the actual volume or value of sales of each product. Suppose the actual figures are as follows.

	Sales this year	*Sales last year*	*Growth in sales*
	£	£	%
Hods	3,000	2,000	50
Zods	110,000	100,000	10

Which would *you* regard as the more successful product here, hods with 50% sales growth to £3,000 or zods with 10% sales growth to £110,000?

Statement (b) might also be true, but again it might be untrue. It all depends on how many accidents there were last year and this year. Is the actual number a significant amount? Were last year's accident figures abnormally low? If the number of accidents rose from just 1 last year to 3 this year, we might conclude that safety at work is still very good, particularly if the workforce is very large.

Statement (c) is highly misleading.The rate of increase in absenteeism has gone down from 20% to 19% to 18% per annum, but absenteeism is still rising, by 600 in 19X2, 684 in 19X3 and 771 in 19X4. The actual annual increase in days lost through absenteeism is rising each year, a sign that the situation is far from being brought under control.

Seasonal variations

2.9 Seasonal variations are short-term fluctuations in recorded values, due to different circumstances which affect results at different times of the year, on different days of the week, at different times of day, or whatever. Here are some examples.

(a) Sales of ice cream will be higher in summer than in winter, and sales of overcoats will be higher in autumn than in spring.

(b) Shops might expect higher sales shortly before Christmas, or in their winter and summer sales.

(c) Sales might be higher on Friday and Saturday than on Monday.

(d) The telephone network may be heavily used at certain times of the day (such as mid-morning and mid-afternoon) and much less used at other times (such as in the middle of the night).

2.10 'Seasonal' is a term which may appear to refer to the seasons of the year, but its meaning in time series analysis is somewhat broader, as the examples given above show.

Example: seasonal variations

2.11 The number of customers served by a company of travel agents over the past four years is shown in the following historigram.

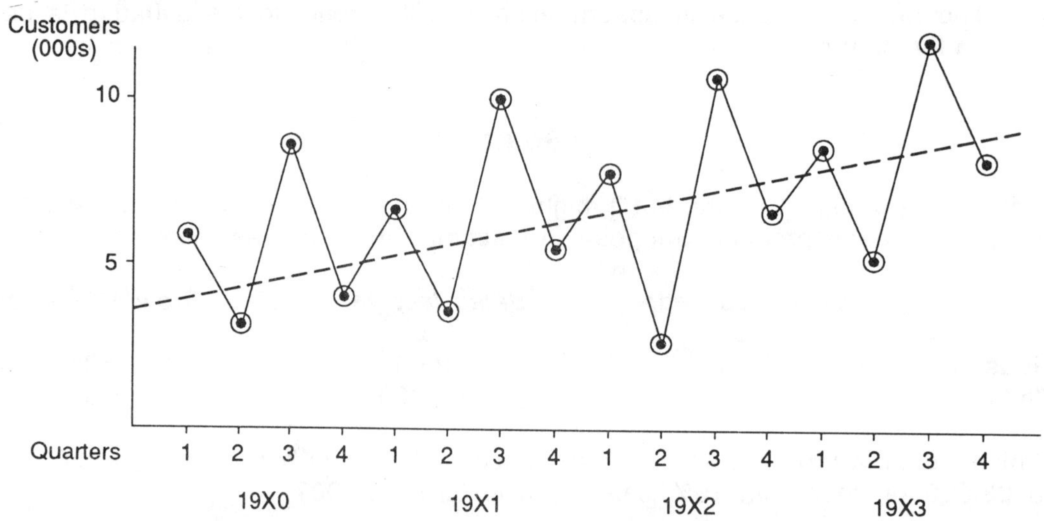

In this example, there would appear to be large seasonal fluctuations in demand, but there is also a basic upward trend.

Cyclical variations

2.12 Cyclical variations are changes in results caused by circumstances which repeat in cycles. In business, cyclical variations are commonly associated with economic cycles, successive booms and slumps in the economy. Economic cycles may last a few years. Cyclical variations are longer-term than seasonal variations.

3. Finding the trend and seasonal variations

3.1 The main problem we are concerned with in time series analysis is how to identify the trend, seasonal variations, cyclical variations and random one-off variations in a set of results over a period of time.

3.2 There are three principal methods of finding a trend and seasonal variations.

(a) *Inspection.* The trend line can be drawn by eye on a graph in such a way that it appears to lie evenly between the recorded points.

(b) *Regression analysis by the least squares method.* This is a statistical technique to calculate the 'line of best fit'. This method, which we shall not discuss in detail here, makes the assumption that the trend line, whether up or down, is a straight line. Periods of time (such as quarters for which sales figures are given) are numbered, commonly from 0, and the regression line of the data on those period numbers is found. That line is then taken to be the trend.

(c) *Moving averages.* This method attempts to remove seasonal (or cyclical) variations by a process of averaging.

Moving averages

3.3 A moving average is an average of the results of a fixed number of periods. Since it is an average of several time periods, it is related to the mid-point of the overall period.

3.4 Moving averages could, for example, cover the sales of a shop over periods of seven days (Monday to the next Sunday, Tuesday to the next Monday, Wednesday to the next Tuesday, and so on), or a business's costs over periods of four quarters, or whatever else was appropriate to the circumstances.

Example: moving averages

3.5

Year	*Sales (units)*
19X0	390
19X1	380
19X2	460
19X3	450
19X4	470
19X5	440
19X6	500

Task

Take a moving average of the annual sales over a period of three years.

Solution

3.6 (a) Average sales in the three year period 19X0 - 19X2 were

$$\left(\frac{390 + 380 + 460}{3}\right) = \frac{1,230}{3} = 410.$$

This average relates to the middle year of the period, 19X1.

(b) Similarly, average sales in the three year period 19X1 - 19X3 were

$$\left(\frac{380 + 460 + 450}{3}\right) = \frac{1,290}{3} = 430.$$

This average relates to the middle year of the period, 19X2.

(c) The average sales can also be found for the periods 19X2 - 19X4, 19X3 - 19X5 and 19X4 - 19X6, to give the following.

Year	*Sales*	*Moving total of 3 years sales*	*Moving average of 3 years sales (÷ 3)*
19X0	390		
19X1	380	1,230	410
19X2	460	1,290	430
19X3	450	1,380	460
19X4	470	1,360	453.3
19X5	440	1,410	470
19X6	500		

Note the following points.

(i) The moving average series has five figures relating to the years from 19X1 to 19X5. The original series had seven figures for the years from 19X0 to 19X6.

(ii) There is an upward trend in sales, which is more noticeable from the series of moving averages than from the original series of *actual* sales each year.

3.7 The above example averaged over a three year period. Over what period should a moving average be taken? The answer to this question is that the moving average which is most appropriate will depend on the circumstances and the nature of the time series. Note the following points.

(a) A moving average which takes an average of the results in many time periods will represent results over a longer term than a moving average of two or three periods.

(b) On the other hand, with a moving average of results in many time periods, the last figure in the series will be out of date by several periods. In our example, the most recent average related to 19X5. With a moving average of five years results, the final figure in the series would relate to 19X4.

(c) When there is a known cycle over which seasonal variations occur, such as all the days in the week or all the seasons in the year, the most suitable moving average would be one which covers one full cycle.

Moving averages of an even number of results

3.8 In the previous example, moving averages were taken of the results in an *odd* number of time periods, and the average then related to the mid-point of the overall period.

3.9 If a moving average were taken of results in an *even* number of time periods, the basic technique would be the same, but the mid-point of the overall period would not relate to a single period. For example, if an average were taken of the following four results:

Spring	120	
Summer	90	
Autumn	180	average 115
Winter	70	

the average would relate to the mid-point of the period, between summer and autumn.

3.10 The trend line average figures need to relate to a particular time period; otherwise, seasonal variations cannot be calculated. To overcome this difficulty, we take a moving average of the moving average. An example will illustrate this technique.

Example: moving average trend line

3.11 Calculate a moving average trend line of the following results.

Year	*Quarter*	*Volume of sales* '000 units
19X5	1	600
	2	840
	3	420
	4	720
19X6	1	640
	2	860
	3	420
	4	740
19X7	1	670
	2	900
	3	430
	4	760

Solution

3.12 A moving average of four will be used, since the volume of sales would appear to depend on the season of the year, and each year has four quarterly results.

The moving average of four does not relate to any specific period of time; therefore a second moving average of two will be calculated on the first moving average trend line.

Year	*Quarter*	*Actual volume of sales* '000 units (A)	*Moving total of 4 quarters sales* '000 units (B)	*Moving average of 4 quarters sales* '000 units (B ÷ 4)	*Mid-point of 2 moving averages* TREND LINE (C)
19X5	1	600			
	2	840			
	3	420	2,580	645	650
	4	720	2,620	655	657.5
19X6	1	640	2,640	660	660
	2	860	2,640	660	662.5
	3	420	2,660	665	668.75
	4	740	2,690	672.5	677.5
19X7	1	670	2,730	682.5	683.75
	2	900	2,740	685	687.5
	3	430	2,760	690	
	4	760			

3.13 By taking a mid point (a moving average of two) of the original moving averages, we can relate the results to specific quarters (from the third quarter of 19X5 to the second quarter of 19X7).

The trend and seasonal variations

3.14 Once a trend has been established, by whatever method, we can find the seasonal variations. Two examples will show how this is done.

Example: seasonal variations (1)

3.15 Output at a factory appears to vary with the day of the week. Output over the last three weeks has been as follows.

	Week 1 '000 units	*Week 2* '000 units	*Week 3* '000 units
Monday	80	82	84
Tuesday	104	110	116
Wednesday	94	97	100
Thursday	120	125	130
Friday	62	64	66

With the days numbered from 0 to 14, a trend line has been found using regression analysis (see paragraph 3.2). It is $y = 0.42x + 92.70$.

Find the seasonal variation for each of the 15 days, and the average seasonal variation for each day of the week.

Solution

3.16 The regression line indicates an upward trend in daily output. Actual results fluctuate up and down according to the day of the week. The difference between the actual result on any one day and the trend figure for that day will be the seasonal variation for the day. The trend figures themselves are found simply by putting the day numbers (0 to 14) as values of x in the equation y = 0.42x + 92.70.

3.17 The seasonal variations for the 15 days are as follows.

		Day	*Actual*	*Trend*	*Seasonal variation*
Week 1	Monday	0	80	92.70	- 12.70
	Tuesday	1	104	93.12	+ 10.88
	Wednesday	2	94	93.54	+ 0.46
	Thursday	3	120	93.96	+ 26.04
	Friday	4	62	94.38	- 32.38
Week 2	Monday	5	82	94.80	- 12.80
	Tuesday	6	110	95.22	+ 14.78
	Wednesday	7	97	95.64	+ 1.36
	Thursday	8	125	96.06	+ 28.94
	Friday	9	64	96.48	- 32.48
Week 3	Monday	10	84	96.90	- 12.90
	Tuesday	11	116	97.32	+ 18.68
	Wednesday	12	100	97.74	+ 2.26
	Thursday	13	130	98.16	+ 31.84
	Friday	14	66	98.58	- 32.58

3.18

	Monday	*Tuesday*	*Wednesday*	*Thursday*	*Friday*
Week 1	- 12.70	+ 10.88	+ 0.46	+ 26.04	- 32.38
Week 2	- 12.80	+ 14.78	+ 1.36	+ 28.94	- 32.48
Week 3	- 12.90	+ 18.68	+ 2.26	+ 31.84	- 32.58
Average	- 12.80	+ 14.78	+ 1.36	+ 28.94	- 32.48

The variation between the actual results on any one particular day and the trend line average is not the same from week to week, but an average of these variations can be taken.

3.19 Our estimate of the 'seasonal' or daily variation is almost complete, but there is one more important step to take. Variations around the basic trend line should cancel each other out, and add up to 0. At the moment, they do not.

	Monday	*Tuesday*	*Wednesday*	*Thursday*	*Friday*	*Total*
Estimated daily variation	- 12.80	+ 14.78	+ 1.36	+ 28.94	- 32.48	- 0.2
Adjustment to reduce total variation to 0	+ 0.04	+ 0.04	+ 0.04	+ 0.04	+ 0.04	+ 0.2
Final estimate of daily variation	- 12.76	+ 14.82	+ 1.40	+ 28.98	- 32.44	0

These might be rounded up or down as follows.
Monday −13; Tuesday +15; Wednesday +1; Thursday +29; Friday −32; Total 0.

Example: seasonal variations (2)

3.20 Calculate a four quarter moving average trend centred on actual quarters and then find seasonal variations from the following.

	Sales in £'000			
	Spring	*Summer*	*Autumn*	*Winter*
19X7	200	120	160	280
19X8	220	140	140	300
19X9	200	120	180	320

Solution

3.21

		Sales £'000	*4-quarter total*	*4-quarter moving average*	*Average of mid-points to centre on an actual qtr = trend*	*Seasonal variations = actual minus trend*
19X7	Spring	200				
	Summer	120				
			760	190		
	Autumn	160			192.5	- 32.5
			780	195		
	Winter	280			197.5	+ 82.5
			800	200		
19X8	Spring	220			197.5	+ 22.5
			780	195		
	Summer	140			197.5	- 57.5
			800	200		
	Autumn	140			197.5	- 57.5
			780	195		
	Winter	300			192.5	+107.5
			760	190		
19X9	Spring	200			195.0	+ 5.0
			800	200		
	Summer	120			202.5	- 82.5
			820	205		
	Autumn	180				
	Winter	320				

3.22 We can now average the seasonal variations.

	Spring	*Summer*	*Autumn*	*Winter*
19X7			- 32.5	+ 82.5
19X8	+22.5	- 57.5	- 57.5	+107.5
19X9	+ 5.0	- 82.5		
	+27.5	-140.0	- 90.0	+190.0
Average variation (in £'000)	+13.75	-70.0	-45.0	+95.0
Adjustment so sum is zero	+1.69	+1.69	+1.69	+1.68
Adjusted average variations	+14.94	-68.31	-43.31	+96.68

4. Forecasting

4.1 Forecasting is an essential but difficult task of management. Many forecasts are made by guessing, but they are unlikely to be reliable.

4.2 There are several mathematical techniques of forecasting which could be used. These techniques will not necessarily provide accurate forecasts, but on the whole, they are likely to provide more reliable estimates than guesswork. Techniques cannot eliminate uncertainty about the future, but they can help to ensure that managers take account of all known facts in the preparation of their forecasts.

4.3 The technique which will be discussed here is that of extrapolating a trend and then adjusting for seasonal variations.

4.4 Forecasts of future values should be made by:

(a) calculating a trend line;

(b) using the trend line to forecast future trend line values;

(c) adjusting these values by the average seasonal variation applicable to the future period, to determine the forecast for that period.

4.5 Extending a trend line outside the range of known data, in this case forecasting the future from a trend line based on historical data, is known as *extrapolation*.

Example: forecasting

4.6 Sales of product X each quarter for the last three years have been as follows (in thousands of units). Trend values, found by a moving averages method, are shown in brackets.

Year	*1st quarter*		*2nd quarter*		*3rd quarter*		*4th quarter*	
1	18		30		20	(18.75)	6	(19.375)
2	20	(20)	33	(20.5)	22	(21)	8	(21.5)
3	22	(22.125)	35	(22.75)	25		10	

Average seasonal variations for quarters 1 to 4 are –0.1, +12.4, +1.1 and –13.4 respectively.

Task

Use the trend line and estimates of seasonal variations to forecast sales in each quarter of year 4.

Solution

4.7 The trend line indicates an increase of about 0.6 per quarter. This can be confirmed by calculating the average quarterly increase in trend line values between the third quarter of year 1 (18.75) and the second quarter of year 3 (22.75). The average rise is

$$\frac{22.75 - 18.75}{7} = \frac{4}{7} = 0.57\text{, say } 0.6.$$

4.8 Taking 0.6 as the quarterly increase in the trend, the forecast of sales for year 4, *before* seasonal adjustments (the trend line forecast) would be as follows.

Year	*Quarter*		*Trend line*
3	*2nd (actual trend)	22.75, say	22.8
	3rd		23.4
	4th		24.0
4	1st		24.6
	2nd		25.2
	3rd		25.8
	4th		26.4

* last known trend line value.

4.9 Seasonal variations should now be incorporated to obtain the final forecast.

	Quarter	*Trend line forecast*	*Average seasonal variation*	*Forecast of actual sales*
		'000 units		'000 units
Year 4	1st	24.6	- 0.1	24.5
	2nd	25.2	+12.4	37.6
	3rd	25.8	+ 1.1	26.9
	4th	26.4	-13.4	13.0

4.10 Note that if the trend had been given as a regression line, trend values could have been obtained simply by inserting the numbers for the quarters as values of x in the regression line equation.

Residuals

4.11 A *residual* is the difference between the results which would have been predicted (for a past period for which we already have data) by the trend line adjusted for the average seasonal variation and the actual results.

4.12 The residual is therefore the difference which is not explained by the trend line and the seasonal average variation. The residual gives some indication of how much actual results were affected by other factors. Large residuals suggest that any forecast is likely to be unreliable.

4.13 In the above example, the 'prediction' for the third quarter of year 1 would have been 18.75 + 1.1 = 19.85. As the actual value was 20, the residual was only 20 - 19.85 = 0.15. The residual for the fourth quarter of year 2 was 8 - (21.5 - 13.4) = 8 - 8.1 = -0.1.

Key points in this chapter

- An average is a *measure of central tendency.* The three main types of average are:
    - the arithmetic mean
    - the mode
    - the median
- The arithmetic mean is widely understood and well suited to further statistical analysis. The value of every item is included in the computation of the mean.
- The mode is a more appropriate average to use than the mean where it is useful to know the most common value.
- The median is of interest only where there is a range of values and the middle item is of some significance.
- We also looked at weighted average.
- A time series is a series of figures or values recorded over time.
- A graph of a time series is called a historigram.
- The trend in a time series is the underlying long term movement over time in the values of the data recorded. Trends must always be interpreted with care.
- Seasonal variations are short-term fluctuations in recorded values, resulting from different circumstances which affect results in different periods.
- Cyclical variations are medium-term changes resulting from circumstances which repeat in cycles.
- The trend, seasonal variations and cyclical variations need to be distinguished from random or one-off variations in a set of results over a period of time. Methods of finding a trend and seasonal variations are inspection, regression analysis by the least squares method and moving averages.

For practice on the points covered in this chapter you should now attempt the Exercises in Session 6 of the Cost Accounting II Workbook

7. Allowing for changing price levels

1. **Indexation**
2. **Multi–item price indices**
3. **Chain based index numbers**
4. **Limitations of index numbers**
5. **Using index numbers in comparing results**

1. Indexation

The need for index numbers

1.1 If we are making comparisons of costs and revenues over time to see how well an organisational unit is performing, we need to take account of the fact that the unit is operating within an economic environment in which general shifts in costs (ie prices) take place. If a business achieves an increase in sales of 10% in monetary (cash) terms over a year, this result becomes less impressive if we are told that there was general price inflation of 15% over the year. If the business has raised its prices in line with this inflation rate of 15%, then a 10% increase in sales in cash terms indicates a fall in the physical volume of sales. The business is now selling less at the new higher prices.

1.2 In the financial accounting field, there has been much debate over whether the financial results declared in the annual report of companies should be adjusted to reflect inflation. Understandably the amount of debate on this subject has tended to be greater in periods of high inflation. In 1974, the professional accounting bodies of the UK recommended that a supplementary statement should be attached to the financial reports of companies showing figures adjusted in terms of their current purchasing power (CPP) at the closing day of the accounting period. They recommended that the Retail Prices Index (RPI) be used to effect this adjustment of historic cost values into current purchasing power equivalents. However, the recommendation was withdrawn in 1978.

1.3 When results of a business are being compared over a period of time for internal management purposes, it is up to managers of the business to agree and use an appropriate method of allowing for changing price levels. The usual method is to use a series of index numbers.

What is an index number?

1.4 An index is a measure, over a period of time, of the average *changes* in the values (prices or quantities) of a group of items.

1.5 An example is the 'cost of living' index. This is made up of a large variety of items including bread, butter, meat, rent, insurance etc. The raw data giving the prices of each commodity for successive years would be confusing and useless to most people; but a simple index stating that the cost of living index is 145 for 1987 compared with 100 for 1980 is easily understood.

Price indices and quantity indices

1.6 An index may be a price index or a quantity index.

(a) A *price index* measures the change in the money value of a group of items over a period of time. Perhaps the most well-known price index in the UK is the Retail Price Index (RPI) which measures changes in the costs of items of expenditure of the average household, and which used to be called the 'cost of living' index. Another example which you may have heard reported in the news is the FT share index, which measures how share prices in general have performed from one day to the next.

(b) A *quantity index* measures the change in the non-monetary values of a group of items over a period of time. A well-known example is a productivity index, which measures changes in the productivity of various departments or groups of workers.

As we shall see, a suitable price index provides a method of allowing for changing price levels when comparing costs or revenues over time.

Index points

1.7 The term 'points' is used to measure the difference in the index value in one year with the value in another year. In the example given above the cost of living index rose 45 points between 1980 and 1987 (ie rose from an index of 100 to 145).

1.8 Points are used for measuring changes in an index because they provide an easy method of arithmetic. The alternative is to use percentages, because indices are based on percentages, as we shall see.

The base period, or base year

1.9 Index numbers are normally expressed as percentages, taking the value for a base date as 100. The choice of a base date or base year is not significant, except that it should normally be 'representative'. In the construction of a price index, the base year preferably should not be one in which there were abnormally high or low prices for any items in the 'basket of goods' making up the index.

Calculation of an index

1.10 Suppose sales for a company over the last five years were as follows.

Year	*Sales (£'000)*
19X5	35
19X6	42
19X7	40
19X8	45
19X9	50

The managing director decided that he wanted to set up a sales index (ie an index which measures how sales have done from year to year), using 19X5 as the base year. The £35,000 of sales in 19X5 is given the index 100%. What are the indices for the other years?

1.11 If £35,000 = 100%, then:

(a) £42,000 = $\frac{42,000}{35,000} \times 100\% = 120\%$

(b) £40,000 = $\frac{40,000}{35,000} \times 100\% = 114\%$

(c) £45,000 = $\frac{45,000}{35,000} \times 100\% = 129\%$

(d) £50,000 = $\frac{50,000}{35,000}$ × 100% = 143%

1.12 Now the table showing sales for the last five years can be completed, taking 19X5 as the base year.

Year	*Sales (£'000)*	*Index*
19X5	35	100
19X6	42	120
19X7	40	114
19X8	45	129
19X9	50	143

Example: price index

1.13 If the price of a cup of coffee in the Hilton Hotel was 40p in 19X0, 50p in 19X1 and 76p in 19X2, using 19X0 as a base point the price index numbers for 19X1 and 19X2 would be:

19X1 price index = $\frac{50}{40}$ × 100 = 125

19X2 price index = $\frac{76}{40}$ × 100 = 190

Example: quantity index

1.14 Similarly, if the Hilton Hotel sold 500,000 cups of coffee in 19X0, 700,000 cups in 19X1, and 600,000 in 19X2, then quantity index numbers for 19X1 and 19X2, using 19X0 as a base year, would be:

19X1 quantity index = $\frac{700,000}{500,000}$ × 100 = 140

19X2 quantity index = $\frac{600,000}{500,000}$ × 100 = 120

2. Multi-item price indices

2.1 In the examples we have seen so far in this chapter, it is not really necessary to calculate an index, because only one product or item has been under consideration. Knowing that sales have risen by 20% from £35,000 to £42,000, for instance, is just as informative as knowing that the index has risen 20 points (from 100 to 120). There was no real need to calculate the index.

2.2 Most practical indices are made up of more than one item. For example, suppose that the cost of living index is calculated from only three commodities: bread, tea and caviar, and that the prices for 19X1 and 19X5 were as follows.

	19X1	*19X5*
Bread	20p a loaf	40p a loaf
Tea	25p a packet	30p a packet
Caviar	450p an ounce	405p an ounce

2.3 An examination of these figures reveals three main difficulties.

(a) Two prices have gone up and one has gone down. The index number must be a compromise.

(b) The prices are given in different units.

(c) There is no indication of the relative importance of each item.

Nothing can be done about difficulty (a) - it is a feature of index numbers and must always be borne in mind - but (b) and (c) can be overcome by *weighting*.

Weighting the index

2.4 To decide the weighting of different items in an index it is necessary to obtain information, perhaps by market research, about the relative importance of each item. In our example of a simple cost of living (or retail price) index, it would be necessary to find out how much the average person or household spends per week (or month) on each item in the 'basket' of goods.

2.5 Research may suggest that the average spending by each household in a week was as follows in 19X1.

	Quantity	*Price per unit*	*Total spending*	*% of total spending*
		£	£	
Bread	6 loaves	20p	1.20	60
Tea	2 packets	25p	0.50	25
Caviar	0.067 ounces	450p	0.30	15
			2.00	100 %

The weighting of each item in the index will depend on the proportion of total weekly spending taken up by the item. In our example, the weighting of bread, tea and caviar would be 60%, 25% and 15% respectively.

2.6 If 19X1 is a base year, the index for 19X5 could be obtained as follows.

(a) Calculate the price of each item in 19X5 as a percentage of the price in 19X1. This percentage figure is called a *price relative*, because it shows the new price level of each item relative to the base year price.

(b) Multiply the price relative by the weighting for each item in the 'basket of goods'. The result for all items is added together to give a weighted average total for 19X5.

(c) Make a similar weighted average total for the base year.

(d) If the base year index = 100, the 19X5 index will be:

$$\frac{\text{weighted average total in 19X5}}{\text{weighted average total in 19X1}} \times 100$$

2.7 There is an important assumption, ie that the relative quantities of bread, tea and caviar consumed each week by the average household did not change between 19X1 and 19X5, and that the 'basket of goods' - ie bread, tea and caviar, is still representative of the average household's consumption pattern.

2.8 In our example:

(a) 19X5 price relatives (ie 19X5 prices as a percentage of 19X1 prices):

(i) Bread $\frac{40p}{20p} \times 100 = 200$

(ii) Tea $\frac{30p}{25p} \times 100 = 120$

(iii) Caviar $\frac{405p}{450p} \times 100 = 90$

(b) Multiply the 19X5 price relative of each item by the index weighting of the item.

Item	*Weighting*	*Price relative*	*Product*
Bread	60%	200	120
Tea	25%	120	30
Caviar	15%	90	13.5
	100%		163.5

(c) The 19X1 equivalent total is 100, ie

Item	*Weighting*	*Price relative*	*Product*
Bread	60%	100	60
Tea	25%	100	25
Caviar	15%	100	15
	100%		100

(d) The 19X5 index is:

$$\frac{163.5}{100} \times 100 = 163.5$$

2.9 The formula for a price index of this type is

$$\text{Price index} = \frac{\Sigma p_1 w}{\Sigma p_0 w} \times 100$$

where p_1 represents prices in the 'new' year, p_0 represents prices in the base year and w is the weighting factor.

2.10 A quantity index measures the change in the *non-monetary* values of a group of items. It is calculated in much the same way as a price index, but because it deals with non-monetary values, it ignores any changes in price: there is no need to work out price relatives when calculating a quantity index. We do not look at quantity indices further here.

3. Chain based index numbers

3.1 In all the previous examples in this chapter, we have used a *fixed base* method of indexing, whereby a base year is selected (index 100) and all subsequent changes are measured against this base.

3.2 The *chain base* method of indexing is an alternative approach, whereby (in a price index), the changes in prices are taken as a percentage of the period immediately before.

3.3 This method is suitable where weightings are changing rapidly, and new items are continually being brought into the index and old items taken out.

Example: the chain base method

3.4 The price of a particular model of car varied as follows over the years 19X5 to 19X8.

Year	19X5	19X6	19X7	19X8
Price	£5,000	£5,560	£6,100	£6,940

Tasks

(a) Construct a fixed base index for the years 19X5 to 19X8, using 19X6 as the base year.

(b) Construct a chain base index for the years 19X5 to 19X8.

Round all answers to the nearest index point.

Solution

3.5 Constructing a fixed base index is exactly the same sort of problem we have already met in this chapter.

Year		*Index*
19X5	$\frac{5,000}{5,560} \times 100 =$	90
19X6		100
19X7	$\frac{6,100}{5,560} \times 100 =$	110

19X8	$\frac{6,940}{5,560}$	×	100	=	125

3.6 Constructing a chain base index is almost the same, except that the index is always calculated using the percentage increase (or decrease) on the previous year, rather than on a base year.

Year					*Index*
19X5					100
19X6	$\frac{5,560}{5,000}$	×	100	=	111
19X7	$\frac{6,100}{5,560}$	×	100	=	110
19X8	$\frac{6,940}{6,100}$	×	100	=	114

3.7 The chain base index shows the rate of change in prices from year to year, whereas the fixed base index shows the change more directly against prices in the base year.

4. Limitations of index numbers

4.1 Index numbers are easy to understand and fairly easy to calculate, so it is not surprising that they are frequently used. However, they are not perfect and it is as well to bear in mind the following points.

(a) Index numbers are usually only approximations of changes in price (or quantity) over time, and must be interpreted with care and reservation.

(b) Weightings become out of date as time passes. Unless a chain base index is used, the weightings will gradually cease to reflect the current 'reality'.

(c) New products or items may appear, and old ones cease to be significant. For example, spending has changed in recent years, to include new items such as colour television, domestic computers and video recorders, whereas the demand for large black and white televisions and twin-tub washing machines has declined. These changes would make the weightings of a retail price index for consumer goods out of date and the base of the index would need revision.

(d) Sometimes, the data used to calculate index numbers might be incomplete, out of date, or inaccurate. For example, the quantity indices of imports and exports are based on records supplied by traders which may be prone to error or even falsification.

(e) The base year of an index should be a 'normal' year, but there is probably no such thing as a perfectly normal year. Some error in the index will be caused by untypical values in the base period.

(f) The 'basket of items' in an index is often selective. For example, the Retail Prices Index (RPI) is constructed from a sample of households and, more importantly, from a basket of only about 600 items.

(g) A national index cannot necessarily be applied to an individual town or region. For example, if the national index of wages and salaries rises from 100 to 115, we cannot necessarily state the following.

(i) The wages and salaries of people in, say, Glasgow, have gone up from 100 to 115.

(ii) The wages and salaries of each working individual have gone up from 100 to 115.

(h) An index may exclude important items; for example, the RPI excludes payments of income tax out of gross wages.

Misinterpretation of index numbers

4.2 You must be careful not to misinterpret index numbers. Several possible mistakes will be explained using the following example of a retail price index.

19X0		*19X1*		*19X2*	
January	340.0	January	360.6	January	436.3
		February	362.5	February	437.1
		March	366.2	March	439.5
		April	370.0	April	442.1

(a) It would be wrong to say that prices rose by 2.6% between March and April 19X2. It is correct to say that prices rose 2.6 points, or

$$\frac{2.6}{439.5} = 0.6\%$$

(b) It would be wrong to say that because prices are continually going up, then there must be rising inflation. If prices are going up, then there must be inflation. But is the *rate* of price increases going up, or is the rate slowing down? In our example, it so happens that although the trend of prices is still upwards, the *rate* of price increase (inflation) is slowing down. For example:

(i) Annual rate of inflation, March 19X1 to March 19X2

$$\frac{439.5 - 366.2}{366.2} \times 100 = 20\%$$

(ii) Annual rate of inflation, April 19X1 to April 19X2

$$\frac{442.1 - 370.0}{370.0} \times 100 = 19.5\%$$

The rate of inflation has dropped from 20% per annum to 19.5% per annum between March and April 19X2, even though prices went up in the month between March and April 19X2 by 0.6%.

(c) It is also wrong to state that the average annual rate of inflation between January 19X0 and January 19X2 is:

$$\frac{1}{2} \text{ of } \frac{436.3 - 340.0}{340.0} = 14.2\% \text{ per annum}$$

The reason for this is that the annual increase has been compounded, ie it has been multiplied by itself. To calculate the average annual increase over the two years we must use a square root.

$$\text{Average annual increase} = \left(\sqrt{\frac{436.3}{340.0}} - 1\right) \times 100 = 13.3\% \text{ per annum}$$

5. Using index numbers in comparing results

5.1 For the purpose of internal management reporting, results recorded over a number of periods can be adjusted using an appropriate price index to convert the figures from money terms to 'real' terms.

5.2 As well as the Retail Prices Index (RPI) - also known as the General Index of Retail Prices - which measures the average level of prices of goods and services purchased by most households in the United Kingdom, the Central Statistical Office publishes a large number of producer price indices for different sectors of industry as well as index numbers of agricultural prices. These indices track changes in prices facing businesses in different industries. Annual average figures for these indices covering the previous five years are published in the Annual Abstract of Statistics. Someone needing to track the trend in prices of raw material inputs could use the Index of Producer Prices: Materials and Fuels, which measures prices of goods as they enter the factory. The price of finished manufactured goods is tracked by the Index of Producer Prices: Manufactured Products, which is sometimes called a measure of 'factory gate prices'.

5.3 The various price indices for specific industry sectors will usually provide a more useful way of comparing results in different periods than more general indices such as the RPI. The RPI measures price changes over a varied 'basket' of retail goods and services, including housing costs. The price trends facing a wholesaler or producer in any particular industry may be very different.

5.4 Once the index to be used is agreed, the index is 'rebased' to the period required and the various data are adjusted by the rebased index.

Example: using index numbers

5.5 PA Footwear Limited manufactures a range of footwear for the home (UK) market and for export. UK sales for the period 19X5 to 19Y0 were as follows.

	£'000
19X5	3,422
19X6	3,608
19X7	3,862
19X8	4,036
19X9	4,072
19Y0	4,114

5.6 The trend in UK sales is to be expressed at 19Y0 prices, using the producer price index numbers for footwear (home sales) set out below (the base year is 19X5). The year-on-year 'real' change in sales is then to be calculated.

	Producer price index
19X5	100.0
19X6	106.3
19X7	110.4
19X8	115.4
19X9	120.1
19Y0	125.7

Solution

5.7

	Rebased index (19Y0=100)	*Sales*	*Sales at 19Y0 prices*	*Real year-on-year increase*
	£'000	£'000	%	
19X5	79.6	3,422	4,299	
19X6	84.6	3,608	4,265	- 0.8
19X7	87.8	3,862	4,399	+ 3.1
19X8	91.8	4,036	4,397	0.0
19X9	95.5	4,072	4,264	- 3.0
19Y0	100.0	4,114	4,114	- 3.5

5.8 Each index number is rebased to 19Y0 by dividing it by the 19Y0 index number and multiplying by 100. For example:

$$19X9: \quad \frac{120.1}{125.7} \times 100 = 95.5$$

5.9 Sales at 19Y0 prices are calculated by dividing the sales figures in cash terms by the rebased index and multiplying by 100. The real year-on-year increase is the percentage change in sales at 19Y0 prices over the previous year.

5.10 Costs in a business may be adjusted in a similar way, using an appropriate index.

'Cash' and 'real' terms in the public sector

5.11 It is recognised in the public sector as well as the private sector that in order to form a judgement about what has happened to unit costs in real terms over a period of years, it may be necessary to show the past figures on a consistent price basis by applying a price index.

5.12 The Treasury recommends that public sector agencies use for this purpose an index called the GDP deflator, which measures the extent of price change year by year in the economy as a whole. Other indices may be used to measure productivity, but in accordance with long-standing mandatory government decisions, in the public sector 'real terms' applies only to figures which are 'deflated' by the GDP deflator.

5.13 A target for the unit cost of output of a public sector agency might be expressed in cash or in 'real' terms. Cash figures will need to be adjusted to real terms in order to assess whether such a target has been reached.

Example: unit cost targets in real terms

5.14 The Certification Agency (a fictitious government agency) has been set a target for 19X1-X2 of reducing the unit cost of issuing a certificate by 2.5% in real terms. The unit cost in cash terms was £8.62 in 19X1-X2, compared with £8.42 in 19X0-X1. The GDP deflator had an average value of 104.6 for 19X1-X2 (19X0-X1 = 100). Did the agency meet its target?

Solution

5.15

	Unit cost £	*GDP deflator*	*Real unit cost* £	*Real unit cost decrease*
19X0-X1	8.42	100.0	8.42	
19X1-X2	8.62	104.6	8.24	2.1%

5.16 The real unit cost is shown at 19X0-X1 prices by dividing the 19X1-X2 unit cost by the GDP deflator and multiplying by 100. The real unit cost has decreased by 2.1%, but the agency has failed to meet its target of a 2.5% decrease.

Recent price index values

5.17 The values of some of the main price indices in recent years are set out in the table below.

Year	*General Index of Retail Prices*	*Producer prices: Materials and fuels*	*Producer prices: Manufactured products*	*GDP deflator*	*Inflation rate**
1980	70.6	72.6	71.2	72.3	17.9
1981	79.1	79.3	78.6	79.5	12.0
1982	85.8	85.1	84.6	85.2	8.5
1983	89.7	91.0	89.2	90.0	4.5
1984	94.3	98.9	95.0	94.9	5.1
1985	100.0	100.0	100.0	100.0	6.0
1986	103.4	92.3	104.3	102.6	3.4
1987	107.7	95.3	108.3	107.8	4.2
1988	113.0	98.4	113.2	114.8	4.9
1989	121.8	104.0	119.0	123.1	7.8
1990	133.3	103.8	126.0	133.8	9.5
1991	141.1	102.6	133.0	142.3	5.9

* Percentage change in the RPI over the same period in the previous year.

Key points in this chapter

- An index is a measure of the average changes in the prices or quantities of a group of items over a period of time.

- A base year is chosen as a representative year and is assigned the index 100. Values for subsequent - or preceding - years are taken as a percentage of the base year value. That percentage is their index.

- A chain based index number can be used whereby the previous year is used as the base for each year's index number.

- An index number series appropriate to the data concerned provides a means of adjusting cost and revenue figures for a number of periods from cash to 'real' terms, thus allowing for changing price levels.

For practice on the points covered in this chapter you should now attempt the Exercises in Session 7 of the Cost Accounting II Workbook

8. Writing reports and completing forms

1. **Written reports**
2. **Planning a report**
3. **General points on style**
4. **The format of formal and informal reports**
5. **Standard forms**

1. Written reports

Introduction

1.1 The standards of competence for Unit 7: *Preparing reports and returns* require you to be able to prepare written reports in a clear and intelligible form. The term 'reports' here embraces the periodic performance reports of an enterprise which you may be required to prepare by a manager. External agencies of various kinds, such as grant-awarding agencies, may also require written reports, as well as forms and other returns, to be submitted to them. The standards of competence expect you to be able to deal with written reports on specific issues as well as reports of a more routine nature.

1.2 Sections 1 to 4 of this chapter are designed to guide you in the effective marshalling and presentation of information in a written report format. We go on to look at the completion of forms in Section 5.

What is a report?

1.3 'Report' is a general term and one that may suggest a wide range of formats. If you give someone a verbal account, or write him a message in a letter or memorandum informing him of facts, events, actions you have taken, suggestions you wish to make as a result of an investigation and so on, you are 'reporting'. In this sense the word means simply 'telling' or 'relating'.

1.4 There will be variety in the format and style of a report.

(a) *Formal or informal.* You may think of reports as huge documents with sections, subsections, paragraphs, subparagraphs, indexes, appendixes and so on. There *are* extensive, complex reports like this, but a single sheet ordinary memorandum may be sufficient in many contexts.

(b) *Routine* reports are produced at regular intervals. Examples of routine reports are budgetary control reports, sales reports or progress reports. *Occasional* reports include an accident report or a disciplinary report. Special reports may be commissioned for *'one-off'* planning and decision-making such as a market research report, or a report on a proposed project or particular issue.

(c) Reports may be *professional,* or for a *wider audience* of laymen or people from other backgrounds, who will not necessarily understand or require the same information or language.

1.5 Reports are meant to be *useful.* There should be no such thing as 'information for information's sake' in an efficient organisation: information is stored in files and retrieved for a purpose. The information contained in a business report might be used in several ways.

(a) *To assist management.* Higher levels of management rarely have time to carry out their own detailed investigations into the matters on which they make decisions; their time, moreover, is extremely expensive. If all (and only) the information relevant to their needs can be gathered and 'packaged' by report writers, managerial time and money will be saved.

A report may consist of:

(i) *information,* retrieved from files or other sources as a basis for management activity;

(ii) *narrative* or *description,* for example of one-off events or procedures, such as an accident, or the installation of new equipment;

(iii) *analysis,* which means making a further processing of information to render it more useful; or

(iv) *evaluation* and *recommendation,* directly assisting in the decision-making process.

(b) *As a permanent record and source of reference*, should details need to be confirmed or recalled in the future.

(c) *To convey information* or suggestions/ideas to other interested parties (eg in a report on a presentation, for a staff journal, for a committee or for a grant awarding agency).

1.6 As a report writer you should be aware that there are different types of information that might be given in a report.

(a) *Descriptive or factual information.* This consists of a description of facts and is objective: inferences can be drawn from the facts, but they must be logical and unbiased.

(b) *Instructive information.* This is information that tells the report user how to do something, or what to do. A recommendation in a report is a form of advice, and is therefore instructive information.

(c) *Evaluative information.* This consists of opinions and ideas, based on an objective assessment of the facts and with reasons explaining why these opinions and ideas have been reached.

Reports and their purpose

1.7 Reports will usually be communications that are intended to initiate a decision or action by the person or group receiving the report. The decisions or actions might be the following types.

(a) *Control action.* If the report describes what has happened in the past, it might indicate a need for control action, or alternatively it might indicate that there is no need for control action. The purpose of the report would in either case be to provide control information.

Budgetary control reports are examples of these reports. Reports that are intended to review events that have happened in the past (eg reports arising out of investigations into high labour turnover, a substantial loss on a major contract or the loss of a major customer to a competitor) are also examples of control reports;

(b) *Planning decisions.* Reports that are commissioned to advise on a certain course of action will include a *recommendation* about what decision should be taken.

1.8 Reports might be routine or non-routine.

(a) Many accounting reports are produced at frequent and regular intervals - such as budgetary control reports.

(b) Some reports are specially commissioned, to assist with 'one-off' planning or control decisions. An example is a report on the financial merits of a proposed capital expenditure project, a feasibility report on the introduction of a new system, or a report on the merits of alternative office layouts on locations.

The report and the report users

1.9 A report is usually made by someone who is instructed to do so by a superior.

(a) A special 'one-off' report will be commissioned by a manager, who will then expect to make a decision on the basis of what the report tells him. For example, the board of directors of a company might call for a report on the financial viability of a new product or investment, and they will expect to decide whether or not to undertake the product development or the investment on the basis of the report's findings.

(b) Routine reports, such as performance reports, might be required because they are a part of established procedures. The managers receiving the reports will not have commissioned them specifically, but they will be expected to act on anything out-of-the-ordinary that the report tells them.

(c) Some reports arise out of a particular event, on which regulations prescribe the writing of a report. For example, a leaving report must be written following an employee's resignation; any accident in the workplace must be reported.

(d) Individual responsibilities often include the requirement to write reports - a representative on a committee, or the secretary at a meeting, will have to report to members, or other committees, the procedures and decisions taken.

1.10 Whether the report is 'one-off' or routine, there is an *obligation on the part of the person requesting the report* to *state the use to which it will be put.* In other words, the purpose of the report must be clear to both its writers and its users.

1.11 In the case of routine reports, the purpose of each and how it should be used ought to be specified in a procedures manual. 'One-offs' will require 'terms of reference', explaining the purpose of the report and any restrictions on its scope. For example, the terms of reference of a management report might be to investigate the short-term profit prospects for a particular service, with a view to recommending either the withdrawal of the service or its continuation. These terms of reference would exclude considerations of long-term prospects for the service, and so place a limitation on the scope and purpose of the report.

Be aware of this in any assessment tasks. You do not have time to write about irrelevancies.

1.12 There is also *an obligation on the part of the report writer to communicate information in an unbiased way.* The report writer knows more about the subject matter of the report than the report user (otherwise there would be no need for the report in the first place). It is important that this information should be communicated impartially, so that the report user can make his own judgements.

This means that:

(a) any assumptions, evaluations and recommendations by the report writer should be clearly 'signalled' as such;

(b) points should not be over-weighted (or omitted as irrelevant) without honestly evaluating how objective the selection is;

(c) facts and findings should be balanced against each other;

(d) a firm conclusion should, if possible, be reached. It should be clear *how* and *why* it was reached.

1.13 Finally, there is an *obligation on the part of the report writer to recognise the needs and abilities of the report user.*

(a) Beware of 'jargon', overly technical terms and specialist knowledge the user may not share.

(b) Keep your vocabulary, sentence and paragraph structures as simple as possible, for clarity (without patronising an intelligent user).

(c) Bear in mind the type and level of detail that will interest the user and be relevant to his/her purpose.

(d) In a business context, the user may range from senior manager to junior supervisor, to non-managerial employee (such as in the case of minutes of a meeting, or general bulletin) to complete layman (customer, press etc). Your vocabulary, syntax and presentation, the amount of detail you can go into, the technical matter you can include and the formality of your report structure should all be influenced by such concerns.

Timeliness

1.14 As with all information, we stress again that a report may be of no use at all if it is not produced *on time,* however well researched and well presented it is. There is no point in presenting a report to influence a decision if the decision has already been made by the time the report is issued. The timescales within which the report user is working must be known, and the time available to produce the report planned accordingly.

2. Planning a report

2.1 Whether you are completing an assignment for your course of studies, compiling a report at work or researching a hobby of your own, you will need to know how to put information together effectively. Unless you have an *extremely* orderly mind, this will take *planning.* Before you can even begin to think about what information you will need and where you will find it (that is, to formulate your information search strategy), you need to consider:

(a) who is the user?

(b) what type of report will be most useful to him/her?
(c) what exactly does he/she need to know, and for what purpose?
(d) how much information is required, how quickly and at what cost?
(e) do you need to give judgements, recommendations etc (or just information)?

2.2 If you know who the user is, what he or she wants and why, and if you are aware of particular constraints imposed on you in terms of report size, time and money, you will have a good framework for going on to plan the structure and content of your report.

2.3 When you then come to plan a report in detail, you can ask yourself questions such as:

(a) What information do I need to provide? What is relevant to the user's requirements?

(b) Do I need to follow a line of reasoning? If so, what is the most logical way in which data can be grouped, and sequenced, to make my reasoning clear?

(c) Do I need to include my own personal views? If so, at what point: final recommendation, throughout?

(d) What can I do to make the report easier to read?

  (i) Are there suitable section or sub-headings I can use to indicate effectively each stage of the information/argument?

  (ii) Is the subject of the report too technical for the user? What vocabulary should I use to help him understand?

  (iii) Do I have a clear introduction to 'ease' the reader in to the subject, and a clear conclusion that will draw everything together for him or her?

2.4 You could use the above questions as a *checklist* for planning your report. If you can then jot down a 'skeleton' of the headings and sub-headings you have decided to use (with notes of any particular points that occur to you as you go along) you will be ready to write. The formal headings of standard business reports may be useful to help you to organise your thoughts - but may not be necessary or even advisable, if they simply act as a constraint on what you actually want to say, and how you want to 'shape' it. You should not worry at this stage about having 'Terms of Reference', 'Procedures', 'Findings' (discussed below), unless they provide a relevant framework for your report.

Example: report plan

2.5 An example of report planning follows.

A manager would like your views on the use of flexible working hours in your organisation. In due course, you are to write him a report considering the advantages and disadvantages to all concerned, and give your conclusions. Your task now is to prepare a plan for the report.

Solution

2.6 *Note:* again, a hint is given as to what is required. A *brief* introduction to flexible working hours may not be amiss (as if the manager has not considered how flexi-time might work). The central section of the report might be structured: *Advantages* - Party 1, party 2, party 3.

Disadvantages - Party 1, party 2, party 3. We have chosen to take the 'concerned' parties in turn, and consider the advantages and disadvantages for each. *Don't* just consider yourself and the staff, but *'all* concerned.'

The plan below is only a suggestion: the ideas for content should be your own.

Suggested plan

I INTRODUCTION

How flexible working hours operate (briefly), core period and flexible hours. Debit/credit of hours per week or month.

II EFFECTS

1. *Staff*

(a) *Advantages*

(i) reduced stress: vagaries of traffic etc. no longer a major worry
(ii) flexibility: fitting in with family patterns, shop hours etc
(iii) morale enhanced by discretion in own work patterns
(iv) favourable results for morale, attendance etc. in trial schemes

(b) *Disadvantages*

(i) reduced discipline: some staff may take advantage
(ii) fluctuating work patterns may be psychologically disruptive
(iii) friction may result from scheduling to cover non-core periods

2. *Management*

(a) *Advantages*

(i) morale and attendance advantages (for staff) ⇛ help management as well
(ii) fewer idle staff (wastage) during quieter periods

(b) *Disadvantages*

(i) planning, administering, controlling scheme
(ii) cost of mechanical logging in/out devices

3. *Customers*

(a) *Advantages*

(i) high morale of staff hopefully ⇛ better service

(b) *Disadvantages*

(i) possible bottlenecks of work during flexi-periods: delays
(ii) possible discontinuity of service: personnel changing through day etc.

III CONCLUSIONS

1. Disadvantages: few and can be overcome with good management.

2. Advantages: fundamental, shown to be effective elsewhere.

3. Recommend trial scheme of flexi-time with a view to introducing it later in full.

3. General points on style

3.1 There are certain stylistic requirements in the writing of reports, formal or informal.

(a) *Objectivity and balance.* Even in a report designed to persuade as well as inform, subjective value judgements and emotions should be kept out of the content and style as far as possible: the bias, if recognised, can undermine the credibility of the report and its recommendations.

(i) Emotional or otherwise loaded words should be avoided.

(ii) In more formal reports, *impersonal constructions* should be used rather than 'I', 'we' etc., which carry personal and possibly subjective associations. In other words, first person subjects should be replaced with third person:

I/we found that...	It became clear that... (Your name) found that... Investigation revealed that...

(iii) Colloquialisms and abbreviated forms should be avoided in formal written English: colloquial (informal) 'I've', 'don't' etc should be replaced by 'I have' and 'do not'. You should not use expressions like 'blew his top': formal phrases should be used, such as 'showed considerable irritation'.

(b) *Ease of understanding.*

(i) This will involve avoiding technical language and complex sentence structures for non-technical users.

(ii) The material will have to be logically organised, especially if it is leading up to a conclusion or recommendation.

(iii) Relevant themes should be signalled by appropriate headings or highlighted for easy scanning.

(iv) The layout of the report should display data clearly and attractively. Figures and diagrams should be used with discretion, and it might be helpful to highlight key figures which appear within large tables of numbers.

3.2 Various display techniques may be used to make the content of a report easy to identify and digest. For example, the relative importance of points should be signalled, each point may be referenced, and the body of text should be broken up to be easy on the eye. These aims may be achieved as follows.

(a) *Headings*

Spaced out or enlarged CAPITALS may be used for the main title.

Important headings, eg of sections of the report, may be in CAPITALS.

Underlining or *Italics* may be used for subheadings.

(b) *References*

Each section or point in a formal report should have a code for easy identification and reference.

Use different labelling for each type of heading	*Alternatively a 'decimal' system may be used:*
Main section headings	
I,II,III,IV,V etc.	
A,B,C,D,E etc.	1 *Heading 1*
	1.1 Subheading 1
Subsections	1.1.1 Point 1
1,2,3,4,5 etc.	1.1.2 Point 2
	1.2 Subheading 2
Points and subpoints	1.2.1 Point 1 etc
(a), (b), (c) etc.	2 *Heading 2*
(i), (ii), (iii) etc.	

(c) *Spacing*

Intelligent use of spacing separates headings from the body of the text for easy scanning, and also makes a large block more attractive and 'digestible'.

4. The format of formal and informal reports

General principles

4.1 When a formal request is made by a superior for a report to be prepared, such as in a formally worded memorandum or letter, the format and style of the report will obviously have to be formal as well: it will be strictly schematic, using impersonal constructions and avoiding emotive or colloquial expressions.

An informal request for a report - 'Can you jot down a few ideas for me about...' or 'Let me know what happens, will you?' - will result in an informal report, in which the structure will be less rigid, and the style slightly more personal (depending on the relationship perceived to exist between the writer and user).

If in doubt, it is better (more courteous and effective) to be too formal than overfamiliar.

4.2 The purpose of reports and their subject matter vary widely, but there are certain generally-accepted principles of report writing that can be applied to most types of report.

(a) *Title*. The report should have a title, and the title should be:

  (i) explicit. In other words, the title should indicate clearly what the report is about;
  (ii) brief. The title should be as short as possible whilst being explicit at the same time.

(b) *Identification of report writer, report user and date*. Reports should indicate in a clear place, possibly before the title itself, whom they are directed at, who has written them and the date of their preparation.

(c) *Confidentiality*. If the report is confidential or 'secret' this fact must be printed at the top of the report and possibly on every page.

(d) *Contents page*. If the report is extensive, it should open with a list of contents.

(e) *Terms of reference*. The introductory section of the report should explain why the report has been written and the terms of reference. The terms of reference will explain not only the purpose of the report but also any restrictions on its scope. For example, an internal auditing report might state that its terms of reference have been to investigate procedures in the credit control section of the accounts department, with a view to establishing whether the existing internal checks are adequate.

Similarly, the terms of reference of a management accounting report might be to investigate the short-term profit prospects for a particular product, with a view to recommending either the closure of the product line or its continued production. These terms of reference would exclude considerations of long-term prospects for the product, and so place a limitation on the scope of the report.

When timescale is important, this should be specified in the terms of reference. For example, the board of directors might call for a report so that they can take a decision by a certain cut-off date, eg whether to put in a tender for a major contract and if so at what price, in a situation where a customer has invited tenders which must be submitted by a certain date.

(f) *Sources of information*. If the report draws on other sources for its information, these sources should be acknowledged in the report. Alternatively, if the report is based on primary research, the nature of the fact-finding should be explained, perhaps in an appendix to the report.

If there is an extensive series of documents referring to one matter, a summary of the history may be provided in the appendix. If the literature includes a lot of correspondence, a uniform code should be used to refer to letters in the summary: for example letters between the Company Secretary and the Companies Registry might be referenced as CS/Reg [date].

(g) *Sections.* The main body of the report should be divided into sections. The sections should have a logical sequence, and each section should ideally have a clear heading. These headings (or sub-headings) should if possible be standardised when reports are produced regularly (eg audit reports). Paragraphs should be numbered, for ease of reference. Each paragraph should be concerned with just one basic idea.

(h) *Appendices.* To keep the main body of the report short enough to hold the reader's interest, detailed explanations, charts and tables of figures should be put into appendices. The main body of the report should make cross-references to the appendices in appropriate places.

(i) *Summary of recommendations.* A report will usually contain conclusions or recommendations about the course of action to be taken by the report user. These conclusions or recommendations should perhaps be stated at the beginning of the report (after the introduction and statement of terms of reference). The main body of the report can then follow, in its logically-progressive sections, and should lead the report user through the considerations that led the report writer to these conclusions.

The conclusions or recommendations should then be re-stated at the end of the main body of the report. For example, a management accounting report into the performance of an operating division might summarise its findings at the beginning, in terms of:

	Plan	*Actual*
Sales turnover	X	X
Profit	X	X
Cash movement	X	X
Capital employed	X	X
Return on capital employed	X	X

The following sections of the report would then go on to look at each of these items in more detail, concluding with an assessment of the division's performance and perhaps recommendations as to how it needs to be improved.

Any assumptions, forecasts or conjectures should be signalled as such, and not passed off as fact.

(j) *Prominence of important items.* The most significant items in a report should be given prominence.

(k) *Report summaries.* Long reports should be summarised in brief. However, as suggested already it is often better to keep the main report itself brief, with the detail in appendices; a report summary would probably not then be necessary.

(l) *Implications for management.* Reference should be made where appropriate to costs, savings and other benefits that might accrue, and to any other implications for management in the report's recommendations (eg implications for staff recruitment, training or redundancies and so on).

(m) *Completeness.* The qualities of information - reliability, objectivity, timeliness, clarity, completeness, and relevance - have been discussed earlier in this text. However, it is worth stressing that a report should be logically complete and should not overlook any item or consideration so that its recommendations are called into question.

4.3 The main types of report you might have to deal with are:

(a) the short formal report;
(b) the short informal report; and
(c) the memorandum report.

You should not feel bound to use the following headings in a report for an assessment task, but the guidelines on report sections may be helpful, should you wish to follow them.

The short formal report

4.4 The short formal report is used in formal contexts such as where middle management is reporting to senior management. It should be laid out according to certain basic guidelines. It will be split into logical sections, each referenced and headed appropriately:

TITLE

I TERMS OF REFERENCE (or INTRODUCTION)
II PROCEDURE (or METHOD)
III FINDINGS
  1 Section heading
  2 Section heading — if required
    (a) sub heading
      (i) sub point
IV CONCLUSIONS
V RECOMMENDATIONS — if asked for

SHORT FORMAL REPORT

TITLE At the top of every report (or on a title page, for lengthy ones) appears the *title* of the report (its subject) and, as appropriate, *who* has prepared it, *for whom* it is intended, the *date* of completion, and the *status* of the report ('Confidential' or 'Urgent').

I TERMS OF REFERENCE

Here is laid out the scope and purpose of the report: what is to be investigated, what kind of information is required, whether recommendations are to be made etc. This section may more simply be called **'Introduction'**, and may include the details set above under 'Title'. The title itself would then give only the subject of the report.

II PROCEDURE or METHOD

This outlines the steps taken to make an investigation, collect data, put events in motion etc. Telephone calls or visits made, documents or computer files consulted, computations or analyses made etc. should be briefly described, with the names of other people involved.

III FINDINGS

In this section the information itself is set out, with appropriate headings and sub-headings, if the report covers more than one topic. The content should be complete, but concise, and clearly structured in chronological order, order of importance, or any other *logical* relationship.

IV CONCLUSIONS

This section allows for a summary of main findings (if the report is complex and lengthy). For a simpler report it may include **action taken** or decisions reached (if any) as a result of the investigation, or an expression of the overall 'message' of the report.

V RECOMMENDATIONS

Here, if asked to do so in the terms of reference, the writer of the report may suggest the solution to the problem investigated so that the recipient will be able to make a decision if necessary.

The short informal report

4.5 The short informal report is used for less complex and lower level information. You, as Senior Accounts Clerk (or similar) could be asked to prepare such a report for the Accounts Manager.

4.6 The structure of the informal report is less developed: it will be shorter and less complex in any case, so will not require elaborate referencing and layout. There will be three main sections, each of which may be headed in any way appropriate to the context in which the report is written.

TITLE

1. BACKGROUND/INTRODUCTION/SITUATION
2. FINDINGS/ANALYSIS OF SITUATION
3. ACTION/SOLUTION/CONCLUSION

SHORT INFORMAL REPORT

Title Again, the subject title, 'to', 'from', 'date' and 'reference' (if necessary) should be provided, perhaps in the same style as memorandum headings.

1. **Background** or **Introduction** or **Situation**
This sets the context of the report. Include anything that will help the reader to understand the rest of the report: the reason why it was requested, the current situation, and any other background information on people and things that will be mentioned in the following detailed section. This section may also contain the equivalent of 'terms of reference' and 'procedure' ('method').

2. **Findings** or **Analysis of the situation**
Here is set out the detailed information gathered, narrative of events or other substance of the report as required by the user. This section may or may not require subheadings: concise prose paragraphs may be sufficient.

3. **Action** or **Solution** or **Conclusions**
The main thrust of the findings may be summarised in this section and conclusions drawn, together with a note of the outcome of events, or action required, or recommendations as to how a problem might be solved.

Examples

Short informal report

REPORT

Confidential

To: M Ployer, Accounts Manager
From: M Ployee, Senior Accounts Clerk
Date: 13 June 19--
Subject: Customer complaint by F R Vessent

1. **Background**

I have thoroughly investigated the situation with regard to Mr Vessent, and the correspondence provided. Mr Vessent is Accounts Clerk for Dibbin & Dobbs Ltd. who have had an account with us since June 19--: account number 39867. Credit terms were agreed with the firm whereby 10% discount is credited to their account for payment within two weeks of the statement date, payment in any case to be made within 30 days.

I have questioned the Accounts Clerk concerning the Dibbin & Dobbs account for April, and we have together consulted the records. In addition I telephoned the third party, Doobey & Sons to make enquiries about payments received from them.

2. **Findings**

The substance of Mr Vessent's complaint was that he had received from us a reminder that an amount of £1,306.70 was outstanding on the Dibbin & Dobbs account for April: according to Mr Vessent, a cheque payment for that amount had been sent on the 12th April, ie within 10 days of receiving the statement on 3rd April.

Records show no payment credited to the Dibbin & Dobbs account. However, an amount of £1,306.70 was credited to the account of Doobey & Sons on the same day, and payment duly acknowledged. Doobey & Sons when consulted admitted to having been puzzled by the acknowledgement of a payment they had never made.

The Accounts Clerk was absent through illness that week, and a temporary Clerk employed.

3. **Conclusion**

It would appear that the temporary Clerk credited the payment to the wrong account.

The entries have been duly corrected, and 10% prompt payment discount credited to Dibbin & Dobbs as usual.

I am writing an appropriate letter of apology and explanation to Mr Vessent.

Obviously this is a matter of some concern in terms of customer relations. I suggest that all clerks be reminded of the need for due care and attention, and that temporary staff in particular be briefed on this matter in the future.

Short formal report

REPORT ON DISC STORAGE, SAFETY AND SECURITY

I INTRODUCTION
This report details the findings of an investigation into methods of computer disc storage currently employed at the Head Office of the firm. The report, to include recommendations for the improvement of current procedure, was requested by Mr M Ployer, Accounts Department Manager, on 3rd September 19--. It was prepared by M Ployee, Senior Accounts Clerk, and submitted to Mr Ployer on 3rd October 19--.

II METHOD
In order to evaluate the present procedures and to identify specific shortcomings, the following investigatory procedures were adopted:

1 interview of all data processing staff
2 storage and indexing system inspected
3 computer accessory firm consulted by telephone and catalogues obtained (appendix I refers)

III FINDINGS

1 Current system

(a) Floppy discs are 'backed up' or duplicated irregularly and infrequently.

(b) Back-up discs where they exist are stored in plastic containers in the accounts office, ie in the same room as the discs currently in use.

(c) Discs are frequently left on desk tops during the day and even over night.

2 Safety and security risks

(a) There is no systematic provision for making copies, in the event of loss or damage of discs in use.

(b) There is no provision for separate storage of copies in the event of fire in the accounts office, and no adequate security against fire or damage in the containers used.

(c) There appears to be no awareness of the confidential nature of information on disc, nor of the ease with which discs may be damaged by handling, the spilling of beverages, dust etc.

IV CONCLUSIONS

The principal conclusions drawn from the investigation were that there was insufficient awareness of safety and security among the DP staff, that there was insufficient formal provision for safety and security procedure, and that there was serious cause for concern.

V RECOMMENDATIONS

In order to rectify the unsatisfactory situation summarised above, the author of the report recommends that consideration be given as a matter of urgency to the following measures:

1 immediate backing-up of all existing discs
2 drafting of procedures for backing up discs at the end of each day's work
3 acquisition of a fire-proof safe to be kept in separate office accommodation
4 communication to all DP staff of the serious risk of loss, theft and damage arising from careless handling of computer discs

Signed: M. Ployee

The memorandum report

4.7 In informal reporting situations within an organisation, the 'short informal report' may well be presented in A4 memorandum format, which incorporates title headings and can thereafter be laid out at the writer's discretion. An ordinary memorandum may be used for flexible, informal reports: aside from the convenient title headings, there are no particular requirements for structure, headings or layout. The writer may consider whatever is logical, convenient and attractive for the reader.

Form reports

4.8 Some commonly prepared reports have certain standard content requirements, and can therefore be preprinted with appropriate format and headings and filled in when the need arises: an accident report form, for example, or a damaged goods report (for incoming orders found to be faulty). Another example is the personnel profile (like a curriculum vitae). Pre-printed forms allow the details of the report to be presented under the relevant headings, and in the space available. (This is largely a matter of common sense, plus the ability to summarise information within formal constraints.) Even if an organisation does not have formatted reports pre-printed, and each report has to be drafted for the occasion, the common elements will still be required.

5. Standard forms

5.1 In recording data and in presenting routine reports to management, accountants and others in organisations make frequent use of forms. A form can be defined as a schedule which is to be filled in with details and has a prescribed layout, arrangement and wording. Forms are standard documents which are used regularly to 'capture' data and communicate information.

5.2 Using forms, rather than collecting data or providing information on non-standard documents, has several important advantages.

(a) Forms ensure that all the information required is actually obtained, or at least that any gaps in the information can be easily recognised. In other words, they help to ensure *completeness* of the data or information when the form is initially filled in.

(b) Because they are in a standard format, they are more easily understandable. Users of forms know where to look on the form for items of information, and if there is anything they do not understand, they can check the meaning in an office procedures manual, which should describe the functions of forms used by the organisation.

(c) Using forms helps management to regulate the flow of information within the organisation, by planning what forms there should be, who should fill them in, how frequently they should be filled in and who should receive and use them.

General principles of good form design

5.3 For Unit 7: *Preparing reports and returns* you are expected to be able to complete standard forms. Competent handling of standard forms will be easier if you are aware of some of the basic principles of form design.

5.4 Form design, like form filling, is largely a matter of common sense and experience, but there are certain principles that should be applied to ensure that there are suitable well-designed forms in use within the organisation. The purpose served by a form is to ensure the effective transmission of necessary information.

5.5 A good form is one which is designed so that information can be easily:

(a) *obtained:* the layout of the form and instructions on how to fill it in should be clear to the user. As much information as possible should be pre-printed to avoid error and reduce the work-load and sentence completion, tick boxes and deletion used where possible to cut down on the amount of writing required. Forms should request and contain all the data required, but no more. In other words the form must be easy to use;

(b) *transmitted:* the form must be capable where necessary of easy handling and transmission;

(c) *interpreted:* the layout of information on the form must be in a clear, logical sequence so that it can be readily understood by the reader. Related items should be grouped together and separated from other areas. A good title will help, and colour coding and typeface may also clarify the purpose of the form and each of its sections;

(d) *filed:* the size of filing cabinets or trays should be considered for forms stored for a long period as hard copy. Each document should have a clear title, and usually a code or identifying colour or number;

(e) *retrieved:* the problems of retrieving a form from file should also be considered. The position of the serial number or identification of the record may be important.

5.6 Every form must have a purpose. When designing a form, the designer must ask himself:

(a) what this purpose is; and
(b) whether the form is really necessary.

He must ensure that there is no other form either existing or proposed which serves the same purpose, or could be made to do so.

5.7 In designing a form there are a number of decisions to be made, about:

(a) content;
(b) layout;
(c) make-up;
(d) printing; and
(e) paper.

Content

5.8 Generally, the content of a form will be determined by the use to which it will be put. There are, however, some items which appear on most forms:

(a) title;
(b) serial number;
(c) date;
(d) narrative ie instructions for filling, subsidiary headings etc;
(e) unit titles: hours, £s, tons etc;
(f) signature (perhaps an authorisation);
(g) distribution of copies (eg copy 1 - accounts; copy 2 - stores; copy 3 - production).

5.9 The title of a form is of great importance. It must be descriptive as well as easy to remember, and preferably concise: forms often have to become known by a nickname. The narrative, ie the headings or instructions relating to spaces where entries are required, must also be given careful consideration. The words used must be matched to the educational and technical level of both the originator (ie the person filling in the information) and the interpreter (ie the person retrieving that information from the form). Different types of entry headings include:

(a) instruction, eg 'Write your name in this space';
(b) question, eg 'What is your name?';
(c) title, eg 'Name'.

5.10 The content of a form can be planned by starting with a checklist of all the data or information that the form should include.

The specific data contents can then be grouped into:

(a) *heading data* - ie data which ought to appear towards the top of the form, somewhere below or to the side of the title. Much of this may be 'static' or unchanging and may therefore be pre-printed; eg on a stores 'bin card' record, permanent items such as maximum and minimum stock levels, re-order levels, location of the product in the store;

(b) *line entries* - ie the main substance of the form, data which will be inserted repeatedly, either all at the same time (eg items listed on a sales order form) or at different times (eg the on-going stock movements on a stores 'bin card' record: quantities, dates etc);

(c) '*trailer data*' - ie data which do not constitute line entries and are less immediately important than heading data, and which might therefore be put at the bottom of a form to prevent the heading data becoming too long eg background or 'other' details.

Layout

5.11 Points of layout include:

(a) *direction:* information should usually be laid out from left to right and top to bottom;

(b) *position of title:* the title will have to be prominently displayed, usually at the top;

(c) *position of reference numbers:* these should normally be placed near a corner so that the document can be easily identified in a file;

(d) *position of entry headings:* these should always be near the space to which they relate. Never leave space *without* a heading, as this encourages misplaced or irrelevant entries.

If data is to be presented in columns, there may not be space for column headings to be written horizontally: they may instead be vertical or diagonal.

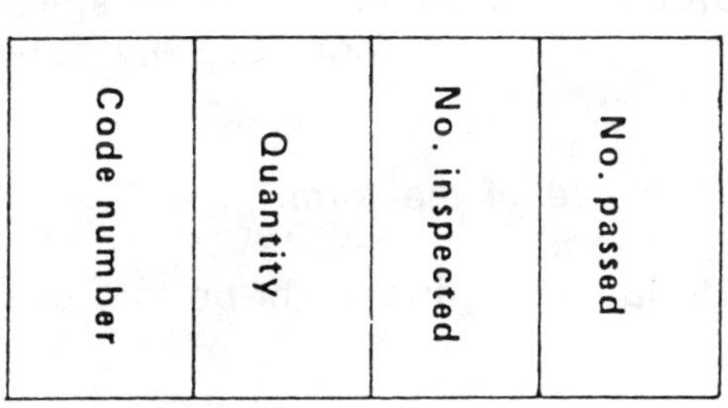

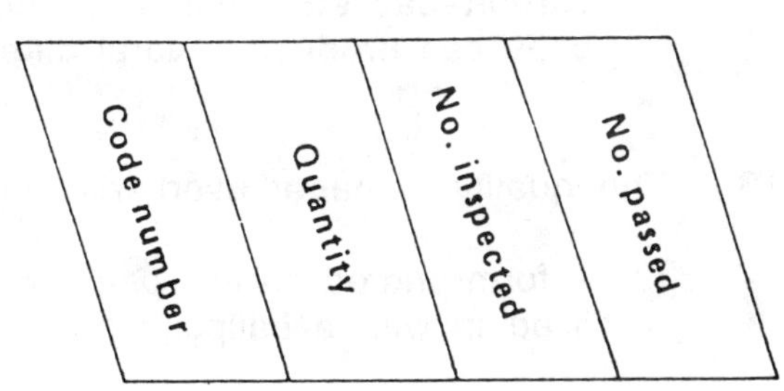

(e) *entry sequence.* Entries should always follow a logical sequence. This is particularly important when the forms will be completed by several different people;

(f) *spacing and separation.* Thin straight lines should surround each area of information, marking its boundaries clearly. There should be adequate spacing, horizontally and vertically, to suit the likely amount and method of entry. For example, if forms are to be handwritten, spaces should be larger than if they are to be produced by machines;

(g) *brief, clear and prominent instructions.* If the form is to be filled in by an organisation's own staff, these instructions may be kept separately in an office manual, but if it is to be filled in by outsiders then explicit, helpful instructions should be clearly displayed on the form itself.

Make-up

5.12 The make-up of the form concerns its size, colour and the number of copies in a multi-part set.

(a) *Size of the form.* This should be suitable for:

(i) *handling.* The form as a whole must be large enough to contain all the information likely to be required and spaces for each entry should be adequate. If the form is to be posted, the size should allow it to be fitted into a standard envelope, perhaps after folding once or twice;

(ii) *filing.* Forms should be of a size that will suit the filing and retrieval system used by the organisation.

Most forms are of a standard document size, eg A4 or A5.

(b) *Colour.* Coloured paper or printing can provide a system of colour-coding in order to:

(i) differentiate easily between copies. Forms might be produced in multi-part sets, with each copy being routed differently - eg top copy (white) to the customer, second copy (pink) to the buying department, third copy (yellow) to accounts etc.

(ii) differentiate between different forms that are similar in design and used by the same office: errors may occur when clerks start filling in the wrong form by mistake, and have to re-copy the data. Colour coding, as well as the title and form number (P45, UB40 etc) can help to reduce such identification errors.

(NB The colours chosen should minimise the likelihood of eye strain. This is why pale pastel colours are usually used, rather than black print on deep orange or red paper!)

(c) *Number of copies.* Keeping the number of copies in a multi-part to a minimum saves on printing costs. Sets, however, can save time and money, where similar forms have different uses. By varying the pre-printed data on each copy in the set, and using carbon-backed paper or interleaved carbon paper sheets, a single entry onto the top copy can produce several different forms eg an order form, delivery note, invoice etc.

5.13 The quality of paper used will depend on the use of the form.

(a) A form printed on thin paper is unlikely to last long, and might be torn or marked if it is filled in with a ballpoint pen or pencil.

(b) Forms used in a factory or out of doors (bearing in mind the uncertain climate) should be made from a suitably sturdy material.

(c) Printing forms that will be posted overseas on thin paper can reduce the costs of airmail postage.

Form filling

5.14 A well-designed form should be easy to fill in. It may not *look* very easy, if it requires a large amount of complex information, but you should find the required items indicated for you, and sufficient instruction to enable you to insert the desired data in the right place and manner. Many forms do the work for you, leaving you only with small insertions, crosses or ticks in 'choice' boxes, either/or deletions etc.

As noted above under 'form reports', however, some forms do simply leave space and ask you to 'give details of....': summarising will be necessary here, since you will probably not have as much space as you initially think you need.

5.15 Some hints for form-filling include the following.

(a) Scan the form first, for main headings and topic areas. That way, you will not put into Section A information that more properly fits into Section D later on.

(b) Obey any instructions about *what to include*. For example, the rubric on an accident report might be: 'Give a full account of the accident explaining as far as possible how it happened and how those killed or hurt received their injuries. Give name and type of any plant, equipment, machinery or vehicle involved and note whether it was in motion.'

(c) Obey instructions about *how* to provide data eg

(i) the level or type of detail required: 'Precise place eg South Warehouse, No 2 Machine Shop, canteen kitchen';

(ii) the method of entry: 'Please complete in block capitals', 'tick the appropriate box' etc.

(d) Plan any prose descriptions or narratives requested. Forms will usually offer you the chance to use 'continuation sheets' if required, but you should practise providing necessary information within the constraints of formality and limited space. Draft an account with all the details you want to include, then delete any items that seem irrelevant to the purpose of the form. Finally, prune your prose of unnecessary circumlocutions (ie using three words when one would do) and superfluous expressions. Then you will be able to write the information 'clean' into the form.

(e) Remember who is going to use the information and why. This will help you to keep to a relevant content and clear written style.

Forms in computer systems

5.16 In computer systems source documents may have to be transcribed into a machine readable medium (eg magnetic disk or tape) but they may have other functions than merely data capture for computer processing. For example, a sales invoice has to function as a sales invoice and so its contents may contain data which is not required for computer processing. The layout of the invoice must:

(a) give a clear indication of which data is to be transcribed for computer input;

(b) make sure that the data required is entered on the invoice in keying-in sequence (eg from left to right, top to bottom of the sheet). The keying-in sequence should preferably be the sequence in which the data will be used by the computer program.

5.17 Computer-produced forms or even other printed forms might be turn-round documents - which start by providing output to a user, are then used (filled in) and re-input to a computer, and so re-processed. Examples of turn-round documents are bank giro payment slips (as at the bottom of telephone bills and electricity bills).

Timeliness

5.18 Like reports, returns made on standard forms must be presented on time. In the case of a form for an external agency, there will usually be a deadline by which the form must be submitted. As with reports, lateness may make a standard return worthless or may lead to sanctions for late submission being exercised. For example, a late VAT return may attract penalties, and a late grant application might not be accepted at all.

Key points in this chapter

- A report may be routine or 'one-off'. The purpose of the report must be clear, and certain general principles should be followed in planning and giving structure to the report.
- Stylistic qualities of reports include objectivity and balance, and ease of understanding.
- Completion of standard forms requires careful following of instructions. The better designed the form, the easier it will be to fill in.

For practice on the points covered in this chapter you should now attempt the Exercises in Session 8 of the Cost Accounting II Workbook

Read cover in unit 6

9. Costs, standard costs and performance

1. **Cost accounting**
2. **Direct costs and overheads (indirect costs)**
3. **Functional costs**
4. **Cost centres and cost units**
5. **Cost codes**
6. **Standard costs**
7. **Standard costing as a cost accounting system**
8. **Standard costs and performance**
9. **Productivity ratios**

1. Cost accounting

1.1 To measure performance effectively the managers of a business must be provided with sufficiently accurate and detailed information - ie periodic performance reports - and the cost accounting system should provide this. *Cost accounting* is a management information system which analyses past, present and future data to provide the basis for managerial action. In this chapter we introduce some of the basic concepts of cost accounting. Various aspects of this subject are dealt with in Unit 6: *Recording cost information*, and more detail is to be found in the BPP *Cost Accounting I* Tutorial Text.

1.2 The cost accountant is interested in providing the answers to the following types of questions.

(a) What has been the cost of goods produced or services provided, or what has been the cost of a department or work section? What have revenues been? Knowing about costs and revenues that are being/have been incurred and earned enables management to do the following.

   (i) Assess the profitability of a product, a service, a department, or the organisation in total.

   (ii) Perhaps, set selling prices with some regard for the costs of sale.

   (iii) Put a value to stocks of goods (raw materials, work in progress, finished goods) that are still held in store at the end of a period, for preparing a balance sheet of the company's assets and liabilities.

(b) What are the future costs of goods and services (and operations etc) likely to be? Costing is an integral part of budgeting (planning) for the future.

(c) How do actual costs compare with budgeted costs? If an organisation plans for its revenues and costs to be a certain amount, but they actually turn out differently, the differences can be measured and reported. Management can use these reports as a guide to whether corrective action (or 'control' action) is needed to sort out a problem revealed by these differences between budgeted and actual results. This system of control is often referred to as budgetary control.

(d) What information does management need in order to make sensible decisions about profits and costs?

1.3 It would be wrong to suppose that cost accounting systems are restricted to manufacturing operations, although they are probably more fully developed in this area of work. Service industries, government departments and welfare activities can all make use of cost accounting information. Within a manufacturing organisation, the cost accounting system should be applied not only to manufacturing but also to administration, selling and distribution, research and development and so on.

The work of the cost department

1.4 The cost department is responsible for keeping the cost accounting records.

(a) These records should analyse production, administration, marketing costs and so on in such a way as to fulfil all of the requirements set out in paragraph 1.2 above.

(b) The systems should cater for the production of regular performance statements which are necessary to management for control purposes.

(c) The system should also be capable of analysing:

(i) past costs (for profit measurement, stock valuation);

(ii) present costs (for control, for example by means of comparing current results against the budget);

(iii) future costs (for budgeting and decision making).

1.5 If a company did not have a costing system, management would not have adequate information on the following.

(a) The profitability of individual products, services or jobs.

(b) The profitability of different departments or operations.

(c) The cost behaviour of the various items of expenditure in the organisation. This would mean that cost estimation would not be as accurate as it could be.

(d) The differences between actual results and expected results. With an efficient costing system, such differences can be traced to the manager responsible.

(e) How to set prices so as to cover costs and generate an acceptable level of profit.

(f) The effect on profits of increases or decreases in output, or the shutdown of a product line or department.

The relationship with financial accounting

1.6 The *financial accounting* and *cost accounting* systems in a business both record the same basic data for income and expenditure, but each set of records may analyse the data in a different way. This is because each system has a different purpose.

(a) Financial accounting is primarily a method of reporting the results and financial position of a business. Although the financial accounts may be of interest to management, their principal function is to satisfy the information needs of persons not involved in the day-to-day running of the business. Shareholders, for instance, may use them to assess how well the directors have carried out their stewardship function. Other outsiders whose information needs are satisfied wholly or in part by the financial accounts are suppliers, customers, employees and the Inland Revenue. In addition, the financial accounts must be prepared in accordance with strict guidelines which are laid down in company law and in accounting standards.

(b) Cost accounting is an *internal* reporting system for the organisation's own management. It provides them with the information which they need to manage the business. Outsiders will not see this information, and there are no strict rules which govern the way in which cost accounting information should be prepared and presented. Each organisation can develop the system which is best suited to its needs.

1.7 Since the cost accounting system and the financial accounting system have different purposes and analyse the data in different ways, they are often kept separately in two sets of accounts. However, it is possible to maintain a single integrated set of accounts containing both cost and financial accounting information.

1.8 Finally, there is a legal requirement for a financial accounting system. Companies are obliged to prepare annual accounts for external reporting purposes. There is no legal requirement for a costing system, which is only necessary if management believes that cost information will help them to plan and control the resources of the organisation more efficiently than if no formal costing system existed. There is no point in having a costing system if its costs outweigh the benefits it provides.

2. Direct costs and overheads (indirect costs)

2.1 Total costs of a product or service consist of the following costs.

(a) The cost of materials consumed in making the product or providing the service.

(b) The cost of the wages and salaries of employees of the organisation, who are directly or indirectly involved in producing the product or providing the service.

(c) The cost of other expenses, apart from materials and labour costs. These include items such as rent and rates, electricity bills, gas bills, depreciation, interest charges, the cost of contractors' services (for example sub-contractors, office cleaners and so on), telephone bills etc.

2.2 Materials, labour costs and other expenses can be classified as direct costs or as indirect costs.

(a) A *direct cost* is a cost that can be traced in full to the product or service (or department etc) that is being costed.

(i) *Direct materials* costs are the costs of materials that are known to have been used in making and selling a product (or providing a service), ie 'the cost of materials entering into and becoming constituent elements of a product or saleable service, and which can be identified separately in product cost'.

(ii) *Direct labour costs* are the specific costs of the workforce used to make a product or provide a service, for the 'remuneration for employees' effort and skills applied directly to a product or saleable service and which can be identified separately in product cost'. Direct labour costs are established by measuring the time taken for a job, or the time taken in 'direct production work'. Traditionally, direct labour costs have been restricted to wage-earning factory workers, but in recent years, with the development of systems for costing services ('service costing') the costs of some salaried staff might also be treated as a direct labour cost.

(iii) Other *direct expenses* are those expenses that have been incurred in full as a direct consequence of making a product, or providing a service, or running a department (depending on whether a product, a service or a department is being costed).

(b) An *indirect cost* is a cost that is incurred in the course of making a product, providing a service or running a department, but which cannot be traced directly and in full to the product, service or department.

2.3 Total expenditure may be analysed as follows.

Material cost	=	Direct material cost	+	Indirect material cost
+		+		+
Wages	=	Direct wages	+	Indirect wages
+		+		+
Expenses	=	Direct expenses	+	Indirect expenses
Total cost	=	Prime cost	+	Overhead

3. Functional costs

3.1 In a 'traditional' costing system for a manufacturing organisation, costs are classified as:

(a) production or manufacturing costs;
(b) administration costs;
(c) marketing, or selling and distribution costs.

Many expenses fall comfortably into one or other of these three broad classifications. Manufacturing costs are associated with the factory, selling and distribution costs with the sales, marketing, warehousing and transport departments and administration costs with general office departments (such as accounting and personnel).

Other expenses that do not fall fully into one of these classifications might be categorised as 'general overheads' or even listed as a classification on their own (for example research and development costs).

3.2 In costing a small product made by a manufacturing organisation, direct costs are usually restricted to some of the production costs (although it is not uncommon to find a salesman's commission for selling the product as a direct selling cost). A common analysis of costs might look like this.

	£
Production costs	
Direct materials	A
Direct wages	B
Direct expenses (if any)	C
Prime cost	A+B+C
Production overheads	D
Full factory cost	A+B+C+D
Administration overheads	E
Selling and distribution overheads	F
Full cost of sales	A+B+C+D+E+F

Functional costs, in more detail

3.3 Functional costs include the following.

(a) *Production costs:* the costs which are incurred by the sequence of operations beginning with the supply of raw materials, and ending with the completion of the product ready for warehousing as a finished goods item; packaging costs are production costs where they relate to 'primary' packing (for example boxes, wrappers, and so on).

(b) *Administration costs:* the costs of managing an organisation, ie planning and controlling its operations, but only insofar as such administration costs are not related to the production, sales, distribution or research and development functions.

(c) *Selling costs,* sometimes known as *marketing costs*, are the costs of creating demand for products and securing firm orders from customers.

(d) *Distribution costs:* the costs of the sequence of operations beginning with the receipt of finished goods from the production department and making them ready for dispatch and ending with the reconditioning for re-use of returned empty containers.

(e) *Research and development costs*

(i) Research costs are the costs of searching for new or improved products.

(ii) Development costs are the costs incurred between the decision to produce a new or improved product and the commencement of full, formal manufacture of the product.

4. Cost centres and cost units

Allocation of costs to cost centres

4.1 Costs consist of the costs of direct materials, direct labour, direct expenses, production overheads, administration overheads and general overheads. But how does a cost accountant set about recording in practice the actual expenses incurred as any one of these classifications?

4.2 To begin with, all costs should be recorded as a direct cost of a *cost centre*. Even 'overhead costs' are directly traceable to an office or an item of expense and there should be an overhead cost centre to cater for these costs.

A cost centre is a location, person or item of equipment for which costs may be ascertained and related to cost units for control purposes.

4.3 Suitable cost centres might be as follows.

(a) In a production department: the department itself, a machine within the department or group of machines, a foreman's work group, a work bench and so on.

(b) Production 'service' or 'back-up' departments, such as the stores, maintenance, production planning and control departments.

(c) Administration, sales or distribution departments, such as the personnel, accounting or purchasing departments; a sales region or salesman; or a warehouse or distribution unit.

(d) Shared costs (for example rent, rates, electricity or gas bills) may require cost centres of their own, in order to be directly allocated. Shared cost items may be charged to separate, individual cost centres, or they may be grouped into a larger cost centre (for example *factory occupancy costs*, for rents, rates, heating, lighting, building repairs, cleaning and maintenance of a particular factory).

4.4 Charging costs to a cost centre simply involves two steps.

(a) Identifying the cost centre for which an item of expenditure is a direct cost.

(b) Allocating the cost to the cost centre (usually by means of a *cost code* - discussed below).

Cost centres, therefore, provide a basis for collection and then further analysis of actual costs, and are a means of building up estimated costs in budgeting.

4.5 Cost centres are an essential 'building block' of a costing system. They are the starting point:

(a) for classifying actual costs incurred;
(b) for preparing budgets of planned costs;
(c) for comparing actual costs and budgeted costs, for management control information.

Cost per unit

4.6 Once costs have been traced to cost centres, they can be further analysed in order to establish a cost per cost unit. Alternatively, some items of cost may be charged directly to a cost unit, for example direct materials and direct labour costs.

A cost unit is 'a unit of product or service in relation to which costs are ascertained'.
(CIMA: *Official Terminology*)

4.7 The unit selected must be appropriate to the business and one with which expenditure can be readily associated. Care must be taken in non-manufacturing operations to ensure that the unit is a meaningful measure. For instance in transport undertakings the cost per tonne transported may not be particularly useful. The cost per tonne carried from London to Glasgow would probably be greater than the cost per tonne from London to Dover, and it would not be easy to make comparisons for control purposes. If the cost unit was changed to a tonne-mile (the cost of transporting one tonne for one mile) then a comparison between the two journeys would be valid.

4.8 Some examples of cost units are shown in the table below. (Source: *CIMA Official Terminology*).

Examples of cost units

Business	*Cost unit*
Brewing	Barrel/hectolitre
Brick-making	1,000 bricks
Coal mining	Ton/tonne
Electricity	kWh
Engineering	Contract, job
Gas	Therm
Paper	Ream
Petroleum	Barrel, tonne, litre
Sand and gravel	Cubic yard/metre
Steel	Tonne/ton/sheet (a) Rolled (b) Cast (c) Extruded
Timber	100 ft/standard/stere
Airline	Available tonne km
Hotel and catering	Room/cover
Professional service (accountants, architects, lawyers, surveyors)	Chargeable hour
Education	(a) Enrolled student (b) Successful student (c) School meal
Healthcare (hospitals)	(a) Bed occupied (b) Out-patient
Activity	
Building service	Square metre
Credit control	Account maintained
Materials/storage/handling	(a) Requisition (b) Unit issued/received (c) Value issued/received
Personnel administration	Employee
Selling	(a) £ of turnover (b) Call made (c) Order taken (a) Number (b) Value
Telephone service	(a) Call made (b) Extension

5. Cost codes

5.1 We have seen that charging costs to a cost centre involves two steps.

(a) Identifying the cost centre for which an item of expenditure is a direct cost.
(b) Allocating the cost to the cost centre.

5.2 The allocation of the cost to the cost centre is usually by means of a *cost code*. A code is 'A system of symbols designed to be applied to a classified set of items to give a brief accurate reference, facilitating entry, collation and analysis' (CIMA *Official Terminology*).

5.3 In order to provide accurate management information, it is vital that costs are allocated correctly. Each individual cost should therefore be identifiable by its code. This is possible by building up the individual characteristics of the cost into the code.

5.4 The characteristics which are normally identified are as follows.

(a) The nature of the cost (materials, wages, hire charges and so on) which is known as a *subjective classification*

(b) The type of cost (direct or indirect and so on)

(c) The cost centre to which the cost should be allocated

(d) The department which the particular cost centre is in

Features of a good coding system

5.5 An efficient and effective coding system, whether manual or computerised, should incorporate the following features.

(a) The cost must be easy to use and communicate.

(b) Each item should have a unique code.

(c) The coding system must allow for expansion.

(d) If there is a conflict between the ease of using the code by the people involved and its manipulation on a computer, the human interest should take priority.

(e) The code should be flexible so that small changes in item classification can be incorporated without major changes to the coding system itself.

(f) The coding system should provide a comprehensive system, whereby every recorded item can be suitable coded.

(g) The coding system should be brief, to save clerical time in writing out codes and to save storage space in computer memory and on computer files. At the same time codes must be long enough to allow for appropriate coding of all items.

(h) The likelihood of errors going undetected should be minimised.

(i) There should be a readily available index or reference book of codes.

(j) Existing codes should be reviewed regularly and out-of-date codes removed.

(k) Code numbers should be issued from a single central point. Different people should not be allowed to add new codes to the existing list independently.

(l) The code should be either entirely numeric or entirely alphabetic. In a computerised system, numeric characters are preferable. The use of dots, dashes, colons and so on should be avoided.

(m) Codes should be uniform (that is, have the same length and the same structure) to assist in the detection of missing characters and to facilitate processing.

(n) The coding system should avoid problems such as confusion between I and 1, O and 0 (zero), S and 5 and so on.

(o) The coding system should, if possible, be *significant* (in other words, the actual code should signify something about the item being coded).

(p) If the code consists of alphabetic characters, it should be derived from the item's description or name (that is, mnemonics should be used).

Types of code

5.6 The main coding methods are listed below.

(a) *Sequence (or progressive) codes*
Numbers are given to items in ordinary numerical sequence, so that there is no obvious connection between an item and its code. For example:

000042	2" nails
000043	office stapler
000044	hand wrench

(b) *Group classification codes*
These are an improvement on simple sequence codes, in that a digit (often the first one) indicates the classification of an item. For example:

4NNNNN	nails
5NNNNN	screws
6NNNNN	bolts

(*Note.* 'N' stands for another digit; 'NNNNN' indicates there are five further digits in the code.)

(c) *Faceted codes*
These are a refinement of group classification codes, in that each digit of the code gives information about an item. For example:

(i) The first digit:
1 Nails
2 Screws
3 Bolts
etc...

(ii) The second digit:

1 Steel
2 Brass
3 Copper
etc...

(iii) The third digit:

1 50 mm
2 60 mm
3 75 mm
etc...

A 60mm steel screw would have a code of 212.

(d) *Significant digit codes*
These incorporate some digit(s) which is (are) part of the description of the item being coded. For example:

5000	screws
5050	50 mm screws
5060	60 mm screws
5075	75 mm screws

(e) *Hierarchical codes*
This is a type of faceted code where each digit represents a classification, and each digit further to the right represents a smaller subset than those to the left. For example:

3	=	Screws
31	=	Flat headed screws
32	=	Round headed screws
322	=	Steel (round headed) screws

and so on.

5.7 A coding system does not have to be structured entirely on any one of the above systems - it can mix the various features according to the items which need to be coded. But the system eventually chosen should always be simple to use and understand and it should be flexible (so that it can readily accommodate changes within an organisation, especially expansion).

5.8 For accounting purposes, the coding system most commonly used is a form of hierarchical code. The code will need to show whether an item is an asset (and what sort of an asset) or a liability (and what sort of a liability) and the cost centre to which it is attributable (if the code is to be used for cost accounting).

6. Standard costs

Definitions

6.1 A *standard cost* is an estimated unit cost, prepared in advance and calculated from management's expectations of:

(a) efficiency levels in the use of materials and labour;
(b) the expected price of materials, labour and expenses;
(c) budgeted overhead costs and budgeted volumes of activity.

It is a planned cost, and so is the cost that should be incurred in making the unit. Differences between actual and standard costs are called *variances*.

6.2 *Standard costing* is the preparation of standard costs:

(a) for use in cost accounting as a means of valuing stocks and the cost of production. It is an alternative method of valuation to FIFO, LIFO, replacement costing etc;

(b) for use in budgetary control (variance analysis).

6.3 The use of standard costs to simplify the keeping of cost accounting records should not be overlooked, but the CIMA's *Official terminology* stresses the control and variance analysis aspect of standard costing. Study the following definitions carefully, bearing in mind that subjective judgements go into establishing standards and standard costs.

(a) *Standard:* 'a predetermined measurable quantity set in defined conditions. Standards are finally set by human judgement and consequently are subject to the same fallibility which attends all human activity. Thus a standard for 100 per cent machine output can be fixed by its geared input/output speeds, but the effective realisable output standard is one of judgement.'

(b) *Standard cost:* 'a standard expressed in money. It is built up from an assessment of the value of cost elements. Its main uses are providing bases for performance measurement, control by exception reporting, valuing stock and establishing selling prices.'

(c) *Standard costing:* 'a control technique which compares standard costs and revenues with actual results to obtain variances which are used to stimulate improved performance.'

6.4 A standard cost card (or standard cost sheet) will be prepared for each product. The card will normally show the quantity and price of each direct material to be consumed, the time and rate of each grade of direct labour required, the overhead recovery and the full cost. The standard selling price and the standard profit per unit may also be shown.

7. Standard costing as a cost accounting system

7.1 You should be aware that standard costs make the task of recording costs in books of account a relatively simple matter.

Example: standard costs

7.2 Suppose that the standard cost card of product Y is as follows.

		£
Direct material	6 kg of material A at £3	18.00
Direct labour	3 hours at £2.50	7.50
Production overhead	3 hours at £3.50	10.50
		36.00

The standard cost per unit for administration, selling and distribution is £4.

During one month the following results were recorded.

Opening stocks of raw material, WIP and finished goods are nil. (Stocks in a manufacturing business comprise raw materials, work in progress (WIP) and finished goods. We return to these terms later in the text.)

Purchases	10,000 kg of material A
Used in production	8,000 kg of material A
Units of product Y made	1,500 units
Units of product Y sold	1,200 units

There was no closing stock of work in progress.

What costs would be entered in the books of account for:

(a) the value of closing stocks of raw materials;
(b) the value of closing stocks of finished goods;
(c) the cost of units produced;
(d) the cost of units sold?

Solution

7.3 (a) Closing stocks of material A are valued at standard cost.
2,000 kg × £3 = £6,000

(b) Closing stocks of finished goods (product Y) are valued at standard production cost.
300 units × £36 = £10,800

(c) Units produced are valued at standard production cost.
1,500 units × £36 = £54,000

(d) Units sold are valued at the standard cost of sales.
1,200 units × £40 = £48,000

Any variance arising because actual costs are different from standard costs will be recorded in the cost accounts as a variance. Variances will be included in the profit and loss account at the end of a period as an adjusting item. In this example it may be seen that the materials actually used (8,000 kg) were less than expected to make 1,500 units of product Y (9,000 kg); therefore a favourable materials usage variance has occurred. The cost of this variance would be recorded in the books of account.

8. Standard costs and performance

Standard costs and budgets

8.1 A budget is a financial and/or quantitative plan of operations for a forthcoming accounting period. Many *functional budgets* (a budget of income or expenditure for individual functions of a business, such as the sales budget, production budget, direct labour budgets etc) are summarised and incorporated into a *master budget* (or a *summary budget).*

8.2 The purposes of a budget are:

(a) to *co-ordinate* the activities of all the different departments of an organisation into a single master plan; in addition, through participation by employees in preparing a budget, it may be possible to motivate them to raise their targets and standards and to achieve better results;

(b) to *communicate* the policies and targets to every manager in the organisation responsible for carrying out a part of that plan;

(c) to establish a system of *control* by having a plan against which actual results can be progressively compared;

(d) to *compel planning.* By having a formal budgeting procedure, management is forced to look to the future instead of 'living hand-to-mouth' without any clear idea of purpose.

8.3 The budget period is the time period to which the budget relates. Except for capital expenditure budgets, the budget period is commonly the accounting year (sub-divided into 12 or 13 control periods).

8.4 Standard costing and budgetary control are interlinked. When standard costs have been determined it is relatively easy to compute budgets for production costs and sales. On the other hand, in determining standard costs it is necessary to ascertain the budgeted level of output for the period in order to prepare a standard fixed production overhead cost per unit.

8.5 When actual costs differ from standard costs we call these differences cost variances. Similarly, we get sales variances when actual sales are different from budgeted sales either due to the number sold (volume variance) or to a different price (price variance). These variances will affect our budgeted profit because our budgeted profit is based on standard costs and standard selling prices.

Determining standards and performance

8.6 The responsibility for setting standard costs should be shared between managers able to provide the necessary levels of expected efficiency, prices and overhead costs.

8.7 It is common for standard costs to be revised once a year to allow for changes in prices, wage rates and any expected alterations in such factors as volume of output, efficiency levels and standard practices.

Standard cost rates

8.8 (a) Direct materials costs per unit of raw material will be estimated by the purchasing department from their knowledge of the following.

(i) Purchase contracts already agreed.
(ii) The forecast movement of prices in the market.
(iii) The availability of bulk purchase discounts.

(b) Direct labour rates per hour will be set by reference to the payroll and to any agreements on pay rises.

(i) A separate hourly rate will be set for each different labour grade/type of employee.

(ii) The hourly rate will probably be an average to incorporate not only basic hourly wages, but also bonus payments, holiday pay, employers' National Insurance contributions etc.

(iii) An average rate will be applied for each grade (even though rates of pay of individual employees may vary according to age and experience).

Performance standards

8.9 It is also necessary to estimate the materials required to make each product (material usage) and the labour hours required (labour efficiency).

Technical specifications must be prepared for each product by production experts (either in the production department or the work study department).

(a) The *Standard production specification* for materials lists the quantities required per unit of each material in the product. These standard input quantities must be made known to the operators in the production department (so that control action by management to deal with excess material wastage will be understood by them).

(b) The *Standard operation sheet* for labour specifies the expected hours required by each grade of labour in each department to make one unit of product. These standard times must be carefully set (for example by work study) and must be understood by the labour force. Where necessary, standard procedures or operating methods should be stated.

8.10 Standards are averages. Even under ideal working conditions, it would be unrealistic to expect every unit of activity or production to take exactly the same time, using exactly the same amount of materials, and at exactly the same cost. Some variations are inevitable, but for a reasonably large volume of activity, it would be fair to expect that on average, standard results should be achieved.

8.11 The CIMA's *Official Terminology* gives specific acknowledgement to the averaging process, with the following definitions.

(a) Standard performance for labour is 'the rate of output which qualified workers can achieve as an average over the working day or shift, without over-exertion, provided they adhere to the specified method and are motivated to apply themselves to their work'.

(b) Standard time is 'the total time in which a task should be completed at standard performance, ie basic time plus contingency allowance plus relaxation allowance'.

Revision of standards

8.12 When there is a sudden change in economic circumstances, or in technology or production methods, the standard cost will no longer be accurate. In practice, changing standards frequently is an expensive operation and can cause confusion. For this reason standard cost revisions are usually only made once a year. From the point of view of providing a target, however, an out-of-date standard is useless and some revision may be necessary.

8.13 At times of rapid price inflation, many managers have felt that the high level of inflation forced them to change price and wage rate standards continually. This, however, leads to a reduction in the value of the standard as a yardstick. At the other extreme is the adoption of 'basic' standards which will remain unchanged for many years. They provide a constant base for comparison, but this is hardly satisfactory when there is technological change in working procedures and conditions.

Problems of setting standard costs

8.14 The problems involved in setting standard costs, apart from the inevitable problems of forecasting errors, include the following.

(a) Deciding how to incorporate inflation into planned unit costs.

(b) Agreeing a labour efficiency standard (for example should current times, expected (improved) times or ideal times be used in the labour efficiency standard?).

(c) Deciding on the quality of materials to be used, because a better quality of material will cost more, but perhaps reduce material wastage.

(d) Deciding on the appropriate mix of component materials, where some change in the mix is possible (for example in the manufacture of foods and drink).

(e) Estimating materials prices where seasonal price variations or bulk purchase discounts may be significant.

(f) Possible 'behavioural' problems; managers responsible for the achievement of standards might resist the use of a standard costing control system for fear of being 'blamed' for any adverse variances.

(g) The cost of setting up and maintaining a system for establishing standards.

Management by exception

8.15 A standard cost, when established, is an *average expected unit cost*. Because it is only an average, actual results will vary to some extent above and below the average. Variances should only be reported where the difference between actual and standard is significant, ie the principle of *reporting by exception* should be used.

Standards for control and motivation

8.16 You will have realised that when setting standards, managers need to be aware of two requirements, the need to establish a useful control measure, and the need to set a standard that will have the desired motivational effect. These two requirements are often conflicting, so that the final standard cost might be a compromise between the two.

9. Productivity ratios

Production and productivity

9.1 It is important to distinguish between the terms 'production' and 'productivity'.

(a) *Production* is the quantity or volume of output produced. It is the number of units produced, or the actual number of units produced converted into an equivalent number of 'standard hours of production'.

(b) *Productivity* is a measure of the efficiency with which output has been produced.

9.2 For example, suppose that an employee is expected to produce three units in every hour worked. The standard rate of productivity is three units per hour, and one unit is valued at $\frac{1}{3}$ of a standard hour of output. If, during one week, the employee makes 126 units in 40 hours of work:

(a) production in the week is 126 units;

(b) productivity is a relative measure of the hours actually taken and the hours that should have been taken to make the output; either:

(i)	126 units should take	42 hours
	But did take	40 hours
	Productivity ratio = 42/40 × 100% =	105%
(ii)	or alternatively:	
	In 40 hours, production should be (× 3)	120 units
	But was	126 units
	Productivity ratio = 126/120 × 100% =	105%

A productivity ratio greater than 100% indicates that actual efficiency is better than the expected or 'standard' level of efficiency.

9.3 Management will wish to plan and control both production levels and labour productivity.

(a) *Production levels* can be raised by working overtime, hiring extra staff, sub-contracting some work to an outside firm or by raising productivity - ie managing the work force so as to achieve more output in a given number of hours worked. Production levels can be reduced by cancelling overtime, or laying off staff; if possible, managers will wish to avoid paying employees (in full) for doing nothing (ie idle time payments) and will also wish to avoid a drop in productivity.

(b) *Productivity*, if improved, will enable a company to achieve its production targets in fewer hours of work, and therefore at a lower cost.

Productivity and its effect on cost

9.4 Improved productivity is an important means of reducing total unit costs. In order to make this point clear, a simple example will be used.

Clockwork Zombies Ltd has a production department in its factory consisting of a work team of just two men, Rob Ottley and Cy Burnett. Rob and Cy each work a 40 hour week and refuse to do any overtime. They are each paid £100 per week and production overheads of £400 per week are charged to their work.

(a) In week one, they produce 160 units of output between them. Productivity is measured in units of output per man hour.

Production	160 units
Productivity (80 man hours)	2 units per man hour
Total cost	£600 (labour plus overhead)
Cost per man hour	£7.50
Cost per unit	£3.75

(b) In week two, management pressure is exerted on Rob and Cy to increase output and they produce 200 units in normal time.

Production	200 units (up by 25%)
Productivity	2.5 units per man hour (up by 25%)
Total cost	£600
Cost per man hour	£7.50 (no change)
Cost per unit	£3.00 (a saving of 20% on the previous cost)

(c) In week three, Rob and Cy agree to work a total of 20 hours of overtime for an additional £50 wages. Output is again 200 units and overhead charges are increased by £100:

Production	200 units (up 25% on week one)
Productivity (100 man hours)	2 units per hour (no change on week one)
Total cost (£600 + £50 + £100)	£750
Cost per unit	£3.75

(d) *Conclusions*

(i) An increase in production without an increase in productivity will not reduce unit costs (week one compared with week three).

(ii) An increase in productivity will reduce unit costs (week one compared with week two).

9.5 Labour cost control is largely concerned with productivity. Rising wage rates, however, have accelerated the trend towards greater automation as the best means of improving productivity and reducing costs.

9.6 Where automation is introduced, productivity is often, but misleadingly, measured in terms of output per man-hour.

Suppose for example, that a work-team of six men (240 hours per week) is replaced by one machine (40 hours per week) and a team of four men (160 hours per week), and as a result output is increased from 1,200 units per week to 1,600 units.

	Production	*Man hours*	*Productivity*
Before the machine	1,200 units	240	5 units per man hour
After the machine	1,600 units	160	10 units per man hour

Labour productivity has doubled because of the machine, and employees would probably expect extra pay for this success. For control purposes, however, it is likely that a new measure of productivity is required, output per machine hour, which may then be measured against a standard output for performance reporting.

Measuring productivity in service industries

9.7 In a service industry, productivity measures need to be based on measures of output appropriate to the service being provided.

(a) For example, a supermarket chain's main activity is selling, and an appropriate productivity measure might be sales per employee.

(b) In a professional service organisation, such as a firm of accountants, the product may be best measured in terms of hours of time chargeable to clients. One appropriate productivity measure would be chargeable hours per employee in a particular period.

The examples of cost units we looked at earlier in this chapter provide further examples. (Look back now to the table on page 164.)

Key points in this chapter

- The cost accounting system is a management information system designed to assist in the efficient management of a business. The system provides information for internal use only, which is the main feature that distinguishes a cost accounting system from a financial accounting system.
- A cost unit is the basic unit of product or service used for cost control in a business.
- A cost centre acts as a collecting place for costs before further analysis is carried out.
- A standard cost is an estimated unit cost used for planning and control purposes. Differences between actual and standard costs are called variances.
- A standard cost is set as an average expected unit cost. The actual cost of individual items may fluctuate around this average.
- Measurement of productivity assists in the effective control of direct labour costs. Improvements in productivity enable a company to achieve its production targets in fewer hours of work, and therefore at a lower cost.

For practice on the points covered in this chapter you should now attempt the Exercises in Session 9 of the Cost Accounting II Workbook

10. Reporting performance. Analysing results

1. **Management accounts**
2. **Accounting for separate organisational units**
3. **Profit centres and transfer pricing**
4. **Analysis of results**

1. Management accounts

1.1 Most financial accounts have as their aim the provision of summarised information about the progress or state of a business as a whole. Such information is generally of limited use for those who manage the business, because it is retrospective and does not distinguish between different sections of the same business. Therefore most large businesses also produce internal accounts periodically for the purposes of management control. Such accounts are generally referred to as 'management accounts' and are an important practical aspect of accounting, especially in larger organisations where managers tend to need more formal regular reports to learn what is happening in business operations.

1.2 There is no obligation to produce management accounts and no set layout; they are solely for internal consumption and are produced in whatever format is convenient. The main reasons for producing such accounts are:

(a) to generate up-to-date information for management purposes (because if a business is making a loss action must be taken soon, not six months after the end of the accounting period, when the profit and loss account is published); and

(b) to provide analysis of results from various sections of the business (because some sections might be profitable and others not).

1.3 Because management accounts are primarily concerned with the analysis of costs they are also known as 'cost accounts' and the person who produces them is sometimes referred to as a cost accountant.

1.4 Management accounts might be presented in the format below.

June management accounts

				Budget for year	
	Month (a)	*Budget (b)*	*YTD (c)*	*Year (d)*	*Plan (e)*
	£'000	£'000	£'000	£'000	£'000
Sales	95	100	1,000	2,400	2,800
Purchases	48	45	460	1,000	1,000
Gross profit	47	55	540	1,400	1,800
Production overheads	8	9	85	220	260
Sales overheads	10	9	90	210	240
Administrative overheads	11	12	101	245	260
Net profit	18	25	264	725	1,040

1.5 The following notes explain the purpose of each column.

(a) *Month.* These are the actual figures for the month of June.

(b) *Budget.* The budgeted figures for the month may have been seasonally adjusted or they may be just the total figure for the year, divided by twelve.

(c) *Year to date.* These are the actual figures for the year up to the end of June.

(d) *Budget for year.* This is, say, the budgeted figure for the year adjusted for the actual figures to date.

(e) *Year plan.* This is the original budget for the year.

1.6 The breakdown of costs and expenses shown in management accounts is at the discretion of the management. The way the figures are presented will depend on what kind of information the managers require to control the business. The allocation of costs to the various profit and loss account categories in a published profit and loss account, as all companies are required to produce, will be much more restricted.

1.7 It is common for management accounting reports to be issued monthly. For certain types of report, weekly or quarterly reporting may be more appropriate.

1.8 It may be helpful to include running annual totals, adding the last month or quarter and dropping the equivalent month or quarter from the previous year each time. This can be particularly worthwhile if there are seasonal patterns and can help to indicate whether a longer-term trend is developing.

Degrees of details

1.9 Internal management reports often include too much detail. In particular, it is common for too many digits to be included, even in reports prepared for public record. For example, up to 1975, the largest manufacturing company in the world, General Motors Corporation, showed the figures in its annual report to the nearest dollar. Having said that, there may be certain figures (such as the emoluments of the highest paid director) which need to be reported to the nearest pound in order to meet the relevant disclosure requirements.

1.10 Why should too high a level of detail be avoided?

(a) Too many figures may make it difficult for the reader to understand the main messages conveyed by the report.

(b) Too much detail may convey a spurious impression of accuracy. General Motors' accounts could certainly not have been claimed to be accurate to the nearest $1.

1.11 In general, the first two significant digits of a number are those which matter. For example, for most reporting purposes, the important part of the figure £29,120 are the figures 2 and 9: the figure might as well be rounded to £29,000. A third digit may be included to avoid too much rounding: for example, the figure might be presented as 29.1 in a £'000 column. However, additional digits are probably excessive for effective appraisal of the figures.

1.12 Where information on costs and revenues from different units of the organisation is aggregated (or 'consolidated') together, it will be necessary to make sure that the resulting consolidated figures are compiled in a consistent way. This may involve ensuring that costs are categorised in a reasonable way and adopting the methods which have been used in past management reports. Note in particular that VAT should be excluded from sales turnover. The current VAT position is reflected in the accounts by showing in the balance sheet net amounts due to or repayable by HM Customs and Excise.

Manufacturing accounts

1.13 A manufacturing account might be prepared by a manufacturing company, in order to establish the cost of the work it has produced during a period of time. When a manufacturing account is prepared, it precedes the trading, profit and loss account, so that there is:

(a) a manufacturing account, to establish the cost of goods produced;

(b) a trading account, to establish the cost of goods sold and gross profit;

(c) a profit and loss account, to establish the net profit, before appropriations for corporation tax and dividends etc.

1.14 Manufacturing accounts are not obligatory for manufacturing companies, because they can prepare a trading, profit and loss account without a manufacturing account if they wish to do so. However, a manufacturing account is needed if management want to know what the cost of producing goods has been, for 'internal' information.

Component elements in the manufacturing process

1.15 A manufacturing account is basically a list of the costs of producing the work in a factory, or in several factories, during a period. These costs consist of:

(a) the cost of raw materials and components that are used to make up the products ('direct materials');

(b) the cost of the labour that makes the products. As this is labour that is directly involved in producing an item of output, it is called 'direct labour';

(c) other costs incurred in the factory, which cannot be attributed to the production of any specific output but which are incurred to keep the factory running. These 'indirect costs', or overheads, include the salaries of supervisors, factory rent, depreciation of the factory building, depreciation of plant and machinery, factory rates, cleaning materials and other general expenses relating to the factory.

1.16 The total direct costs of production are often known as prime cost, and the total of direct costs plus overheads is known as factory cost or works cost.

1.17 A further distinction is often made between:

(a) *variable costs*. These are costs that vary with the number of goods produced, or the number of hours worked. For example, if a unit of production has a variable cost of £10, the total variable cost of 10 such units would be £100, and the total variable cost of 20 such units would be £200 etc; and

(b) *fixed costs*. These are the costs which are the same total amount for a period of time, regardless of the number of units produced or the number of hours worked. Factory rent and rates, and depreciation of factory premises are examples of fixed costs.

1.18 Some kinds of cost have both fixed and variable elements. For example, utility charges (gas, electricity and so on) often include a basic fixed charge as well as a variable charge based on usage. In general, direct costs are variable costs. Most overhead costs, or even all overhead costs, are regarded as fixed costs, although there are often some variable overhead costs too.

2. Accounting for separate organisational units

Departmental and branch accounts

2.1 A large proportion of organisations are large enough for a certain degree of divisionalisation to make sense. Organisations and businesses of different kinds may be divided into departments, sales areas, divisions or branches.

2.2 Where an organisation is increasing in size and/or is intending to diversify its activities, it may find it necessary or advantageous to control operations more precisely by instituting a system of departmental or branch accounting. As each department or branch is established as a separate cost and/or accounting centre, the net profit per branch can be found and accumulated to arrive at the profit for the whole business.

2.3 A profit target can be set for each unit of the organisation. These targets will form part of a larger plan: the company's long-term profit target. The profit earned by separate parts of the enterprise can each be compared with its own target.

2.4 Various types of organisations may operate through branches; examples include banks, building societies, estate agents, accountants, travel agents, as well as retailing businesses such as department stores or chain stores.

2.5 Divisional or branch accounts may be considered to fall into three main categories.

(a) Departmental accounts are prepared where a large retail store is divided into various departments.

(b) Branch accounts may be prepared to show the performance of both a main trading centre (the head office) and subsidiary trading centres (the branches), but with all accounting records being maintained by the head office.

(c) 'Separate entity' branch accounts are prepared where branches maintain their own records, which must therefore be combined with head office records in order to prepare accounts for the whole business.

Departmental accounts

2.6 In retail store accounting, although all departments may be in the same building, it is useful to control operations by finding the net profit per department as well as for the total business. Usually, trading and profit and loss accounts are prepared in columnar form for each department and the business as a whole.

2.7 An important aspect of departmental accounting is the allocation and apportionment of expenses to the various departments. Direct department expenses are easily allocated as separate records are usually kept for each department. However, where a number of departments share in the use of facilities, such as a canteen service, or administration for processing invoices and other documents, some method must be found to apportion the expenses (overheads) on the most equitable basis to the departments. In practice, several bases of apportionment are used depending upon some relationship of the expense to the benefit derived by the respective departments.

Typical overheads	*Usual bases of apportionment*
• Supervisor's salary	• Time spent in respective departments, or production output
• Power, heating and lighting	• Measured units of electricity or floor area
• Rent and rates	• Floor area
• Insurance	• Average book value of assets insured
• Canteen services	• Number of employees
• Advertising and selling expenses	• Sales value
• General administration expenses	• Number of employees, or the sum of expenses purchases and costs/sales values (linked to the volume of paperwork involved)

Example: apportionment of overheads

2.8 Bracedep Ltd has two production departments, which both do work on three products, sirks, varks, and zooks.

(a) Wages costs in each department for the year to 31 December 19X7 were:

	£
Assembly department	70,000
Finishing department	30,000
	100,000

(b) Manufacturing overheads in total for the year were £150,000. These are to be apportioned between departments in proportion to wages costs incurred during the year.

(c) Departmental overhead costs are to be apportioned between products as follows:

	Assembly dept	*Finishing dept*
Sirks	30%	50%
Varks	40%	10%
Zooks	30%	40%

Calculate the overhead cost attributable to each product during the year.

Solution

2.9

		Assembly Dept		Finishing Dept	Total
		£		£	£
Manufacturing overhead	(70%)	105,000	(30%)	45,000	150,000
Apportioned as follows:					
Sirks	(30%)	31,500	(50%)	22,500	54,000
Varks	(40%)	42,000	(10%)	4,500	46,500
Zooks	(30%)	31,500	(40%)	18,000	49,500
		105,000		45,000	150,000

Example: departmental accounts

2.10 Departmental trading and profit and loss accounts for a retailer could be presented in the following format.

ALLSALES LIMITED
DEPARTMENTAL TRADING AND PROFIT AND LOSS ACCOUNTS
FOR THE YEAR ENDED 31 DECEMBER 19X0

	Furniture dept		*Electrical goods dept*		*Total*	
	£	£	£	£	£	£
Sales		180,000		270,000		450,000
Cost of sales:						
Opening stock	36,000		45,000		81,000	
Purchases	105,000		162,000		267,000	
	141,000		207,000		348,000	
Less closing stock	39,000		54,000		93,000	
		102,000		153,000		255,000
Gross profit		78,000		117,000		195,000
Less expenses:						
Selling & distribution (in sales ratio 2:3)	22,800		34,200		57,000	
Administration (in employee ratio)	17,450		26,450		43,900	
Lighting & heating (as measured)	1,000		4,800		5,800	
Rent & rates (in floor area ratio of 2:1)	19,000		9,500		28,500	
		60,250		74,950		135,200
Net profit		17,750		42,050		59,800

2.11 The normal problems of preparing accounts (such as calculating provisions for bad debts, accruals and prepayments) have to be dealt with. Indeed, records may be incomplete and 'unknowns' may have to be calculated before the accounts can be fully prepared.

2.12 Note the different bases of apportioning costs used in the above example. These bases are essentially arbitrary, and different methods are possible. What is important is that within one business, the methods applied are consistent, unless there is good reason to change the basis of apportionment at some stage.

Accounting for branches

2.13 When a branch is established, considerable trust is placed in its manager, where stocks are despatched to his sole control. One way in which Head Office can check the manager's honesty and performance and deter him from fraud and outright theft is to establish an internal audit department, whose staff, amongst other duties, will visit branches to check the records and to count the stock, ensuring that all material differences from the expected value are accounted for.

2.14 It is the responsibility of a business's managers to establish an adequate system of *internal control* so that the business is carried on efficiently and the assets are safeguarded. One way of doing this is for Head Office to keep records of stock and other assets sent to the branch and for the branch manager to record sales proceeds in memorandum only, forwarding his sales and stock returns daily, weekly or monthly and banking the sales proceeds intact (probably daily). Expenses will probably be paid centrally from Head Office (except for petty cash items, like staff refreshments). Head office staff can see from the branch returns whether the branch is meeting its sales targets and whether there has been any unusual stock wastage. Internal and external audit procedures should confirm the accuracy of the branch returns.

2.15 You do not need to learn the specific techniques involved in branch accounting for the purposes of Unit 7. You should however have a general awareness of branch accounting as one means of accounting for transactions between separate units of an organisation.

Preparation of final accounts

2.16 Where a complete and independent set of records is maintained by the branch (or branches) trading and profit and loss accounts and balance sheets can be prepared for each branch and the head office. Accounts for the business as a whole can then be produced by combining the individual accounts.

2.17 At the end of an accounting period trial balances are extracted from the head office and branch ledgers. Using the trial balances accounts may be prepared for:

(a) the head office;
(b) the branch;
(c) the combined firm or company.

2.18 Generally, the trading and profit and loss accounts and balance sheets are produced in columnar form, the head office and branch being treated almost as if they were separate legal entities. The organisation is only regarded as a single concern in the 'combined' columns which are arrived at by totalling appropriate items in the head office and branch columns. In the combined balance sheet the branch current account is replaced by the underlying assets and liabilities.

3. Profit centres and transfer pricing

3.1 In some businesses, management establishes 'profit centres' of operations, with each centre held accountable for making a profit, and the manager of the centre made responsible for its good or bad results.

3.2 Where there are transfers of goods or services between divisions of a divisionalised organisation, the transfers could be made 'free' or 'as a favour' to the division receiving the benefit. For example, if a garage and car showroom has two divisions, one for car repairs and servicing and the other for car sales, the servicing division will be required to service cars before they are sold and delivered to customers. There is no requirement for this service work to be charged for: the servicing division could do its work for the car sales division without making any record of the work done. However, unless the cost or value of such work is recorded, management cannot keep a proper check on the amount of resources (like labour time) being used up on new car servicing. It is necessary for control purposes that some record of the inter-divisional services should be kept, and one way of doing this is through the accounting system. Inter-divisional work can be given a cost or charge: a transfer price.

3.3 It is particularly important in the case of transferred *goods* that a transfer price should be charged. A proper system of accounting demands that goods should be costed as they progress through work in progress to finished goods and so the need for a transfer cost or transfer price should be clear.

3.4 A transfer price is defined in the CIMA *Official terminology* as 'The price at which goods or services are transferred from one process or department to another or from one member of a group to another.'

The bases on which transfer prices might be set

3.5 A transfer price may be based upon:

(a) marginal cost (at marginal cost or with a gross profit margin on top);
(b) full cost (at full cost, or at a full cost plus);
(c) market price;
(d) at a discount to the market price;
(e) negotiated price, which could be based on any of (a) to (d) above.

3.6 A transfer based on *cost* might be at marginal cost or full cost only but in a profit centre system of divisionalisation, is more likely to be a price based on marginal cost or full cost plus a margin for contribution or profit. This is to allow profit centres to make a profit on work they do for other profit centres, and so earn a reward for their effort and use of resources on the work.

3.7 Transfers based on *market price* might be:

(a) the actual market price at which the transferred goods or services could be sold on an external market;

(b) the actual external market price, minus an amount that reflects the savings in costs (selling costs, bad debts) when goods are transferred internally; or

(c) the market price of similar goods which are sold on an external market, although the transferred goods are not exactly the same and do not themselves have an external market.

The responsibilities of a transfer price

3.8 Transfer prices are important because if one profit centre does work for another a system of profit centre accounting cannot work without them. The size of the transfer price will affect the costs of one profit centre and the revenues of another. Since profit centre managers are held accountable for their costs, revenues, and profits, they are likely to dispute the size of transfer prices with each other, or disagree about whether one profit centre should do work for another or not. Transfer prices affect behaviour and decisions by profit centre managers.

3.9 In a system of profit centre accounting, the transfer price of goods and services between divisions is a focal issue. If managers of individual profit centres are tempted to take decisions that are harmful to other divisions and are not congruent with the goals of the organisation as a whole, the problem is likely to emerge in disputes about the transfer price.

(a) One profit centre manager might be reluctant to transfer goods and services to another division, arguing that he is not paid enough for the work.

(b) Alternatively, one profit centre manager might refuse to accept more transfers of goods from another division, arguing that it is too costly or unprofitable to take the extra transfers.

3.10 The disagreements about output levels would tend to focus on the transfer price. When there are disagreements about how much work should be transferred, and how many external sales the division should make, there is presumably a profit-maximising level of output and sales for the organisation as a whole. However, unless each profit centre also maximises its own profit at this same level of output, there will be inter-divisional disagreements about output levels and the profit-maximising output will not be achieved.

3.11 Ideally a transfer price should be set at a level that overcomes these problems.

(a) The transfer price should provide an 'artificial' selling price that enables the transferring division to earn a return for its efforts, and the receiving division to incur a cost for benefits received.

(b) The transfer price should be set at a level that enables profit centre performance to be measured 'commercially'. This means that the transfer price should be a fair commercial price.

(c) The transfer price, if possible, should encourage profit centre managers to agree on the amount of goods and services to be transferred, which will also be at a level that is consistent with the aims of the organisation as a whole such as maximising company profits.

Service departments and transfer pricing

3.12 In some organisations a service department such as a transport department, a canteen or a personnel department might be turned into a profit centre to encourage its management to control costs and operate efficiently. Under a profit centre arrangement the service department 'sells' its services to user departments at the transfer price. The transfer price should exceed costs, and so the service department should make a profit. User departments would be charged for the service at the transfer price rate and would be free to decide how much of the service they wished to purchase.

3.13 Not all service departments can operate as profit centres since not all departments have a measurable output. Examples of suitable services include a computer department, a printing department and a central management services department.

3.14 Note that except insofar as a profit centre arrangement encourages managers to operate efficiently, the use of transfer prices will not affect the total company profit. The transfer price will be a 'credit' to the service department, and a 'debit' to the user department. The debit and credit will cancel each other out in the accounts, thus having no effect on the total company profit. Don't fall into the trap of thinking that company profits can be increased by simply raising the transfer prices! (*Note.* The taxation effect of transfer pricing in multinational companies can sometimes alter profits, but this point will not be discussed further here.)

4. Analysis of results

4.1 The accounting records maintained for departments and branches provide managers with much useful information. Appropriate management action may need to be taken if certain departments and branches are performing badly. If a branch is unprofitable, for example, it may be necessary to consider cost-cutting measures if there is little prospect of raising the branch revenues significantly. Ultimately, unsuccessful branches may need to be closed.

4.2 Managers may also make use of information on the results of different parts or areas of the organisation analysed in other ways. Two examples which we look at below are the analysis of results by sales areas and the analysis of results by product. It should not be difficult for you to see that broadly similar principles can be applied to the analysis of results in other ways. In all cases, a suitable set of methods for performing the analysis must be agreed and followed.

Example: analysis of results by sales area

4.3 Most sales and marketing activities are organised on a territorial basis. The purpose of making an analysis of the profitability of sales areas or territories is to identify areas in which there are weaknesses or problems. Action taken to correct a weakness might be to increase the number of sales people operating in the area, for example.

4.4 Direct costs will be those incurred in respect of particular sales areas.

4.5 Indirect costs are those incurred for all of the sales areas together. Some kind of apportionment of indirect costs between the various sales areas must be made (see Chapter 9).

4.6 An analysis of results by sales area might look like the table below.

Sierra Limited: analysis of results by sales area

	Area 1	*Area 2*	*Area 3*	*Total*
	£'000	£'000	£'000	£'000
Sales (A)	600	500	150	1,250
Direct costs by areas:				
Cost of goods sold	320	250	60	630
Transport & outside warehousing	60	35	15	110
Regional office expenses	40	45	28	113
Salespeople's expenses	30	25	11	66
Other regional expenses	20	15	8	43
Total direct cost by areas (B)	470	370	122	962
Contribution to head office overheads and profit (A - B)	130	130	28	288
Indirect costs:				
Central administration	44	52	12	108
Central warehousing	16	18	3	37
Advertising	30	30	8	68
Total indirect costs (C)	90	100	23	213
Net profit (A - B - C)	40	30	5	75
Percentage of net profit	53%	40%	7%	100%
Percentage of sales	48%	40%	12%	100%
Contribution/sales % (A - B) ÷ A	22%	26%	19%	23%

4.7 Percentage of net profit, percentage of sales and contribution/sales percentage are all performance indicators which can be used to compare the results of the different sales areas. Can you see how they have been calculated?

Calculating these performance indicators for different areas, divisions or departments may also help to disclose whether costs are being misclassified between different parts of the organisation, as this could lead to unusual or unexpected changes in the indicators.

Example: analysis of results by product and cost centre

4.8 Analysing results of an enterprise by product, or product type, not only indicates the relative profitability of different products or types of product, but also highlights strengths or weaknesses which should be taken into account in future decision-making.

Profitability is not the only basis on which a product should be judged: a major reason for this is that indirect costs must be spread or apportioned across the product range somehow, and this apportionment must be arbitrary to some extent. The analysis below follows the previous analysis in looking at the *contribution* of each product. The contribution can be viewed as the amount which remains after paying direct or variable costs. It is, then, the amount available to pay for (or 'contribute to') indirect costs or fixed costs and profit.

Piper Limited: analysis of results by product

	Product A	*Product B*	*Product C*	*Total*
	£'000	£'000	£'000	£'000
Sales	200	350	250	800
Variable costs of goods sold	95	175	90	360
Gross contribution	105	175	160	440
Variable marketing costs:				
Transport and warehousing	5	26	37	68
Office expenses	8	20	7	35
Sales salaries	15	44	25	84
Other expenses	2	7	6	15
Total variable marketing costs	30	97	75	202
Contribution to fixed costs and profit	75	78	85	238
Fixed costs:				
Manufacturing	15	20	20	55
Administration	25	35	25	85
Marketing	20	30	20	70
Total fixed costs	60	85	65	210
Net profit (loss)	15	(7)	20	28
Contribution/sales %	37%	22%	34%	30%

Variable costs by cost centre

	Cost centre 1	*Cost centre 2*	*Cost centre 3*
	£'000	£'000	£'000
Product A	50	45	30
Product B	115	60	97
Product C	40	50	75
Total	205	155	202

Variable costs by product

	Product A	*Product B*	*Product C*	*Total*
	£'000	£'000	£'000	£'000
Cost centre 1	50	115	40	205
Cost centre 2	45	60	50	155
Cost centre 3	30	97	75	202
	125	272	165	562

4.9 A graphical presentation of some of the key information in this analysis might take the following form.

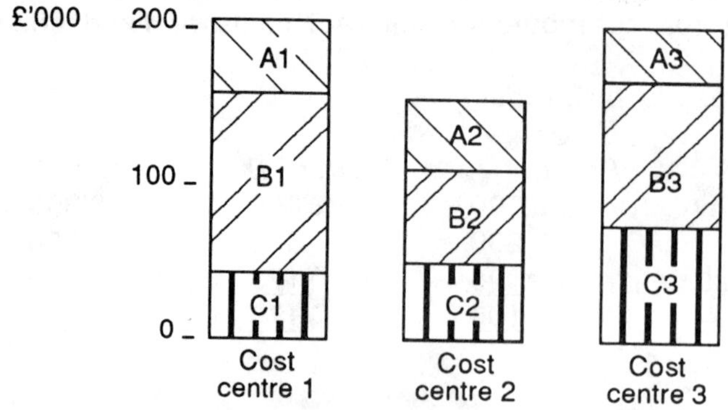

Variable costs by cost centre

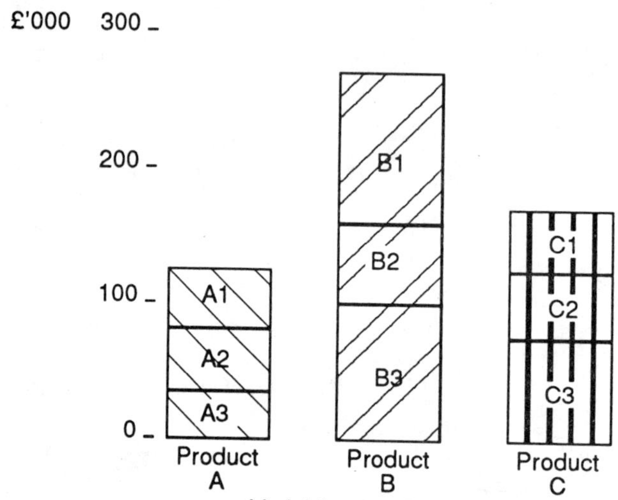

Variable costs by product

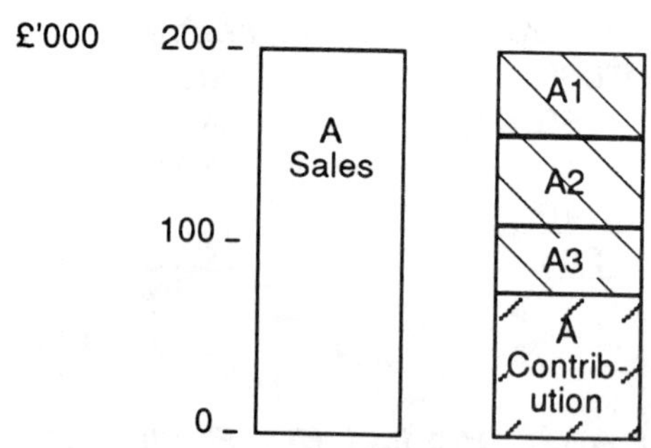

Contribution for Product A

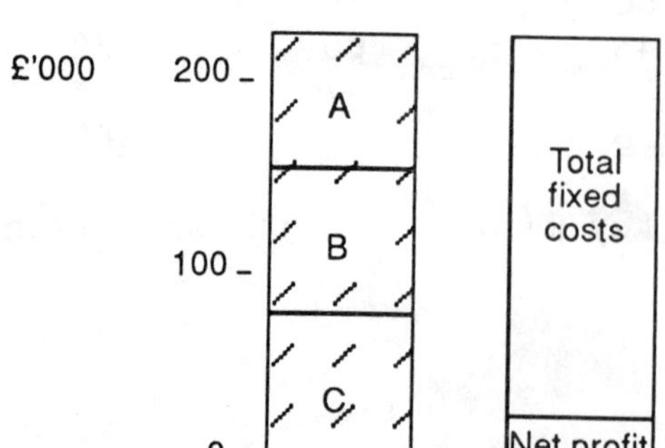

Net profit

4.10 A product may be making a loss after fixed expenses and still be worth producing. Piper Limited's product B above, for example, is shown as making a net loss although it still makes a 'contribution' to fixed expenses. Product B should continue in production, although steps ought to be taken to improve its profitability in future.

4.11 In these analyses, we have made use of some performance indicators, a topic which is covered further in the next chapter.

Key points in this chapter

- Management accounts are important in all kinds of business.
- In a manufacturing industry, manufacturing accounts are prepared for internal management use only. Their purpose is to distinguish between the costs and profitability associated with manufacturing operations and those associated with trading (which are shown in the trading account).
- In this chapter we have looked at aspects of accounting for separate units of an organisation, including an overview of departmental accounts and accounting for branches.
- A transfer price is a price at which goods or services are transferred from one part of the business to another part of the same business.
- For management purposes, results may be analysed in different ways, for example by division, by sales area or by product. When preparing such analyses, the methods agreed by management need to be followed.

For practice on the points covered in this chapter you should now attempt the Exercises in Session 10 of the Cost Accounting II Workbook

11. Ratio analysis. Performance measurement in the public sector

1. **Ratio analysis**

2. **Measuring divisional performance: profit or contribution?**

3. **Performance measurement in the public sector**

1. Ratio analysis

1.1 For Unit 7: *Preparing reports and returns* you are expected to have an awareness of relevant performance and quality measures. You are also expected to be able to calculate accurately ratios and performance indicators in accordance with agreed methods. We looked at productivity ratios in Chapter 9. We also looked earlier at the cost per unit as a performance indicator.

1.2 The profit and loss account, the balance sheet and forms of divisional income statement used by management are all sources of useful information about the condition of a business. The analysis and interpretation of these statements can be done by calculating certain ratios, between one item and another, and then using the ratios for comparison, either:

(a) between one year and the next for a particular business or division, in order to identify any trends, or significantly better or worse results than before; or

(b) between one business or division and another, to establish which has performed better, and in what ways.

Some of the most important ratios concerning the performance of businesses are described below.

Indicators of profitability

1.3 There are three principal ratios which can be used to measure how well the operations of a business are doing. These are:

(a) profit margin;
(b) asset turnover;
(c) return on capital employed.

1.4 Profit margin is the ratio of net profit to sales, and may also be called 'profit percentage' or 'net profit percentage'. For example, if a company makes a net profit of £20,000 on sales of £100,000 its profit percentage or profit margin is 20%. This also means that its costs are 80% of sales. A high profit margin indicates that either:

(a) costs are being kept well under control because if the ratio of costs to sales goes down, the profit margin will automatically go up. For example, if the cost:sales ratio changes from 80% to 75%, the profit margin will go up from 20% to 25%; or

(b) sales prices are high. For example, if a company sells goods for £100,000 and makes a profit of £16,000, costs would be £84,000 and the profit margin 16%. Now if the company can raise selling prices by 20% to £120,000 without affecting the volume of goods sold or their costs, profits would rise by the amount of revenue increase (£20,000) to £36,000 and the profit margin would also rise (from 16% to 30%).

1.5 A gross profit percentage ([sales less cost of sales] ÷ sales) is also often calculated, for example as below.

	£	£	
Sales		140,000	
Cost of sales			
Purchases	62,000		
Less closing stock	6,000		
		56,000	
Gross profit		84,000	60%
Selling and distribution expenses	30,000		
Administrative expenses	24,000		
		54,000	
Net profit		30,000	21%

1.6 *Asset turnover* is the ratio of sales turnover in a year to the amount of capital employed. For example, if a company has sales in 19X4 of £720,000 and has assets of £360,000, the asset turnover will be:

$$\frac{£720{,}000}{£360{,}000} = 2 \text{ times}$$

This means that for every £1 of assets employed, the company can generate sales turnover of £2 per annum. To utilise assets more efficiently, managers should try to create a higher volume of sales and a higher asset turnover ratio. For example, suppose that our firm with assets of £360,000 can increase its sales turnover from £720,000 to £900,000 per annum. The asset turnover would improve to:

$$\frac{£900{,}000}{£360{,}000} = 2.5 \text{ times}$$

The significance of this improvement is that if a business can create more sales turnover from the same amount of assets it should make larger profits (because of the increase in sales) without having to increase the size of its investment.

1.7 *Return on capital employed* (ROCE) is the amount of net profit as a percentage of capital employed. If a company makes a profit of £30,000, we do not know how good or bad the result is until we look at the amount of capital which has been invested to achieve the profit. £30,000 might be a good sized profit for a small firm, but it would not be good enough for a 'giant' firm such as Marks and Spencer, say. For this reason, it is helpful to measure performance by relating profits to capital employed, and because this seems to be the only satisfactory ratio or percentage which judges profits in relation to the size of business, it is sometimes called the primary ratio in financial analysis.

1.8 You may already have realised that there is a mathematical connection between return on capital employed, profit margin and asset turnover:

$$\frac{\text{Profit}}{\text{Capital employed}} = \frac{\text{Profit}}{\text{Sales}} \times \frac{\text{Sales}}{\text{Capital employed}}$$

$$\text{ROCE} = \text{Profit margin} \times \text{Asset turnover}$$

This is important. If we accept that ROCE is the single most important measure of business performance, comparing profit with the amount of capital invested, we can go on to say that business performance is dependent on two separate 'subsidiary' factors, each of which contributes to ROCE:

(a) profit margin;
(b) asset turnover.

For this reason, just as ROCE is sometimes called the primary ratio, the profit margin and asset turnover ratios are sometimes called the secondary ratios.

1.9 The implications of this relationship must be understood. Suppose that a return on capital employed of 20% is thought to be a good level of business performance in the retail trade for electrical goods.

(a) Company A might decide to sell its products at a fairly high price and make a profit margin on sales of 10%. It would then need only an asset turnover of 2.0 times to achieve a ROCE of 20%.

(b) Company B might decide to cut its prices so that its profit margin is only 2½%. Provided that it can achieve an asset turnover of 8 times a year, attracting more customers with its lower prices, it will still make a ROCE of 2½% × 8 = 20%.

1.10 Company A might be a department store and company B a discount warehouse. Each will have a different selling price policy, but each, in its own way, can be effective in achieving a target ROCE. In this example, if we supposed that both companies had capital employed of £100,000 and a target return of 20% or £20,000:

(a) company A would need annual sales of £200,000 to give a profit margin of 10% and an asset turnover of 2 times;

(b) company B would need annual sales of £800,000 to give a profit margin of only 2½% but an asset turnover of 8 times.

The inter-relationship between profit margin and asset turnover

1.11 A higher return on capital employed can be obtained by increasing the profit margin or the asset turnover ratio. The profit margin can be increased by reducing costs or by raising selling prices.

However, if selling prices are raised, it is likely that sales demand will fall, with the possible consequences that the asset turnover will also decline. If higher prices mean lower sales turnover, the increase in profit margin might be offset by the fall in asset turnover, so that total return on capital employed might not improve.

Example: inter-relationship between profit margin and asset turnover

1.12 Suppose that Swings and Roundabouts Ltd achieved the following results in 19X6:

Sales	£100,000
Net profit	£5,000
Capital employed	£20,000

The company's management wish to decide whether to raise its selling prices. They think that if they do so, they can raise the profit margin to 10% and by introducing extra capital of £55,000, sales turnover could be increased to £150,000.

Evaluate the decision in terms of the effect on ROCE, profit margin and asset turnover.

Solution

1.13 At present, ratios are:

Profit margin	5%
Asset turnover	5 times
ROCE (5/20)	25%

With the proposed changes, the profit would be 10% × £150,000 = £15,000, and the asset turnover would be:

$\frac{£150,000}{£\ 75,000}$ = 2 times, so that the ratios might be:

Profit margin	×	Asset turnover	=	ROCE	
10%	×	2 times	=	20%	$\frac{£15,000}{£75,000}$

In spite of increasing the profit margin and raising the total volume of sales, the extra assets required (£55,000) only raise total profits by £(15,000 - 5,000) = £10,000.

The return on capital employed falls from 25% to 20% because of the sharp fall in asset turnover from 5 times to 2 times.

Whose return and whose capital employed?

1.14 Most of the providers of finance to a business expect some return on their investment.

(a) Trade creditors and other current liabilities merely expect to be paid what they are owed.

(b) A bank charges interest on overdrafts.

(c) Interest must be paid to the holders of loan stock and debentures.

(d) Preference shareholders expect a dividend at a fixed percentage rate of the nominal value of their shares.

(e) Ordinary shareholders also expect a dividend. However, any retained profits kept in the business also represent funds 'owned' or 'provided' by them.

1.15 So when we refer to 'return' we must be clear in our mind about which providers of finance we are concerned with, and we should relate the return earned for those providers of finance to the amount of capital they are providing.

(a) If 'return' is profit after tax, it is return earned by ordinary and preference shareholders. The capital employed by these investors is:

(i) the nominal value of preference shares;

(ii) the nominal value of ordinary shares;

(iii) the amount in various reserves, because reserves are surpluses or profits retained in a business and 'owned' by the equity investors - ie the ordinary shareholders in a company.

(b) If 'return' is profit after tax and preference dividend, the left-over return is for ordinary shareholders, and is called 'earnings'. The return on equity capital is:

$$\frac{\text{Earnings}}{\text{Ordinary share capital plus reserves}}$$

(c) If we prefer to consider the business as a whole, then the fixed assets and net current assets are financed by long-term capital which may include loan creditors as well as shareholders. The fund available to satisfy the claims of all these providers of finance is the profit before interest payments and taxation. In this case ROCE may be calculated as:

$$\frac{\text{Profit before interest and tax (PBIT)}}{\text{Loan capital plus share capital plus reserves}}$$

which equals

$$\frac{\text{PBIT}}{\text{Fixed assets plus net current assets}}$$

Example: different ways of calculating ROCE

1.16 Suppose that Draught Ltd reports the following figures:

PROFIT AND LOSS ACCOUNT FOR 19X4 (EXTRACT)

	£
Profit before interest and tax	120,000
Interest	(20,000)
Profit before tax	100,000
Taxation	(40,000)
Profit after tax	60,000
Preference dividend	(1,000)
Profit available for ordinary shareholders (= earnings)	59,000
Ordinary dividend	(49,000)
Retained profits	10,000

BALANCE SHEET AT 31 DECEMBER 19X4

	£	£
Fixed assets: tangible assets		350,000
Current assets	400,000	
Less current liabilities	150,000	
Net current assets		250,000
Total assets less current liabilities		600,000
Creditors: amounts falling due after more than one year:		
10% debenture loans		200,000
		400,000
Capital and reserves:		
Called up share capital:		
5% preference shares		20,000
ordinary shares		80,000
		100,000
Profit and loss account		300,000
		400,000

1.17 Using the three alternatives described in paragraph 1.15, ROCE might be calculated in any of the following ways:

(a) *Return on shareholders' capital*

$$\frac{\text{Profit after tax}}{\text{Share capital plus reserves}} = \frac{£\ 60,000}{£400,000} = 15\%$$

(b) *Return on equity capital*

$$\frac{\text{Profit after tax and preference dividend (earnings)}}{\text{Ordinary share capital plus reserves}} = \frac{£\ 59,000}{£380,000} = 15.5\%$$

(c) *Return on total long-term capital*

$$\frac{\text{Profit before interest and tax}}{\text{Loan capital plus share capital plus reserves}} = \frac{£120,000}{£600,000} = 20\%$$

Turnover periods

1.18 A 'turnover' period is an (average) length of time.

(a) In the case of *stock turnover*, it is the length of time an item of stock is held in stores before it is used.

(i) A raw materials stock turnover period is the length of time raw materials are held before being issued to the production department.

(ii) A work in progress turnover period is the length of time it takes to turn raw materials into finished goods in the factory.

(iii) A finished goods stock turnover period is the length of time that finished goods are held in a warehouse before they are sold.

(iv) When a firm buys goods and re-sells them at a profit, the stock turnover period is the time between their purchase and their resale.

(b) The *debtors turnover* period, or debt collection period, is the length of the credit period taken by customers - ie it is the time between the sale of an item and the receipt of cash for the sale from the customer.

(c) Similarly, the *creditors turnover* period, or period of credit taken from suppliers, is the length of time between the purchase of materials and the payment to suppliers.

1.19 Turnover periods can be calculated from information in a firm's profit and loss account and balance sheet.

Stock turnover periods are calculated as follows:

(a) Raw materials:

$$\frac{\text{(Average) raw material stocks held}}{\text{Total raw materials consumed in one year}} \times 12 \text{ months}$$

(b) Work in progress (the length of the production period):

$$\frac{\text{(Average) finished goods stocks held}}{\text{Total cost of production in the year}} \times 12 \text{ months}$$

(c) Finished goods:

$$\frac{\text{(Average) stocks}}{\text{Total cost of goods sold in one year}} \times 12 \text{ months}$$

(d) Stocks of items bought for re-sale:

$$\frac{\text{(Average) stocks}}{\text{Total (materials) cost of goods bought and sold in one year}} \times 12 \text{ months}$$

The word 'average' is put in brackets because although it is strictly correct to use average values, it is more common to use the value of stocks shown in a balance sheet - ie at one point in time - to estimate the turnover periods.

1.20 For example, if a company buys goods costing £620,000 in one year but uses goods costing £600,000 in production (in regular monthly quantities) and the cost of material in stock at 1 January is £100,000, the stock turnover period could be calculated as:

$$\frac{£100{,}000}{£600{,}000} \times 12 \text{ months} = 2 \text{ months}$$

In other words, stocks are bought two months before they are eventually re-sold.

1.21 The debt collection period is calculated as:

$$\frac{\text{Average debtors}}{\text{Annual credit sales}} \times 12 \text{ months}$$

For example, if a company sells goods for £1,200,000 per annum in regular monthly quantities, and if debtors in the balance sheet are £150,000, the debt collection period is:

$$\frac{£150{,}000}{£1{,}200{,}000} \times 12 \text{ months} = 1.5 \text{ months}$$

In other words, debtors will pay for goods 1½ months on average after the time of sale.

1.22 The period of credit taken from suppliers is calculated as:

$$\frac{\text{Average trade creditors}}{\text{Total purchases in one year}} \times 12 \text{ months}$$

(Notice that the creditors are compared with materials bought whereas for raw material stock turnover, raw material stocks are compared with materials used in production. This is a small, but significant difference.)

For example, if a company sells goods for £600,000 and makes a gross profit of 40% on sales, and if the amount of trade creditors in the balance sheet is £30,000, the period of credit taken from the suppliers is:

$$\frac{£30,000}{(60\%\ \text{of}\ £600,000)} \times 12\ \text{months} = 1\ \text{month}$$

In other words, suppliers are paid in the month following the purchase of goods.

1.23 Stocks, debtors and cash, less creditors, make up what is called the 'working capital' of the business, and the turnover periods for these items are known as 'working capital ratios'.

2. Measuring divisional performance: profit or contribution?

2.1 A principle of what is known as 'responsibility accounting' is that profit centre managers should only be held accountable for those revenues and costs that they are in a position to control (or at least to explain). Short-term controllable costs are mainly variable (although there may be some fixed costs which are discretionary) and it is therefore arguable that a divisional manager's performance should perhaps be measured in terms of total contribution, an idea which we touched on in the previous chapter.

(a) The costs he is capable of reducing (by improvements in efficiency) are mainly variable costs.

(b) Increases in production volume, within the relevant range of output, will raise profit by the amount of increase in contribution.

2.2 A divisional performance statement based on contribution might appear as follows.

	Division A	*Division B*	*Total*
	£'000	£'000	£'000
Sales	80	100	180
Less variable costs	60	50	110
Contribution	20	50	70
Less fixed costs			50
Profit			20

(a) Divisional performance can be improved by increasing the sales price, or volume of sales, or reducing the unit variable costs.

(b) The relative profitability of divisions A and B could be compared by means of their contribution/sales ratio (in this example, 25% and 50% respectively).

Directly attributable fixed costs

2.3 One drawback to using contribution alone as a measure of divisional performance is that although it indicates the short-term controllable results of the division, it gives no indication as to longer-term underlying profitability. Suppose, for example, that a division is closed down. Apart from the 'one-off' effects of closure, such as redundancy payments and receipts from the sale of assets, there would be some reduction of annual running costs.

2.4 The variable costs of production would be avoided, but there would also be a reduction in fixed costs. All the fixed costs which are directly attributable to the division would be saved, so that even if a contribution towards profits is being earned, it might still be profitable to close the division because directly attributable costs exceed the size of the contribution.

2.5 In the following example, closure of division X might be justified, since there would be a net saving in annual running costs of £5,000.

	Division X	*Division Y*	*Total*
	£'000	£'000	£'000
Sales	70	120	190
Less variable costs	50	80	130
Contribution	20	40	60
Less directly attributable fixed costs	25	25	50
Profit of the division	(5)	15	10
Less fixed costs (general)			8
Company profit			2

2.6 The longer-term performance of divisions should therefore be measured after deducting directly attributable fixed costs, but contribution should also be shown, since this indicates short-term controllable results.

3. Performance measurement in the public sector

3.1 In public sector organisations, an increasing volume of information on performance and 'value for money' is produced for internal and external use. The ways in which performance can be measured depends very much upon which organisation is involved.

3.2 The first question which would need to be asked is 'what are the aims and objectives of the organisation?' For example, the objective of Companies House is to maintain and make available records of company reports.

3.3 The next question to ask is 'How can we tell if the organisation is meeting the objectives?' Quantified information - ie information in the form of numbers - will be useful, and this will consist mainly of output and performance measures and indicators. For these, targets can be set. Any individual organisational unit should have no more than a handful of key targets.

3.4 Individual targets are likely to fall under the following broad headings.

(a) Financial performance.
(b) Volume of output.
(c) Quality of service.
(d) Efficiency.

Performance measurement in central government

3.5 Over recent years, much of the work of central government has been reorganised into semi-autonomous 'executive agencies'.

3.6 Targets related to financial performance which you may become aware of, for example if you work for an executive agency, could include ones similar to the following.

(a) Full cost recovery (Civil Service College, Central Office of Information and others), plus unit cost targets.

(b) Commercial revenue to offset costs (Met Office).

(c) Non-Exchequer income as a percentage of total income (National Engineering Laboratory).

3.7 Targets related to output can be difficult to set. While the output of the Vehicle Inspectorate can be measured on the number of tests performed, and the output of the Hydrographic Office consists of charts for navigators, in many other cases the output of executive agencies is less tangible. For example, the Historic Royal Palaces Agency not only deals with visitors, whose numbers can be counted, but is also responsible for maintaining the fabric of royal palaces - an output which is more difficult to measure. In such cases, performance will be best measured by appraising the progress of the 'project' as a whole (called 'project appraisal').

3.8 Example of quality targets set for executive agencies include the following.

(a) *Timeliness*

(i) time to handle applications (Passport Office, Vehicle Certification Agency and many others);

(ii) car driving tests to be reduced to 6 weeks nationally and 10 weeks in London (Driving Standards Agency);

(iii) all cheques to be banked within 35 hours (Accounts Services Agency).

(b) *Quality of product*

(i) number of print orders delivered without fault (HMSO);

(ii) error rate in the value of benefit payments (Employment Service);

(iii) 95% business complaints handled within 5 days (Radio Communications Agency);

(iv) 85% overall customer satisfaction rating (Recruitment and Assessment Services Agency);

(v) hold meetings of creditors within 12 weeks in 90% of cases (Insolvency Service).

3.9 Efficiency improvements may come through reducing the cost of inputs without reducing the quality of outputs. Alternatively, areas of activity affecting total costs may be reduced. Targets related to efficiency include the following.

(a) Percentage reduction in price paid for purchases of stationery and paper (HMSO).

(b) Reduction in the ratio of cost of support services to total cost (Laboratory of the Government Chemist).

(c) 8.7% efficiency increase in the use of accommodation (Recruitment and Assessment Services Agency).

Performance measurement in local government

3.10 The performance measures chosen by local authorities usually consist of comparative statistics and unit costs. These measures do two things.

(a) They give details, statistics and unit costs of an authority's own activities.

(b) They show statistical and cost comparisons with other authorities or clusters of authorities.

3.11 Reporting on comparative statistics is recommended by the Department of the Environment in its 1982 code of practice *Local authority annual reports*.

3.12 The following list illustrates the types of comparative statistics suggested in the code of practice.

For the authority's total expenditure and for each function	Net cost per 1,000 population Manpower per 1,000 population
Primary education, secondary education	Pupil/teacher ratio Cost per pupil
School meals	Revenue/cost ratio Pupils receiving free meals as a proportion of school roll
Children in care	As a proportion of total under-18 population Cost per child in care
Care of elderly	Residents of council homes as a proportion of total over-75 population Cost per resident week
Home helps	Contract hours per 1,000 population over 65
Police	Population per police officer Serious offences per 1,000 population
Fire	Proportion of area at high risk
Public transport	Passenger journeys per week per 1,000 population

Highways	Maintenance cost per kilometre
Housing	Rents as a proportion of total cost Management cost per dwelling per week Rent arrears as a percentage of year's rent income Construction cost per dwelling completed
Trading services	Revenue/gross cost ratio

Key points in this chapter

- Important performance ratios include profit margin, asset turnover and return on capital employed. Stock, debtors and creditors turnover periods reflect the condition of the working capital of the business.
- Divisional performance may be better measured by contribution, which is within the manager's direct control, than by profit.
- Performance measurement is becoming increasingly important in the public sector, although there can be problems in deciding how the 'output' of any particular organisational unit is to be defined.

For practice on the points covered in this chapter you should now attempt the Exercises in Session 11 of the Cost Accounting II Workbook

PART B
Unit 8: Preparing VAT returns

12. The VAT charge and VAT records

1. **Basic principles of VAT**
2. **The scope of VAT**
3. **Invoices and records**
4. **Registration for VAT**

1. Basic principles of VAT

1.1 In Unit 8, you will study value added tax (VAT). VAT applies to a great many business transactions, and you will often see it mentioned on invoices and in price lists and advertisements. In your work as an accounting technician, you will not be able to deal with sales, purchases, receipts and payments correctly unless you understand how VAT works.

1.2 You will find that the style of this part of the Tutorial Text is very different from the style of Part A. This is because VAT, like all taxes, was created by law, and the law has to be very precise and detailed to prevent people from evading the tax. If any loopholes are left in the law, someone will use them so as to pay less tax than they should.

1.3 Because there are a lot of hard and fast rules to learn (instead of recommended approaches), you may find it helpful to try new approaches to study. Here are some suggestions.

(a) Start by reading through the whole of Part B of this Tutorial Text twice quickly. Do not spend time puzzling out the meaning of a paragraph which is not clear to you, but move on so that you get an overall view.

(b) Then read through Part B much more carefully, making sure that you do understand everything as you go. When you come to a rule, try to see the point of it. For example, what could taxpayers get away with if the rule did not exist? (However, not all rules are aimed at the deliberate tax dodger.)

(c) Finally, try the exercises and assignments in the Workbook. Note that Unit 8 is not examined by central assessment, only by devolved assessment. Also note that you can have a copy of the Customs & Excise Notice 700, the VAT Guide, with you during your devolved assessment. The VAT Guide gives quite a lot of detailed information, and is a useful memory-jogger.

Computing VAT due

1.4 VAT is a tax on sales, not on income or profit. Whenever goods or services are sold, VAT (at 17.5%) may be due. The VAT is added to the price, so the money is collected by the seller. The seller then pays over the money to HM Customs & Excise, who administer VAT.

1.5 The system is arranged so that all the VAT on the full value of the item sold is borne by the final consumer, however many stages there are before him. Everybody except the final consumer goes through the following procedure.

(a) Work out the VAT on sales (the *output tax*).

(b) Work out the VAT on purchases (the *input tax*).

(c) Pay to HM Customs & Excise the output tax minus the input tax, or claim from HM Customs & Excise the input tax minus the output tax.

Example: the VAT charge

1.6 Anne makes a table from some wood she has grown herself. She sells it to Bob for £100, who sells it to Christine for £150. Christine sells it to David for £280. All these prices exclude VAT, and David is the final consumer.

Tasks

(a) Show the profits made by Anne, Bob and Christine, ignoring VAT.
(b) Show the effect of imposing VAT at 17.5%.

Solution

1.7 (a)

	Selling price	*Purchase price*	*Profit*
	£	£	£
Anne	100	0	100
Bob	150	100	50
Christine	280	150	130

(b) In the following table, the selling and purchase prices have all been increased by 17.5%, to take account of the VAT. The VAT payable is the output tax minus the input tax. The profit is the selling price minus the purchase price minus the VAT payable.

	Selling price	*Purchase price*	*Output tax*	*Input tax*	*VAT payable*	*Profit*
	£	£	£	£	£	£
Anne	117.50	0	17.50	0	17.50	100
Bob	176.25	117.50	26.25	17.50	8.75	50
Christine	329.00	176.25	49.00	26.25	22.75	130
					49.00	

The imposition of VAT has made no difference to any of Anne, Bob and Christine, each of whom makes the same profit as before. The two parties who are affected are:

(i) David, who pays £329 for the table instead of £280, so he is £49 worse off;

(ii) HM Customs & Excise, who collect £49 in VAT. They collect £17.50 from Anne, £8.75 from Bob and £22.75 from Christine.

Accounting for VAT

1.8 A trader does not in practice work out the VAT due every time he sells something. Instead he works out the total VAT due for a *tax period* (usually three months). He fills in a *VAT return* (form VAT 100) for the period, showing the total output tax, the total input tax and the total VAT due or repayable. He then sends this return to HM Customs & Excise, together with any VAT due. HM Customs & Excise then send him a return for the next period, with his name, address and VAT registration number pre-printed.

Example: VAT for a tax period

1.9 In a tax period, Susan sold goods for £10,000 (excluding VAT). She bought goods for £7,050 (including VAT). Show the tax figures for her VAT return for the period.

Solution

1.10 The output tax is £10,000 × 17.5% = £1,750.

The input tax is 17.5% of the purchases excluding VAT, so it is 17.5/117.5 = 7/47 of the purchases including VAT. This fraction of 7/47, the VAT in an amount including VAT, is called the *VAT fraction.*

The input tax is £7,050 × 7/47 = £1,050.

The VAT payable is £(1,750 - 1,050) = £700.

1.11 Most tax periods last for one quarter (three months). They may end at the ends of June, September, December and March; July, October, January and April; or August, November, February and May. A trader is allocated to one of these groups depending on the type of trade carried on, but may ask to be put into the group which will fit in with his own accounting year.

1.12 Some traders regularly get refunds of VAT (see Section 2 of Chapter 13 below). Such traders can elect to have monthly tax periods, so that they get their refunds more quickly.

1.13 Some traders can have annual tax periods. This *annual accounting scheme* is dealt with in Section 5 of Chapter 13 below.

Paying VAT

1.14 The return is due within one month after the end of the tax period. Any VAT due must be paid within the same time limit. An extra seven days is allowed for submitting the return and for payment if the bank credit transfer system is used, rather than the VAT being sent with the return.

1.15 If a repayment to the trader is due, the trader may receive it through the post or, if he prefers, by credit transfer directly to his bank account.

Substantial traders

1.16 If a trader does not made monthly returns, and the total VAT liability over 12 months exceeds £2,000,000, he must thereafter make payments on account of each quarter's VAT liability during the quarter. Payments are due a month before the end of the quarter and at the end of the quarter, with the final payment due at the usual time, a month after the end of the quarter. An extra seven days is allowed for each payment if the credit transfer system is used.

1.17 For a trader who exceeded the £2,000,000 limit in the 12 months to his last return period end before 1 June 1993, the amount of each of the two payments on account is 1/12 of the total VAT liability of the year ended 31 March, 30 April or 31 May 1993. Other traders must pay 1/12 of the VAT liability for the first 12 months in which they exceeded the £2,000,000 limit. However, if the total VAT liability for any later period of 12 months is less than 80% of the total liability for the 12 months used to compute the payments on account, the trader can apply to use 1/12 of that later total. A later total can even be used if the year has not ended, so long as HM Customs & Excise are satisfied that it will be below the 80% limit. A business can leave the scheme if its latest 12 months' VAT liability was less than £1,600,000.

1.18 If a trader's total annual liability increases to 120% or more of the amount used to calculate the payments on account, then the new higher annual liability is used to calculate new payments on account. The increase applies from the end of the 12 months with the new higher annual liability.

1.19 For the purposes of calculating the payments on account (but not for the purposes of the £2,000,000 limit for entry into the scheme), a trader's tax due on imports from outside the EU is ignored.

The boxes on a VAT return

1.20 The boxes on a VAT return which a trader must fill in are as follows.

(a) *Box 1:* the VAT due in the period on sales and other outputs

(b) *Box 2:* the VAT due on acquisitions from other EU member states

(c) *Box 3:* the total of boxes 1 and 2

(d) *Box 4:* the VAT reclaimed in the period on purchases and other inputs

(e) *Box 5:* the net VAT to be paid or reclaimed: the difference between boxes 3 and 4

(f) *Box 6:* the total value (before cash discounts) of sales and all other outputs in the period, excluding VAT but including the total in box 8

(g) *Box 7:* the total value (before cash discounts) of purchases and all other inputs in the period, excluding VAT but including the total in box 9

(h) *Box 8:* the total value of all sales and related services to other EU member states

(i) *Box 9:* the total value of all purchases and related services from other EU member states

Amounts in boxes 1 to 5 are given in pounds and pence. All other amounts are given to the nearest pound below.

The notes on the back of a return (which are referred to on the front) are reminders of what goes in which box, of how to correct errors and of how to pay VAT.

A VAT return is shown below.

Value Added Tax Return
For the period
01 07 X5 to 30 09 X5

For Official Use

Registration number: 212 7924 36

Period: 09 X5

BERNINI PLC
1 LONG LANE
ANYTOWN
AN4 5QP

Due date: 31 10 X5

For Official Use

Your VAT Office telephone number is 0123-4567

ATTENTION
If this return and any tax due are not received by the due date you will be liable to a surcharge.

If you are using Retail Scheme B1, D or J, please remember to carry out your annual adjustment at the appropriate time.

Before you fill in this form please read the notes on the back and the VAT Leaflet *"Filling in your VAT return"*. Fill in all boxes clearly in ink, and write 'none' where necessary. Don't put a dash or leave any box blank. If there are no pence write "00" in the pence column. Do not enter more than one amount in any box.

For official use

	Box	£	p
VAT due in this period on sales and other outputs	1		
VAT reclaimed in this period on acquisitions from other EU Member States	2		
Total VAT due (the sum of boxes 1 and 2)	3		
VAT reclaimed in this period on purchases and other inputs (including acquisitions from the EU)	4		
Net VAT to be paid to Customs or reclaimed by you (Difference between boxes 3 and 4)	5		
Total value of sales and all other outputs excluding any VAT. Include your box 8 figure	6		00
Total value of purchases and all other inputs excluding any VAT. Include your box 9 figure	7		00
Total value of all supplies of goods and related services, excluding any VAT, to other EU Member States	8		00
Total value of all acquisitions of goods and related services, excluding any VAT, from other EU Member States	9		00

Retail schemes. If you have used any ot the schemes in the period covered by this return, enter the relevant letter(s) in this box.

If you are enclosing a payment please tick this box.

DECLARATION: You, or someone on your behalf, must sign below.

I, ... declare that the
(Full name of signatory in BLOCK LETTERS)
information given above is true and complete.

Signature.. Date .... 19 ....

A false declaration can result in prosecution.

Errors in previous periods

1.21 Where errors have been made in previous periods and the net error (error in tax payable net of error in tax allowable) is £2,000 or less, the error may be corrected on the next VAT return by changing the figures in boxes 1, 2 and 4. If an amount was overstated, the figure must be reduced. If a figure becomes negative because of this, it should be shown in brackets.

1.22 Larger errors must be separately notified to the local VAT office, either on form VAT 652 or by letter.

The time of a supply

1.23 Because sales and purchases (supplies by and to a business) are grouped together in tax periods, rules are needed to fix the time of a supply. It can then be decided which tax period a supply falls into. This time of supply is the *tax point.*

1.24 The basic tax point is the date on which goods are removed or made available to the customer, or the date on which services are completed.

1.25 If a tax invoice (an invoice meeting the conditions set out in Section 3 below) is issued or payment is received before the basic tax point, the earlier of these dates automatically becomes the tax point. If the tax invoice is issued within 14 days after the basic tax point, the invoice date becomes the tax point (although the trader can elect to use the basic tax point for all his supplies if he wishes). This 14 day period may be extended to accommodate, for example, monthly invoicing; the tax point is then the tax invoice date or the end of the month, whichever is applied consistently.

1.26 Goods supplied on sale or return are treated as supplied on the earlier of adoption by the customer or 12 months after despatch. Continuous supplies of services paid for periodically normally have tax points on the earlier of the receipt of each payment and the issue of each tax invoice. However, if one invoice covering several payments is issued in advance for up to a year, the tax point becomes the earlier of each due date or date of actual payment.

2. The scope of VAT

2.1 (a) VAT is charged on supplies of goods and services, provided that they are:

(i) taxable supplies;

(ii) made in the UK;

(iii) made by a taxable person; and

(iv) made in the course or furtherance of any business carried on by that taxable person.

(b) VAT is charged on imports of goods into the UK, whether or not made by a taxable person or for business purposes.

(c) VAT may also be charged on services received from abroad. This is called the *reverse charge*.

Special rules, covered in Chapter 13 below, apply to trade with other European Union countries.

2.2 Supplies may be *taxable* or *exempt*. Exempt supplies (for example insurance) are not subject to VAT. A list of such supplies is given in Section 2 of Chapter 13 below.

2.3 *Taxable supplies* may be *standard rated* or *zero rated*. Standard rated supplies (for example calculators) are subject to tax at 17.5%. Zero rated supplies (for example most food) are subject to tax at 0%. A list of zero rated supplies is given in Section 2 of Chapter 13 below.

2.4 There is a difference between exempt and zero rated supplies. A trader making exempt supplies cannot recover the input tax on his purchases, but a trader making zero rated supplies can.

2.5 A *taxable person* is someone who is or ought to be registered for VAT (see Section 4 below). Such a person may be an individual, a partnership, a company, a club, an association or a charity.

3. Invoices and records

Tax invoices

3.1 A taxable person making a taxable supply to another person registered for VAT must supply a *tax invoice* within 30 days of the time of supply, and must keep a copy. The recipient of a supply can only claim the VAT on the supply as input tax if he holds a valid tax invoice. Tax invoices need not be issued for zero rated supplies except for supplies to other European Union (EU) member states.

3.2 There is no set form for a tax invoice, but it must show:

(a) the supplier's name, address and registration number. A trader who makes supplies to other EU member states will normally show his country code (GB for the UK) before his registration number;

(b) the date of issue, the tax point and an invoice number;

(c) the name and address of the customer;

(d) the type of supply (sale, hire purchase, loan, exchange, hire, goods made from the customer's materials, sale on commission, sale or return etc);

(e) a description of the goods or services supplied, giving for each description the quantity, the rate of tax and the tax exclusive amount;

(f) the rate of any cash discount;

(g) the total invoice price excluding VAT (with separate totals for zero rated and exempt supplies);

(h) each VAT rate applicable, the amount of VAT at each rate and the total amount of VAT.

Credit notes must give the reason for the credit (such as 'returned goods'), and the number and date of the original tax invoice. If a credit note makes no VAT adjustment, it should state this.

3.3 For supplies to other EU member states, item (d) may be omitted but the supplier's VAT registration number must be prefixed by 'GB' and the customer's registration number (including the state code, such as DE for Germany) must be shown.

3.4 A *less detailed tax invoice* may be issued by a retailer where the invoice is for a total including VAT of up to £100 and the supply is not to another EU member state. Such an invoice must show:

(a) the supplier's name, address and registration number;
(b) the date of the supply;
(c) a description of the goods or services supplied;
(d) the rate of tax chargeable;
(e) the total amount chargeable including tax.

Zero rated and exempt supplies must not be included in less detailed invoices.

3.5 Tax invoices are not required for payments of up to £25 including VAT which are for telephone calls or car park fees or are made through cash operated machines. In such cases, input tax can be claimed without a tax invoice.

Records

3.6 Every VAT registered trader must keep records for six years, although HM Customs & Excise may sometimes grant permission for their earlier destruction. They may be kept on paper, on microfilm or microfiche or on computer. However, there must be adequate facilities for HM Customs & Excise to inspect records.

3.7 All records must be kept up to date and in a way which allows:

(a) the calculation of tax due;
(b) officers of HM Customs & Excise to check the figures on VAT returns.

3.8 The following records are needed.

(a) Copies of tax invoices, credit notes and debit notes issued

(b) Tax invoices, credit notes and debit notes received

(c) Records of goods received from and sent to other EU member states

(d) Documents relating to imports from and exports to countries outside the EU

(e) A VAT account (see Paragraph 3.13 below)

(f) Order and delivery notes, correspondence, appointment books, job books, purchases and sales books, cash books, account books, records of takings (such as till rolls), bank paying-in slips, bank statements and annual accounts

(g) Records of zero rated and exempt supplies, gifts or loans of goods, taxable self-supplies (see Paragraphs 3.24 to 3.27 of Chapter 13 below) and any goods taken for non-business use

3.9 A summary of supplies made must be kept, in the same order as the copies of tax invoices retained. It must enable the trader to work out the following totals for each tax period.

(a) The VAT chargeable on supplies

(b) The values of standard rated and zero rated supplies excluding VAT

(c) The value of exempt supplies

(d) The value of all supplies, excluding VAT

(e) The VAT due on goods imported by post and on services received from abroad to which the reverse charge applies

Under (b), (c) and (d), credits allowed should be deducted but cash discounts should not be deducted.

3.10 A summary of supplies received must be kept, in the same order as the tax invoices received. It must enable the trader to work out the following totals for each tax period.

(a) The VAT charged on goods and services received

(b) The VAT due on goods imported by post and on services received from abroad to which the reverse charge applies

(c) The value excluding VAT of all supplies received, deducting credits received from suppliers but not deducting cash discounts

3.11 The summaries described in Paragraphs 3.9 and 3.10 above could be obtained by adding appropriate columns to sales and purchases day books. The cash book can alternatively be used for the summary of supplies received, if the trader normally claims a deduction for input tax when the supplier is paid.

3.12 When credits are given or received, the VAT should be adjusted. Thus if goods are sold for £10,000 plus £1,750 VAT, and goods worth £1,000 plus £175 VAT are returned, the VAT to be accounted for should be shown as £(1,750 - 175) = £1,575. However, no adjustment need be made if both parties agree and the buyer makes no exempt supplies.

3.13 A VAT account must be kept, made up for each tax period.

(a) The *tax payable portion* (the credit side) shows the following.

(i) The output tax due for the tax period (excluding tax under (ii))

(ii) The output tax due on acquisitions from other EU member states for the tax period

(iii) Any corrections to tax payable for previous periods, provided that the net error (error in tax payable net of error in tax allowable) is not more than £2,000. Each error must be separately recorded

(iv) Any adjustments to the tax on supplies made in previous tax periods which are evidenced by credit notes or debit notes

(v) Any other adjustment to the tax payable for the period

(b) The *tax allowable portion* (the debit side) shows the following.

(i) The input tax allowable for the tax period (excluding tax under (ii))

(ii) The input tax allowable on acquisitions from other EU member states for the tax period

(ii) Any corrections to tax allowable for previous periods, provided that the net error (error in tax payable net of error in tax allowable) is not more than £2,000. Each error must be separately recorded

(iv) Any adjustments to the tax on supplies received in previous periods which are evidenced by credit notes or debit notes

(v) Any other adjustment to the tax allowable for the period

Example: A VAT account

3.14 Jane has the following transactions in the tax period from January to March 1994.

	Net	*VAT*	*Gross*
	£	£	£
Sales	15,000	2,625	17,625
Purchases	8,000	1,400	9,400
Credits allowed (current period's sales)	400	70	470
Credits allowed (previous periods' sales)	200	35	235
Credits received (current period's purchases)	800	140	940
Credits received (previous periods' purchases)	600	105	705

Jane discovered in March 1994 that she had under-declared the VAT payable for the tax period from October to December 1993 by £74.

Show Jane's VAT account for the tax period from January to March 1994.

Solution

3.15 VAT ACCOUNT FOR THE TAX PERIOD FROM JANUARY TO MARCH 1994

Tax allowable	£	*Tax payable*	£
Input tax allowable		Output tax due	
£(1,400 - 140)	1,260	£(2,625 - 70)	2,555
Adjustment for credits received	(105)	Correction of error	74
		Adjustment for credits allowed	(35)
	1,155		2,594
Cash (payment to HM Customs & Excise)	1,439		
	2,594		2,594

4. Registration for VAT

4.1 A trader may be *registered* for VAT, and must then charge VAT on sales and may reclaim VAT on purchases. A registered trader has a VAT registration number, which must be shown on all tax invoices issued and quoted in all correspondence with HM Customs & Excise.

4.2 A trader has one registration covering all his business activities. The turnovers of all such activities are added together to determine whether the trader must register (see below).

Compulsory registration

4.3 A trader making taxable supplies becomes liable to register for VAT if, in any period of 12 consecutive calendar months, the value of his taxable supplies (excluding VAT) exceeds £45,000. The trader must notify HM Customs & Excise within 30 days of the end of the 12 month period. HM Customs & Excise will then register the trader with effect from the end of the month following the 12 month period, or from an earlier date if they and the trader agree.

Registration under this rule is not required if HM Customs & Excise are satisfied that the value of the trader's taxable supplies (excluding VAT) in the year starting at the end of the 12 month period will not exceed £43,000.

4.4 A trader is also liable to register at any time if there are reasonable grounds for believing that his taxable supplies (excluding VAT) in the following 30 days will exceed £45,000. HM Customs & Excise must be notified by the end of the 30 day period, and registration will be with effect from the beginning of that period.

Example: Compulsory registration

4.5 A trader had the following monthly turnovers of taxable supplies (excluding VAT) from the start of trade on 1 April 1993.

Period	*Monthly turnover*
	£
1 April - 31 December 1993	3,350
1 January - 30 September 1994	4,200
1 October 1994 onwards	4,800

By what date must the trader notify his liability to register for VAT?

Solution

4.6 9 × £3,350 = £30,150, so the registration limit is clearly not exceeded in 1993.

12 months to end of	*Working*	*Turnover*
		£
January 1994	(9 × 3,350) + 4,200	34,350
February 1994	(9 × 3,350) + (2 × 4,200)	38,550
March 1994	(9 × 3,350) + (3 × 4,200)	42,750
April 1994	(8 × 3,350) + (4 × 4,200)	43,600
May 1994	(7 × 3,350) + (5 × 4,200)	44,450
June 1994	(6 × 3,350) + (6 × 4,200)	45,300

The registration limit is exceeded in the 12 months to 30 June 1994, so the trader must notify his liability to register by 30 July 1994 (not 31 July).

4.7 When determining the value of a trader's taxable supplies for the purposes of registration, supplies of goods and services that are capital assets of the business are disregarded, except for non-zero-rated supplies of interests in land.

4.8 When a trader should have registered in the past, it is his responsibility to pay VAT. If he is unable to collect it from those to whom he made taxable supplies, the VAT burden will fall on him. A trader must start keeping VAT records and charging VAT to customers as soon as he is required to register. However, VAT should not be shown separately on any invoices until the registration number is known. The invoice should show the VAT inclusive price and customers should be informed that a tax invoice will be forwarded once the registration number is known. Formal tax invoices should then be sent to such customers within 30 days of receipt of the registration number.

4.9 Notification of liability to register must be made on form VAT 1. Simply writing to, or telephoning, a local VAT office is not enough.

Voluntary registration

4.10 A trader may decide to become VAT registered even though his taxable turnover falls below the £45,000 limit. Unless a trader is registered he cannot recover the input tax he pays on supplies to him.

4.11 Voluntary registration is advantageous where a person wishes to recover input tax on supplies to him. For example, consider a trader who has one input during the year which cost £1,000 plus £175 VAT; he works on the input which becomes his sole output for the year and he decides to make a profit of £1,000.

(a) If he is not registered for VAT he will charge £2,175 and his customer will obtain no relief for any VAT.

(b) If he is registered for VAT he will charge £2,000 plus VAT of £350. His customer will have input tax of £350 which he will be able to recover if he, too, is registered for VAT.

If the customer is not registered he will prefer (a) as the cost to him is £2,175 instead of £2,350. If he is registered he will prefer (b) as the net cost is £2,000 instead of £2,175. Thus, a decision whether or not to register may depend upon the status of customers.

4.12 Provided that a trader satisfies HM Customs & Excise that he is carrying on a business, and intends to make taxable supplies, he is entitled to be registered for VAT if he chooses. This is called *intending trader registration*. But, once registered, he is obliged to notify HM Customs & Excise within 30 days if he no longer intends to make taxable supplies.

Exemption from registration

4.13 If a trader makes zero rated supplies but no standard rated supplies, he may request exemption from registration. The trader must notify any material change in the nature of his supplies. Exemption is only advisable where the amount of input tax which could otherwise be recovered is small in relation to the administrative effort involved in VAT procedures.

HM Customs & Excise may also allow exemption from registration if only a small proportion of supplies are standard rated, provided that the trader would normally receive repayments of VAT if registered.

Group registration

4.14 Companies under common control may apply for group registration. Broadly, the effects of group registration are as follows.

(a) Each VAT group must appoint a representative member which must account for the group's output tax and input tax. However, all members of the group are liable for any tax due from the representative member.

(b) Any supply of goods or services by a member of the group to another member of the group is disregarded for VAT purposes.

(c) Any other supply of goods or services by or to a group member is treated as a supply by or to the representative member.

(d) Any tax payable on the import of goods by a group member is payable by the representative member.

4.15 Two or more companies are eligible to be treated as members of a group provided that each of them either is resident in the UK or has an established place of business in the UK, and:

(a) one of them controls each of the others;
(b) one person (which could be an individual or a holding company) controls all of them; or
(c) a partnership controls all of them.

4.16 The application for group registration must be made by one of the companies not less than 90 days before the date from which it is to take effect. It is made on form VAT 50.

4.17 Individual companies which are within a group for company law purposes may still register separately and stay outside the VAT group.

Divisional registration

4.18 A company which is divided into several units which each prepare accounts can apply for divisional registration. Divisional registration is for administrative convenience; the separate divisions do not become separate taxable persons and the company is itself still liable for the VAT. Broadly, the conditions for divisional registration are as follows.

(a) Each division must be registered even where that division's turnover is beneath the registration limit.

(b) The divisions must be independent, self-accounting units, carrying on different activities or operating in separate locations.

(c) Input tax attributable to exempt supplies (see the partial exemption rules in Section 3 of Chapter 13 below) by the company as a whole must be less than £600 a month on average.

(d) Each division must make VAT returns for the same tax periods.

(e) Tax invoices must not be issued for supplies between the divisions of the same company as they are not supplies for VAT purposes.

Deregistration

4.19 A trader is eligible for *voluntary deregistration* if HM Customs & Excise are satisfied that the value of his taxable supplies (net of VAT and excluding supplies of capital assets) in the following 12 month period will not exceed £43,000. However, deregistration will not be allowed if the reason for the expected fall in value of taxable supplies is the cessation of trading or the suspension of taxable supplies for a period of 30 days or more in that following year.

4.20 HM Customs & Excise will cancel a trader's registration from the date the request is made or from an agreed later date.

4.21 Traders may suffer *compulsory deregistration*. Failure to notify a requirement to deregister may lead to a penalty. Compulsory deregistration may also lead to HM Customs & Excise reclaiming input tax which has been wrongly recovered by the trader since the date on which he should have deregistered.

4.22 (a) If HM Customs & Excise are misled into granting registration then the registration is treated as void from the start.

(b) A person may be compulsorily deregistered if he is no longer making nor intending to make taxable supplies.

(c) Changes in legal status also require cancellation of registration. For example:

(i) a sole trader becoming a partnership;
(ii) a partnership reverting to a sole trader;
(iii) a business being incorporated;
(iv) a company being replaced by an unincorporated business.

4.23 On deregistration, a special final VAT return (form VAT 193) is completed. The form has the same boxes 1 to 9 as an ordinary return. VAT is chargeable on all stocks and capital assets in a business on which input tax was claimed, because the registered trader is in effect making a taxable supply to himself as a newly unregistered trader. If the tax chargeable does not exceed £250, it need not be paid.

4.24 This special VAT charge does not apply if the business (or a separately viable part of it) is sold as a going concern to another taxable person (or a person who immediately becomes a taxable person as a result of the transfer). Such transfers are generally outside the scope of VAT. If the original owner ceases to be taxable, the new owner of the business may also take over the existing VAT number. If he does so, he takes over the rights and liabilities of the transferor as at the date of transfer.

Pre-registration input tax

4.25 VAT incurred before registration can be treated as input tax and recovered from HM Customs & Excise (on the trader's first VAT return) subject to certain conditions.

4.26 If the claim is for input tax suffered on goods bought prior to registration then both of the following conditions must be satisfied.

(a) The goods were acquired for the purposes of a business which either was carried on or was to be carried on at the time of supply.

(b) The goods have not been supplied onwards or consumed before the date of registration (although they may have been used to make other goods which are still held).

4.27 If the claim is for input tax suffered on a supply of services prior to registration then both of the following conditions must be satisfied.

(a) The services were supplied for the purposes of a business which either was carried on or was to be carried on at the time of supply.

(b) The services were supplied within the six months prior to the date of registration.

Key points in this chapter

- VAT is collected in stages along the production chain, but is effectively a burden on the final consumer.
- VAT is accounted for one tax period at a time. The trader completes a VAT return.
- The tax point for a supply is in practice usually the invoice date.
- Supplies may be standard rated (17.5% VAT), zero rated or exempt.
- Tax invoices must show specified information.
- Traders must keep full records, including a VAT account.
- Registration for VAT is compulsory if annual taxable turnover exceeds £45,000, unless exemption is granted.
- Voluntary registration, group registration and divisional registration are also possible.
- Pre-registration input tax can be reclaimed if certain conditions are satisfied.

For practice on the points covered in this chapter you should now attempt the Exercises in Session 12 of the Cost Accounting II Workbook

13. *The computation and administration of VAT*

1. Finding the VAT on a supply
2. Zero rated and exempt supplies
3. The deduction of input tax
4. Imports and exports
5. Special schemes
6. Administration
7. Penalties

1. Finding the VAT on a supply

1.1 The VAT on a standard rated supply is 17.5% of the price excluding VAT, or 17.5/117.5 = 7/47 of the price including VAT.

1.2 If a discount is offered for prompt payment, VAT is computed on the amount after deducting the discount (at the highest rate offered), even if the discount is not taken. (However, for imports from outside the EU, VAT is computed on the full price unless the discount is actually taken up.) If goods are sold to staff at a discount, VAT is charged on the reduced price.

1.3 If a trader charges different prices to customers paying with credit cards and those paying by other means, the VAT due on each standard rated sale is the full amount paid by the customer × 7/47.

1.4 The rules on the rounding of amounts of VAT are as follows.

(a) If amounts of VAT are calculated for individual lines on an invoice, they must be:

(i) rounded down to the nearest 0.1p, so 86.76p would be shown as 86.7p; or

(ii) rounded to the nearest 0.5p, so 86.76p would be shown as 87p and 86.26p would be shown as 86.5p.

(b) If amounts of VAT are calculated from an amount of VAT per unit or article, the amount of VAT should be:

(i) calculated to the nearest 0.01p and then rounded to the nearest 0.1p, so 0.24p would be rounded to 0.2p; or

(ii) rounded to the nearest 0.5p, but with a minimum of 0.5p for any standard rated item, so 0.24p would be rounded to 0.5p rather than to 0p.

(c) The total VAT shown on an invoice should be rounded down to the nearest 1p, so £32.439 would be shown as £32.43.

Example: The VAT on supplies

1.5 Find the VAT on each of the following supplies.

(a) Goods with a normal retail price of £10,000 excluding VAT are sold net of a trade discount of 20% and a cash discount of 5% (for payment within ten days) or 3% (for payment within 21 days). No cash discount is taken up.

(b) Goods which would be sold for £109 including VAT to a customer paying by cash or cheque, are sold to a customer paying by credit card subject to a 4% surcharge.

Solution

			£
1.6	(a)	Normal retail price	10,000
		Less trade discount £10,000 × 20%	2,000
			8,000
		Less cash discount £8,000 × 5%	400
		Amount on which VAT is calculated	7,600

VAT = £7,600 × 17.5% = £1,330

(b) Price including VAT = £109 × 1.04 = £113.36

VAT = £113.36 × 7/47 = £16.88

1.7 When goods are permanently taken from a business for non-business purposes tax must be accounted for on their market value. If services bought for business purposes are used for non-business purposes (without charge), then tax must be accounted for on their cost, but the tax to be accounted for is not allowed to exceed the input tax deductible on the purchase of the services.

1.8 Different goods and services are sometimes invoiced together at an inclusive price (a *mixed supply*). Some items may be chargeable at the standard rate and some at the zero rate. In such cases the supplier must account for tax separately on the standard rated and zero rated elements by splitting the total amount payable in a fair proportion between the different elements and charging tax on each at the appropriate rate. There is no single way of doing this: one method is to split the amount according to the cost to the supplier of each element, and another is to use the open market value of each element.

An example of a mixed supply which may be sold at an inclusive price is a pack of audio-visual materials containing slides (standard rated) and books (zero rated).

1.9 However, where a supply cannot be split into components, there is a *composite supply*, to the whole of which one VAT rate must be applied. The rate depends on the nature of the supply as a whole. A supply of air transport including an in-flight meal has been held to be a single, composite supply of transport (zero rated) rather than a supply of transport (zero rated) and a supply of a meal (standard rated).

1.10 Gifts of goods must normally be treated as sales at cost (so VAT is due). However, business gifts are not supplies (so VAT need not be accounted for) if:

(a) the cost to the donor is £10 or less and the gift is not part of a series of gifts made to the same person; or

(b) the gift is a sample. However, if two or more identical samples are given to the same person, all but one of them are treated as supplies.

Errors on invoices

1.11 If an invoice shows too much VAT, the full amount shown must be accounted for unless the error is corrected by issuing a credit note to the customer.

1.12 If an invoice shows too little VAT and a supplementary invoice is issued to the customer to collect the extra VAT, the full correct amount of VAT must be accounted for.

1.13 If an invoice shows too little VAT but the extra VAT is not collected from the customer, the VAT which must be accounted for is the gross amount shown × 7/47.

2. Zero rated and exempt supplies

2.1 Zero rated supplies are taxable at 0%. A registered trader whose outputs are zero rated but whose inputs are standard rated will obtain VAT repayments. Here is an example.

	Net	*VAT*	
	£	£	
Sales	160	0	(0%)
Less purchases	100	17.50	(17.5%)
Gross margin	60	17.50	

The trader gets a repayment of the £17.50 of VAT he paid on his purchases, so that his own profit after this repayment is £160 (takings) - £117.50 (paid to supplier) + £17.50 (VAT repayment) = £60.

2.2 However, *exempt supplies* are not so advantageous. In exactly the same way as for a non-registered trader, a trader making exempt supplies is unable to recover VAT on inputs. The exempt trader thus has to shoulder the burden of VAT.

Of course, he may increase his prices to pass on the charge, but he cannot issue a tax invoice which would enable a registered customer to obtain a credit for VAT, because no VAT is chargeable on exempt supplies.

Example: Standard rated, zero rated and exempt supplies

2.3 Here are figures for three traders, the first with standard rated outputs, the second with zero rated outputs and the third with exempt outputs. All their inputs are standard rated. All have purchases of £20,000 excluding VAT and sales of £30,000 excluding VAT.

	Standard rated £	Zero rated £	Exempt £
Inputs	20,000	20,000	20,000
VAT	3,500	3,500	3,500
	23,500	23,500	23,500
Outputs	30,000	30,000	30,000
VAT	5,250	0	0
	35,250	30,000	30,000
Pay/(reclaim)	1,750	(3,500)	0
Net profit	10,000	10,000	6,500

Zero rated supplies

2.4 The following goods and services are zero rated.

(a) Human and animal food, although pet food and certain luxury items, such as confectionery are standard rated. Food supplied in the course of catering (which includes all hot takeaways) is standard rated. Most beverages are standard rated, but milk, tea, coffee and cocoa are zero rated unless supplied in the course of catering

(b) Sewerage services and water (other than such services supplied for industrial activities, which are standard rated)

(c) Periodicals, books and leaflets (not stationery)

(d) Supplies to charities in respect of 'talking books' for the blind and sound recording equipment and cassette recorders used or loaned by charities caring for the blind and severely handicapped

(e) New construction work or the sale of new buildings by builders, where the buildings are to be used for residential or charitable purposes (not repairs, enlargements to existing buildings or alterations)

(f) Sales of substantially reconstructed listed buildings, and alterations to such buildings, where such buildings are to be used for residential or charitable purposes

(g) Services of making arrangements to perform services outside the European Union (the EU), and certain services in relation to goods to be exported from the EU

(h) Passenger transport, but pleasure transport and transport in vehicles seating fewer than 12 passengers are standard rated, unless the reason why there are fewer than 12 seats is that space for wheelchairs has been provided. Freight transport is also zero rated when one end of the journey is outside the EU

(i) Large residential caravans and houseboats

(j) Gold supplied to a central bank. Other supplies of gold bullion and gold coins are standard rated, and a VAT registered buyer who is buying for business purposes must account for the VAT (rather than the seller), to prevent fraud

(k) Bank notes

(l) Drugs and medicines on prescription and aids, building alterations, special motor vehicles, boats and so on for the handicapped

(m) Exports of goods to outside the EU, and supplies to VAT registered traders in other EU states where the purchaser's VAT registration number is shown on the invoice

(n) Sales in tax free shops (for example at airports)

(o) Supplies to charities of advertising, any medical products to treat humans or animals, equipment for use in medical research, drugs and chemicals used directly by a charity for medical research, transport for the ill and telecommunication and other specialised equipment used by rescue and first aid services. Sales to health authorities and medical institutions of certain medical equipment paid for with funds from a charity are also zero rated

(p) Sales by a charity (or by another person who has covenanted all the profits of the sale to a charity) of goods donated for sale

(q) Goods and services for sea rescue

(r) Clothing and footwear for young children and certain protective clothing

Fuel and power for domestic or charity use (except fuel for motor vehicles) is taxed at only 8% until 31 March 1995. Thereafter the 17.5% standard rate applies. Fuel and power for commercial use is standard rated.

Exempt supplies

2.5 The following supplies are exempt.

(a) Sales of freeholds and leaseholds of land (including the surrender of a lease) by someone other than the builder of buildings on the land (although the seller may have an option to charge VAT at the standard rate except in the case of dwellings and charity buildings other than offices)

(b) Transactions in buildings (other than a sale by the builder) where the building is to be used for residential or charitable purposes, including renting, leasing or hiring, except short-term accommodation at hotels and boarding houses and camping and parking facilities

(c) Financial services, including credit card services to retailers, the arrangements for, and underwriting of, capital issues, and securities dealing services. Investment advice is standard rated

(d) Insurance

(e) Postal services provided by the Post Office

(f) Betting and gaming, except admission charges and subscriptions

(g) Education and vocational training supplied by a school, a university or an independent private tutor

(h) Health services, including medical, nursing, dental and ophthalmic treatment and hospital accommodation. The supply of related goods is only exempt if they are dental prostheses or a minor and inseparable part of the service (such as bandages, but not spectacles) or if the supply is made in a hospital

(i) Burial and cremation services

(j) Supplies to members by trades unions and professional bodies if in consideration only of a membership subscription

(k) (i) Entry fees to non-profit making sports competitions

(ii) Services closely related to sport and physical education supplied by non-profit making bodies to members (not visitors), including playing membership subscriptions, equipment hire and charges for the use of changing rooms

(l) Disposals of works of art and other items to public bodies in lieu of capital taxes

(m) Welfare services supplied by charities

(n) Supplies by charities, philanthropic bodies, trade unions, professional associations and non-profit making sports bodies in connection with fund raising events

3. The deduction of input tax

3.1 For input tax to be deductible, the payer must be registered for VAT, with the supply being to him in the course of his business. In addition a VAT invoice must be held (except for payments of up to £25 including VAT which are for telephone calls or car park fees or which are made through cash operated machines).

3.2 There are a few special cases where the input tax is not deductible. These are:

(a) VAT on motor cars, which is never deductible unless a car is acquired new for resale or is acquired for use in or leasing to a taxi business, a self drive car hire business or a driving school. However, VAT on accessories such as car radios is deductible if the accessories are ordered separately and are fitted after delivery of the car. Also, the VAT charged when a car is hired is reclaimable;

(b) VAT on business entertaining, except entertaining staff;

(c) VAT on expenses incurred on domestic accommodation for directors;

(d) VAT on non-business items passed through the business accounts. However, when goods are bought partly for business use, the buyer may:

(i) deduct all the input tax, and account for output tax in respect of the private use; or

(ii) deduct only the business proportion of the input tax.

Where services are bought partly for business use, only method (ii) may be used. If services are initially bought for business use but the use then changes, a fair proportion of the input tax (relating to the private use) is reclaimed by HM Customs & Excise by making the trader account for output tax;

(e) VAT which does not relate to the making of supplies by the buyer in the course of a business.

Where non-deductible input tax arises the VAT inclusive amount will be included in the trader's accounts.

Partial exemption

3.3 A taxable person may only recover the VAT he has paid on supplies to him so far as it is attributable to taxable supplies made by him. Where a trader makes a mixture of taxable and exempt supplies, he is partially exempt, and not all his input tax is recoverable because some of it is attributable to exempt supplies made by him. A person able to recover all input tax (except as in Paragraph 3.2 above) is a *fully taxable person*.

3.4 The standard method of attributing input tax involves the following steps.

(a) Calculate the amount of input tax suffered on supplies made to the taxable person in the period.

(b) Calculate how much of the input tax suffered relates to supplies which are wholly used or to be used by him in making taxable supplies: this input tax is deductible in full.

(c) Calculate how much of the input tax suffered relates to supplies which are wholly used or to be used by him in making exempt supplies: this input tax is not deductible.

(d) Calculate how much of any remaining input tax is deductible by taking the percentage (taxable turnover excluding VAT/total turnover excluding VAT) × 100%, rounded to the nearest whole percentage above.

Example: The standard method of attributing input tax

3.5 Mr A makes both exempt and taxable supplies: £100,000 exempt and £300,000 taxable. Most of the goods purchased are used for both types of supply which means that much of the input tax cannot be directly attributed to either type of supply. After directly attributing as much input tax as possible the following position arises.

	£
Attributed to taxable supplies	1,200
Attributed to exempt supplies	600
Unattributed tax	8,200
	10,000

How much input tax can Mr A recover?

Solution

3.6 The amount of unattributed tax which is attributable to the making of taxable supplies is

$$\frac{300,000}{400,000} \times £8,200 = £6,150$$

Mr A can therefore recover £1,200 + £6,150 = £7,350 of input tax.

3.7 Alternative bases of attributing input tax may be agreed with HM Customs & Excise.

3.8 Where the input tax attributable to exempt supplies is not more than £600 a month on average it is treated as being attributable to taxable supplies and therefore fully recoverable.

3.9 An annual adjustment is made, covering the year to 31 March, 30 April or 31 May (depending on when the return periods end). A computation of recoverable input tax is made for the whole year, using the same method as for individual returns. The '£600 a month on average' test is also applied to the year as a whole, and if it is passed then all input tax for the year is recoverable.

3.10 The result for the whole year is compared with the total of results for the individual return periods.

(a) If the result for the whole year shows that less input tax is recoverable than has been recovered period by period, the difference is accounted for as output tax on the return for the next period after the end of the year.

(b) If the result for the whole year shows that more input tax is recoverable than has been recovered period by period, the difference is claimed as input tax on the return for the next period after the end of the year.

3.11 If the '£600 a month on average' test is passed for every return period in the year, no annual adjustment is made.

3.12 If there was no exempt input tax (that is, input tax attributable to exempt supplies) for the preceding year, the 'year' for the purposes of the annual adjustment starts at the beginning of the first return period in which there was exempt input tax.

In the year of registration, the 'year' starts on the day when exempt input tax was first incurred.

If a trader ceases to be taxable, the 'year' ends when he ceases to be taxable.

Motoring expenses

3.13 The VAT incurred on the purchase of a new car is not recoverable (except as in Paragraph 3.2 (a) above). If accessories are fitted at a later date to the original purchase and a separate invoice is raised then the VAT on the accessories can be treated as input tax (and recovered) so long as the accessories are for business use.

If a car is used for business purposes then any VAT charged on repair and maintenance costs can be treated as input tax. No apportionment has to be made for private use.

3.14 If an employee accepts a reduced salary in exchange for being allowed to use his employer's car privately, there is no supply, so VAT is not due on the salary reduction.

3.15 The VAT incurred on fuel used for business purposes is fully deductible as input tax. If the fuel is bought by employees who are reimbursed for the actual cost or by a mileage allowance, the employer may deduct the input tax.

3.16 Fuel for private use supplied to an individual at less than the cost of that fuel to the business gives rise to output tax using set scale charges per quarter or per month, based on the cylinder capacity of the car's engine.

3.17 The scale charges (from April 1994) are as follows.

Cylinder capacity	*Scale figure (deemed supply including VAT)*		*VAT due (scale figure × 7/47)*	
	Quarter	*Month*	*Quarter*	*Month*
cc	£	£	£	£
Diesel engines				
Up to 2,000	145	48	21.60	7.15
Over 2,000	187	62	27.85	9.23
Non-diesel engines				
Up to 1,400	160	53	23.83	7.89
1,401 - 2,000	202	67	30.09	9.98
Over 2,000	300	100	44.68	14.89

Relief for bad debts

3.18 If a trader supplies goods or services on credit, he may well account for the VAT on the sale before receiving payment. For example, if a trader prepares a VAT return for January to March he will include VAT on sales invoiced in March and will pay that VAT at the end of April, even though the customer may not pay him until May.

3.19 VAT may therefore have to be paid to HM Customs & Excise before the trader knows that he is going to be paid at all. The customer might never pay. Without a special relief, the trader might lose both the amount of the bad debt excluding VAT and the VAT on the sale.

3.20 Under VAT bad debt relief, the trader can reclaim VAT already accounted for on debts which have gone bad. The VAT is reclaimed on the creditor's VAT return, by adding it to the figure for VAT reclaimed on purchases. The amount must be debited to a 'refunds for bad debts' account and the debit is then transferred to the tax allowable portion of the VAT account.

3.21 All of the following conditions must be met for VAT bad debt relief to be available.

(a) The debt is over six months old (measured from the time of supply).

(b) The debt has been written off in the creditor's accounts.

(c) The consideration was money and not in excess of the market value of the goods or services.

(d) If the supply was a supply of goods (as opposed to services) ownership of the goods has passed to the customer.

(e) The creditor has a copy of the tax invoice, and records to show that VAT on the supply has been accounted for and that the debt has been written off.

3.22 If the debtor has paid some, but not all, of what he owes, the most recent debts are treated as the ones still owed.

3.23 If the relief is claimed but some payment from the debtor is later received, a corresponding part of the VAT must be paid back to HM Customs & Excise.

Self supply

3.24 As we have seen, a trader making exempt supplies cannot reclaim input tax charged on goods and services bought to make those supplies. This could lead to distortion of competition, as some traders with exempt outputs could obtain a tax advantage by producing their own goods or making use of their own services rather than buying them. The Treasury has power to deal with such distortion by making regulations taxing self supplies. Regulations have been made covering:

(a) standard rated construction services costing £100,000 or more;

(b) stationery in excess of £45,000 a year. The stationery regulation does not apply to fully taxable persons;

(c) cars.

3.25 The effect is that the trader is treated as supplying the goods or services to himself. Output tax is due to HM Customs & Excise, but if the trader is wholly or partly exempt (or if the goods are cars other than the types on which VAT is recoverable) all or some of that tax cannot be recovered as input tax. Thus the business suffers a VAT cost.

3.26 Regulations prevent the input tax being fully recovered by the trader saying that it is attributable to the (taxable) supply of the goods or services concerned to himself. However, the VAT on materials bought to make self supplies is fully recoverable.

3.27 The amount of the self supply is excluded from both the numerator and the denominator of the fraction used in the partial exemption calculation.

4. Imports and exports

4.1 Imports are chargeable to VAT when the same goods supplied in the home market by a registered trader would be chargeable to VAT, and at the same rate.

4.2 An importer of goods from outside the European Union must calculate tax on the value of the goods imported (the price plus packaging, freight, insurance, commission and customs and excise duties), and account for it at the point of entry into the UK. He can then deduct the tax payable as input tax on his next VAT return. HM Customs & Excise issue monthly certificates to importers showing the VAT paid on imports and these certificates are the evidence required to obtain a deduction for input tax (like tax invoices for supplies obtained in the UK). VAT is chargeable on the sale of the goods in the UK in the normal way. If security can be provided, the deferred payment system can be used whereby VAT and customs duty are automatically debited to the importer's bank account each month rather than payment being made for each import when the goods arrive in the UK.

4.3 There is also a system of paying VAT on imports of services (from inside or outside the EU), known as the *reverse charge*. A registered trader belonging in the UK who obtains services from abroad for business purposes is treated as supplying the services, so that VAT is paid on them.

4.4 Exports of goods are zero rated (even if a sale of the same goods in the UK would be standard rated or exempt), but the exporter should retain evidence of export (such as commercial documents).

Trade within the European Union

4.5 The general approach for trade within the EU is as follows.

(a) For goods sold between registered traders, the seller zero rates the supply. The buyer must pay VAT at his country's rate on the supply to him, and can treat it as input tax. Thus the buyer's country's VAT rate is substituted for the seller's country's VAT rate.

(b) On a sale to an unregistered buyer, the seller simply applies VAT (at his own country's rate) in the same way as he would for a sale within his own country.

(c) However, if the seller makes substantial sales to unregistered buyers in one country, he may have to register in that country and apply its VAT rate.

4.6 VAT is charged on *taxable acquisitions* (the term 'imports' is not used) of goods from other EU member states. An acquisition is taxable if it meets all of the following conditions.

(a) The acquirer is a taxable person.

(b) (i) The goods were acquired in the course or furtherance of a business, or of an activity of any corporate or unincorporated body;

(ii) the acquirer carries on the business or activity; and

(iii) the supplier is taxable on the supply in another member state of the EU.

(c) The supply to the acquirer is not an exempt supply.

4.7 No VAT is charged on an acquisition of zero rated goods.

4.8 If goods are supplied to someone acquiring them in another EU state, the supply is not zero rated or exempt unless:

(a) a supply of the same goods in the UK would be zero rated or exempt; or

(b) the acquirer is VAT registered and his registration number (preceded by a two letter code for his state) is shown on the invoice. The supply is then zero rated. If the number is not shown, but is later given to the supplier, a credit note can then be issued for the VAT charged and the supply can then be treated as zero rated.

4.9 The time of any acquisition, or supply to a trader in another EU state who is liable to VAT as acquirer, is not determined by the usual tax point rules. It is the earlier of:

(a) the date of issue of a tax invoice;
(b) the 15th of the month following removal of the goods.

4.10 When goods are acquired, the VAT due is accounted for as output tax on the return form. If the goods are for business purposes, it may also be treated as input tax so long as a tax invoice issued by the supplier is held, the invoice showing both the supplier's VAT registration number (prefixed by the state code) and the acquirer's VAT registration number (prefixed by GB). However, if the goods are for directors' domestic accommodation the tax may not be treated as input tax.

4.11 Certain advertising, banking, professional and freight transport services are, when supplied to people outside the EU or to VAT registered traders in other EU member states, outside the scope of VAT. No VAT is charged but the services are included in the Box 6 total on the VAT return.

4.12 Traders with substantial trade within the EU must submit monthly statistical returns *(Intrastat forms)*.

4.13 Traders making supplies to registered traders in other EU states must submit *EU sales statements* quarterly (or in some cases monthly or annually). These statements are due 42 days after the period to which they relate, and show the total supplies to each trader. An example, showing supplies to traders in France and Germany, is shown on the next page.

Value Added Tax
EU Sales List
For the period
01 04 X4 to 30 06 X4

VAT Registration Number
GB 1 3 7 2 4 2 8 9 1

Branch/subsidiary identifier

You could be liable to a financial penalty if your completed listing is not received by the due date.

XYZ LTD
1 BROOK ST
LONDON
W20 4DP

Calendar Quarter
2 X 4

Due date: 11 08 X4

For Official Use

Your VAT Office telephone number is 0123-4567

Before you fill in this form please read the notes overleaf.

Country Code	Customer's VAT Registration Number	Total value of supplies £	p	Indicator
FR	86 921285028	80618	00	
DE	370385679	722156	00	
DE	366047560	581049	00	
			00	
			00	
			00	
			00	
			00	
			00	
			00	
			00	
			00	
			00	
			00	
			00	

Number of pages completed 1

Lines completed (this page only) 3

Declaration: You, or someone on your behalf, must sign below.

I, PETER DAVIS declare that the
(Full name of signatory in BLOCK LETTERS)
information given above is true and complete.

Signature P Davis Date 4/8 19 X4

A false declaration can result in prosecution.

Could you please supply a

Contact Name: PETER DAVIS Telephone number 0123-9876

5. Special schemes

The cash accounting scheme

5.1 The cash accounting scheme enables businesses to account for tax on the basis of cash paid and received. That is, the date of payment or receipt determines the return in which the transaction is dealt with. The scheme can only be used by a trader whose annual taxable turnover (excluding VAT) does not exceed £350,000. A trader can join the scheme only if all returns and VAT payments are up to date (or arrangements have been made to pay outstanding VAT by instalments).

5.2 If the value of taxable supplies has exceeded £437,500 in the 12 months to the end of a VAT accounting period and has also exceeded £350,000 in the following 12 months, the trader must leave the scheme and start using the normal method of accounting at the end of the second 12 months.

5.3 A trader using the scheme should use his records of cash paid and received (for example his cash book) to prepare returns.

The annual accounting scheme

5.4 The annual accounting scheme is only available to traders who regularly pay tax to HM Customs & Excise, not to traders who normally get repayments. It is available for traders whose annual taxable turnover (excluding VAT) does not exceed £300,000. The year for which each return is made may end at the end of any calendar month.

5.5 Traders opting for the annual accounting scheme make VAT returns only once a year. However, throughout the year they make payments on account of the ultimate liability. HM Customs & Excise estimate the annual liability based on the past performance of the business. The trader must pay 90% of this estimate during the year by means of nine monthly direct debit payments starting in the fourth month of the year.

5.6 At the end of the year the trader completes an annual VAT return which must be submitted to HM Customs & Excise along with any payment due by two months after the end of the year.

5.7 It is not possible to join the annual accounting scheme if input tax exceeded output tax in the year prior to application. In addition, all returns must have been made up to date.

5.8 If the expected value of a trader's taxable supplies exceeds £375,000 notice must be given to HM Customs & Excise within 30 days and the trader may then have to leave the scheme. If the £375,000 limit is in fact exceeded, the trader must leave the scheme.

If a trader fails to make the regular payments required by the scheme or the final payment for a year, or has not paid all VAT shown on returns made before joining the scheme, he may be expelled from the scheme.

Retail schemes

5.9 A number of special retail schemes exist to facilitate VAT accounting by shops, particularly those making a mixture of standard rated, zero rated and exempt supplies. Some schemes rely on separate totals being kept for different sorts of supply, and others make estimates of VAT due by reference to purchases and/or fixed mark-ups.

If a trader has used a retail scheme during the period covered by a VAT return, he must enter the letter designating the scheme on the return.

Secondhand goods schemes

5.10 The basic idea of the secondhand goods schemes is to restrict the amount of tax due on goods sold under them to tax on the trader's margin, rather than on the entire amount charged on reselling the goods. The trader has to account for tax at 7/47 of the difference between his buying price and his selling price.

5.11 No tax invoice is issued, so a customer cannot reclaim the input tax suffered.

5.12 The following categories of goods can be included within secondhand goods schemes.

(a) Motor cars (except those bought for taxi businesses, self drive car hire businesses and driving schools), motor cycles and caravans

(b) Works of art, antiques and collectors' pieces

(c) Boats, outboard motors and aircraft

(d) Electronic organs

(e) Firearms

(f) Horses and ponies

It is intended to extend secondhand goods schemes to cover almost all secondhand goods from 1 January 1995.

5.13 The schemes can only be applied where the goods have been purchased from a person who did not charge VAT on the supply or from one who was operating a secondhand goods scheme. The goods must be used goods at the time of purchase.

6. Administration

Sources of information

6.1 The sources of law on VAT are as follows.

(a) The Value Added Tax Act 1994 (VATA 1994)
(b) Subsequent legislation contained in finance acts
(c) Statutory instruments
(d) Some sections of HM Customs & Excise Notice 700, *The VAT guide*

6.2 Information on VAT is also available in notices and leaflets obtainable from local VAT offices. *VAT notes* is a newsletter sent with the VAT return.

Local VAT offices

6.3 Local VAT offices are responsible for the local administration of VAT and for providing advice to registered persons whose principal place of business is in their area. They are controlled by regional collectors.

6.4 Completed VAT returns should be sent to the VAT Central Unit at Southend, not to a local VAT office.

6.5 From time to time a registered trader will be visited by staff from a local VAT office to ensure that the law is understood and is being applied properly. If a trader disagrees with any decision by HM Customs & Excise he can ask his local VAT office to reconsider the decision. It is not necessary to appeal formally to a tribunal while a case is being reviewed in this way.

6.6 If a trader's VAT returns are not made on time, or appear to be false or incomplete, HM Customs & Excise can raise assessments charging the VAT which appears to be due.

Appeals to VAT and duties tribunals

6.7 VAT and duties tribunals, which are independent of HM Customs & Excise, provide a method of dealing with disputes. Provided that VAT returns and payments shown thereon have been made, appeals can be heard by a tribunal.

A tribunal can waive the requirement to pay all tax shown on returns before an appeal is heard in cases of hardship.

6.8 An appeal must be lodged with the tribunal (not the local VAT office) within 30 days of the date of any decision by HM Customs & Excise. If instead the trader would like the local VAT office to reconsider their decision he should apply within 30 days of the decision to the relevant VAT office. The local VAT office may, after reconsideration, either:

(a) confirm the original decision, in which case the taxpayer has a further 21 days from the date of that confirmation in which to lodge an appeal with a tribunal; or

(b) send a revised decision, in which case the taxpayer will have a further 30 days from the date of the revised decision in which to lodge an appeal with a tribunal.

There may be a dispute over the deductibility of input tax which hinges on the purposes for which goods or services were used, or on whether they were used to make taxable supplies. The trader must then show that HM Customs & Excise acted unreasonably in refusing a deduction, if the goods or services are in the nature of luxuries, amusements or entertainment.

6.9 If one of the parties is dissatisfied with a decision on a point of law he may appeal to the courts. Tribunals may award costs.

7. Penalties

7.1 There are many different *penalties* for failure to comply with VAT law.

Late notification

7.2 A trader who makes taxable supplies must tell HM Customs & Excise if supplies exceed the registration limit. A penalty can be levied for failure to notify a liability to register by the proper date.

7.3 The penalty for late notification is based on the net tax due from the date when the trader should have been registered to the date when notification is made or if earlier, the date on which HM Customs & Excise become aware of the trader's liability to be registered. The rate varies as follows.

Number of months registration late by	*Percentage of tax*
Up to 9	10%
Over 9, up to 18	20%
Over 18	30%

A minimum penalty of £50 applies.

7.4 The late registration penalty is not due if the trader can show that there is a reasonable excuse for the failure, and the penalty may be mitigated by HM Customs & Excise or by a tribunal.

The unauthorised issue of invoices

7.5 This penalty applies where a person who is not registered for VAT nevertheless issues tax invoices. The penalty is 30% of the VAT involved with a minimum penalty of £50, but this penalty may be mitigated.

Breaches of regulations

7.6 There are penalties for breaches of VAT regulations of any kind. The amount of penalty varies with the type and frequency of the breach concerned.

The default surcharge

7.7 A default occurs when a trader either submits his VAT return late, or submits the return on time but pays the VAT late. If a taxpayer defaults, HM Customs & Excise will serve a *surcharge liability notice* on the taxpayer. The notice specifies a *surcharge period* running from the date of the notice to the anniversary of the end of the period for which the taxpayer is in default.

7.8 If a further default occurs during the surcharge period the original surcharge period will be extended to the anniversary of the end of the period to which the new default relates. In addition, if the default involves a late payment of VAT (as opposed to simply a late return) a surcharge is levied.

7.9 The surcharge depends on the number of defaults involving late payment of VAT which have occurred in the surcharge period, as follows.

Default involving late payment of VAT in the surcharge period	*Surcharge as a percentage of the VAT outstanding at the due date*
First	2%
Second	5%
Third	10%
Fourth and over	15%

Any surcharge of less than £30 is increased to £30, but surcharges at the 2% and 5% rates are not normally demanded unless the amount would be at least £200.

7.10 A trader must submit one year's returns and pay the tax shown on them on time in order to break out of the surcharge liability period and the escalation of surcharge percentages.

7.11 A trader will not be liable to a default surcharge if he can show that the return or payment was sent at such a time, and in such a manner, that it was reasonable to expect that HM Customs & Excise would receive it by the due date. Posting the return and payment first class the day before the due date is generally accepted as meeting this requirement. Nor will he be liable to a penalty if he can give a reasonable excuse for the late submission or payment.

The misdeclaration penalty: very large errors

7.12 The making of a return which understates a person's true liability or overstates the repayment due to him incurs a penalty of 15% of the tax which would have been lost if the return had been accepted as correct. The same penalty applies when HM Customs & Excise issue an assessment of VAT due which is too low and the trader fails to notify the error within 30 days from the issue of the assessment. These penalties apply only where the VAT which would have been lost is at least £1m or is at least 30% of the sum of the true input tax and the true output tax. This sum is known as the *gross amount of tax (GAT)*. (In the case of an incorrect assessment 30% of the true amount of tax, the tax actually due from or to the trader, is used instead of 30% of the GAT.) The penalty may be mitigated.

7.13 Errors on a VAT return of up to £2,000 may be corrected on the next return without giving rise to a serious misdeclaration penalty or interest.

7.14 This penalty does not apply if the trader can show reasonable excuse for his conduct, or if he made full disclosure when he had no reason to suppose that HM Customs & Excise were enquiring into his affairs.

7.15 If conduct leads to a conviction for fraud, or to a penalty for conduct involving dishonesty, it cannot also lead to a misdeclaration penalty.

The misdeclaration penalty: repeated errors

7.16 If a trader submits an inaccurate return, and the VAT which would have been lost if it had been accepted as accurate is at least £500,000 or at least 10% of the GAT, the inaccuracy is *material*.

7.17 Before the end of the fourth tax period following the period of a material inaccuracy, HM Customs & Excise may issue a *penalty liability notice*, specifying a *penalty period*. The period is the eight tax periods starting with the one in which the notice is issued.

7.18 If there are material inaccuracies for two or more tax periods falling within the penalty period, then each such inaccuracy apart from the first one leads to a penalty of 15% of the VAT which would have been lost. The penalty may be mitigated.

7.19 An inaccuracy is not regarded as material in the circumstances set out in Paragraphs 7.14 and 7.15 above, or if a misdeclaration penalty for a very large error is imposed for it. However, even if a misdeclaration penalty for a very large error is imposed, a penalty liability notice may still be issued following the inaccuracy.

Default interest

7.20 Interest (not deductible in computing taxable profits) is charged on VAT which is the subject of an assessment (where returns were not made or were incorrect), or which could have been the subject of an assessment but which was paid before the assessment was raised. It runs from the *reckonable date* until the date of payment.

7.21 The reckonable date is when the VAT should have been paid (one month from the end of the return period), or in the case of VAT repayments to traders which should not have been made, seven days from the issue of the repayment order. However, where VAT is charged by an assessment interest does not run from more than three years before the date of assessment; and where the VAT was paid before an assessment was raised, interest does not run for more than three years before the date of payment.

Repayment supplement

7.22 Where a trader is entitled to a repayment of VAT and the original return was rendered on time (or up to one month late) but HM Customs & Excise do not issue a written instruction for the repayment to be made within 30 days of receiving the return, then the trader will receive a supplement of the greater of £50 and 5% of the amount due.

7.23 If, however, the return states an amount due which differs from the correct refund due by more than the greater of 5% of the correct refund and £250, no supplement is added.

7.24 Days spent in raising and answering reasonable enquiries in relation to the return do not count towards the 30 days allowed to HM Customs & Excise to issue an instruction to make the repayment.

7.25 HM Customs & Excise can deduct from any refund due to a trader any tax, penalty, interest or surcharge due from him. This set off will then discharge the obligations of both parties. They can also refuse to make any repayment which would unjustly enrich the claimant.

Interest on overpayments due to official errors

7.26 If VAT is overpaid or a credit for input tax is not claimed because of an error by HM Customs & Excise, then the trader may claim interest on the amount eventually refunded, running from the date on which he paid the excessive VAT (or from the date on which HM Customs & Excise might reasonably be expected to have authorised a VAT repayment owing to him) to the date on which HM Customs & Excise authorise a repayment.

7.27 Interest must be claimed within six years of the date on which the trader discovered the error or could with reasonable diligence have discovered it. Interest is not available where a repayment supplement is available. Interest does not run for periods relating to reasonable enquiries by HM Customs & Excise into the matter in question.

Key points in this chapter

- VAT is computed on the price after discounts.
- Mixed supplies are split, but composite supplies are not.
- Some supplies are zero rated, while others are exempt.
- Input tax on some supplies, including most cars, is not recoverable.
- If a trader makes some exempt supplies, only a proportion of his input tax may be recoverable.
- VAT bad debt relief is available after six months.
- VAT is generally due on imports, but exports are zero rated.
- Special schemes include the cash accounting scheme and the annual accounting scheme.
- Returns are sent to the VAT Central Unit, but a trader may have dealings with his local VAT office or with a VAT tribunal.
- The most important penalties are the default surcharge and the misdeclaration penalty.

For practice on the points covered in this chapter you should now attempt the Exercises in Session 13 of the Cost Accounting II Workbook

FURTHER READING

BPP publishes a companion Workbook to be worked through in conjunction with this Tutorial Text. The Workbook includes a large number of exercises on topics covered in each chapter of the Text. There are also longer assignments for practice in preparation for devolved assessment, and central assessment exercises, including those set by the AAT.

To order your Workbook, ring our credit card hotline on 081-740 6808. Alternatively, send this page to our Freepost address or fax it to us on 081-740 1184.

To: BPP Publishing Ltd, FREEPOST, London W12 8BR **Tel: 081-740 6808**

Fax: 081-740 1184

Forenames (Mr / Ms): ____________________

Surname: ____________________

Address: ____________________

____

Post code: ____________ Date of central assessment (month/year): ____________

Please send me the following books:	Quantity	Price	Total
AAT *Cost Accounting II* Workbook	....	£10.95	....

Please include postage:

UK: £2.00 for first plus £1.00 for each extra book. ....

Europe (inc ROI): £3.00 for first plus £2.00 for each extra book. ....

Rest of the World: £5.00 for first plus £3.00 for each extra book. ....

I enclose a cheque for £ __________ or charge to Access/Visa

Card number | | | | | | | | | | | | | | | | |

Expiry date ____________ Signature ____________________

To order any further titles in the AAT range, please use the form overleaf.

ORDER FORM

Any books from our AAT range can be ordered by ringing our credit card hotline on 081-740 6808. Alternatively, send this page to our Freepost address or fax it to us on 081-740 1184.

To: BPP Publishing Ltd, FREEPOST, London W12 8BR **Tel: 081-740 6808**
Fax: 081-740 1184

Forenames (Mr / Ms): ____________________

Surname: ____________________

Address: ____________________

____

Post code: ____________

Please send me the following books:

		Price		*Quantity*		*Total*
		Tutorial Text	*Workbook*	*Tutorial Text*	*Workbook*	
Foundation		£	£			£
Unit 1	Cash Transactions	8.95	8.95	....	....	....
Unit 2	Credit Transactions	8.95	8.95	....	....	....
Unit 3	Payroll Transactions	10.95	10.95	....	....	....
Unit 20	Data processing	11.95*		....		....
Units 24-28	Business Knowledge	9.95*		....		....
Intermediate						
Units 4&5	Financial Accounting	11.95	11.95	....	....	....
Unit 6	Cost Accounting I	10.95	10.95	....	....	....
Units 7&8	Cost Accounting II	10.95	10.95	....	....	....
Units 21&22	Information Technology	11.95*		....		....
Technician						
Unit 9	Cash Management & Credit Control	8.95	7.95	....	....	....
Unit 10	Managing Accounting Systems	10.95	7.95	....	....	....
Units 11&12	Management Accounting I	9.95	7.95	....	....	....
Unit 13	Management Accounting II	8.95	7.95	....	....	....
Unit 14	Financial Statements	10.95	7.95	....	....	....
Unit 18	Auditing	8.95	7.95	....	....	....
Unit 19	Taxation	10.95	7.95	....	....	....
Unit 23	Information Management Systems	10.95	7.95	....	....	....
Unit 25	Health and Safety	2.00		....		....

(Price includes postage; this booklet is an extract from Units 24-28 Business Knowledge Combined Text)

* Combined Text

Please include postage:

UK: £2.00 for first plus £1.00 for each extra book.	....	....	....
Europe (inc ROI): £3.00 for first plus £2.00 for each extra book.	....	....	....
Rest of the World: £5.00 for first plus £3.00 for each extra book.	....	....	....
		Total	______

I enclose a cheque for £ __________ **or charge to Access/Visa**

Card number | | | | | | | | | | | | | | | | |

Expiry date ______________ Signature ____________________

REVIEW FORM

Name: ______________________________

How have you used this Tutorial Text?

Home study (book only)	☐	With 'correspondence' package	☐
On a course: college______________	☐	Other______________________	

How did you obtain this Tutorial Text?

From us by mail order	☐	From us by phone	☐
From a bookshop	☐	From your college	☐

Where did you hear about BPP Tutorial Texts?

At bookshop	☐	Recommended by lecturer	☐
Recommended by friend	☐	Mailshot from BPP	☐
Advertisement in ______________	☐	Other ______________________	

Have you used the companion Workbook for this subject? **Yes/No**

Your comments and suggestions would be appreciated on the following areas

Coverage of elements of competence

Errors (please specify, and refer to a page number)

Structure and presentation

Other

Please return to: BPP Publishing Ltd, FREEPOST, London W12 8BR